D1423281

SOHO IN THE EIGHTIES

SOHO IN THE EIGHTIES

Christopher Howse

BLOOMSBURY CONTINUUM

LONDON · NEW YORK · OXFORD · NEW DELHI · SYDNEY

BLOOMSBURY CONTINUUM
Bloomsbury Publishing Plc
50 Bedford Square, London, WC1B 3DP, UK

BLOOMSBURY, BLOOMSBURY CONTINUUM and the Diana logo are trademarks of
Bloomsbury Publishing Plc

First published in Great Britain 2018

A catalogue record for this book is available from the British Library

Library of Congress Cataloguing-in-Publication data has been applied for

ISBN: HB: 978-1-4729-1480-4; EPDF: 978-1-4729-1482-8; EPUB: 978-1-4729-1481-1

4 6 8 10 9 7 5 3

Typeset by Newgen KnowledgeWorks Pvt. Ltd., Chennai, India
Printed and bound in Great Britain by CPI Group (UK) Ltd, Croydon CR0 4YY

To find out more about our authors and books visit www.bloomsbury.com
and sign up for our newsletters.

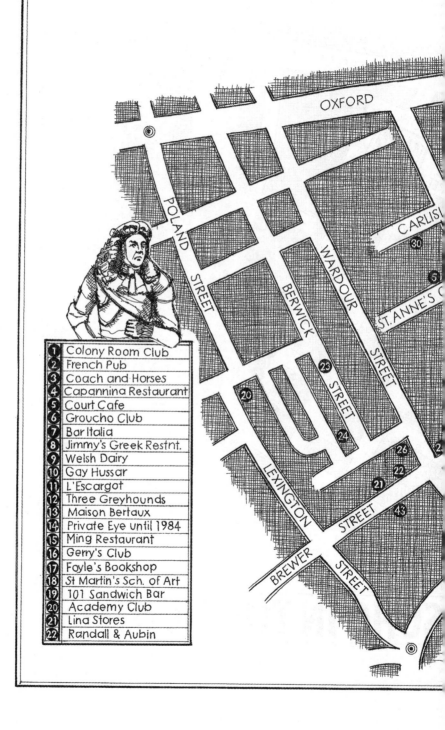

1	Colony Room Club
2	French Pub
3	Coach and Horses
4	Capannina Restaurant
5	Court Cafe
6	Groucho Club
7	Bar Italia
8	Jimmy's Greek Restnt.
9	Welsh Dairy
10	Gay Hussar
11	L'Escargot
12	Three Greyhounds
13	Maison Bertaux
14	Private Eye until 1984
15	Ming Restaurant
16	Gerry's Club
17	Foyle's Bookshop
18	St Martin's Sch. of Art
19	101 Sandwich Bar
20	Academy Club
21	Lina Stores
22	Randall & Aubin

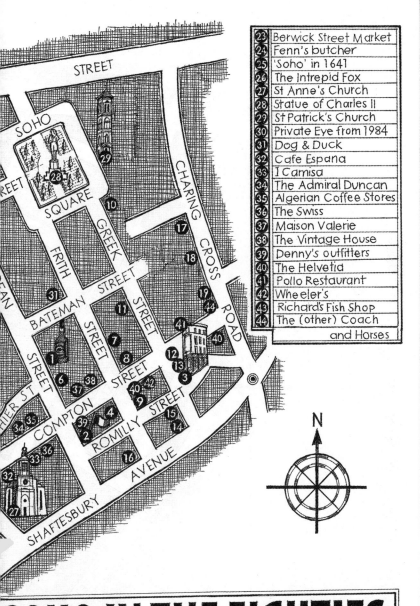

23	Berwick Street Market
24	Fenn's butcher
25	'Soho' in 1641
26	The Intrepid Fox
27	St Anne's Church
28	Statue of Charles II
29	St Patrick's Church
30	Private Eye from 1984
31	Dog & Duck
32	Cafe Espana
33	I Camisa
34	The Admiral Duncan
35	Algerian Coffee Stores
36	The Swiss
37	Maison Valerie
38	The Vintage House
39	Denny's outfitters
40	The Helvetia
41	Pollo Restaurant
42	Wheeler's
43	Richard's Fish Shop
44	The (other) Coach and Horses

SOHO IN THE EIGHTIES

Contents

CONTENTS

CONTENTS

List of Illustrations

walks past my frown, beard and beer. (By kind permission of Michael Heath)

7 'Francis Bacon on the Piccadilly Line' by Johnny Stiletto (1983). Bruce Bernard learned that it was Bacon's favourite photograph of him and arranged for the two to meet. (By kind permission of Johnny Stiletto)

8 On Derby day 1988, just as the big-wheel car came down, with the fairground hand standing by, Bruce Bernard's camera clicked to catch Ann Robson chatting and my knuckles petrified. (Private Collection)

9 Christopher Battye's *Friday Night in the French* shows eighties men and women drinking like monstrous fledglings. (Private Collection)

10 End of the eighties: the Colony Room Club on the day Francis Bacon died, 28 April 1992, in Craig Easton's photograph. (By kind permission of Craig Easton)

Plans

Foreword

In 1987 Daniel Farson threw a party to celebrate the publication of his book *Soho in the Fifties*. It was held upstairs in Kettner's, which had opened up French restaurant food to London diners in the 1860s. By 1987 it was pleasantly faded. The man who had built the house that became Kettner's was in the 1730s the first known landlord of the Coach and Horses public house opposite.

At Daniel's party the usual suspects turned out, from Francis Bacon to young Fred Ingrams, the son of the editor of *Private Eye*, for they liked him although he was, as he knew, a monster, a Jekyll regularly turned Hyde by the application of sufficient gin.

His book came out 30 years after the period it celebrated, and now it is 30 years since the eighties. *Soho in the Eighties* is a memoir. Like a policeman giving evidence, my memory is refreshed by contemporaneous notes. My focus is the places where poets, painters, stagehands, retired prostitutes, actors, criminals, musicians and general layabouts met to drink and converse, or shout at each other.

There is nothing much here about the hospitals of Soho, interesting though they were, or the Marquee, Madame Jojo's or even Ronnie Scott's. Many little worlds throve in Soho and this is mine. It had remarkable inhabitants.

That world has gone. Everyone is dead among the older people, apart from Norman Balon, London's rudest landlord; too many of the younger people are dead, too.

The crowded stages where the nightly tragicomedy was played out were principally the Coach and Horses, the French pub and the Colony Room Club. They had their virtues, and their dangers. It was all very funny indeed, and of course ended in disaster.

London, 26 July 2018

The Coach and Horses

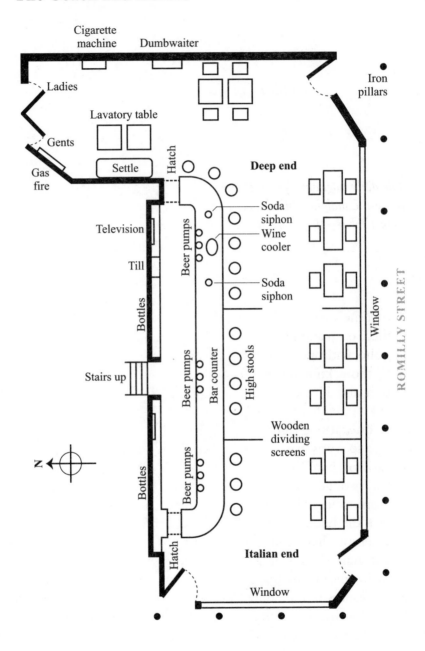

I

The Coach – and Horses

The daily tragicomedy – Fings Ain't Wot They Used T'Be – London's Rudest Landlord – The man in black – 'See you next Thursday' – Stoker Tobin – 'If you had to eat someone here' – Death in the Afternoon

The daily tragicomedy

'Don't mess with those Bernard brothers,' said the drunkest man in the Coach and Horses. But I did, with all three, and much else in Soho, with what effect you may judge.

Without knowing it, I had jumped in at the deep end. The Coach and Horses in Greek Street – the Coach as everyone called it – did have a shallow end and a deep end, although there were no warning signs.

And so it was that, a couple of years later, I was caught up in the Great Coach and Horses Betting Raid, when the Metropolitan Police swooped on Jeffrey Bernard for making an illegal book on horseracing. The funniest part was when Sandy Fawkes tried to save the bookie's bank by sweeping the money from the bar counter into her handbag.

But, wait a moment – if you don't know any of these people, it won't mean anything. The cast was what made the daily performances of the Soho tragicomedy so compelling. I've never laughed as much as I did in that decade. Any television sitcom seemed utterly lame in comparison, even though the long-running comedy of Soho ended in divorce, sickness, poverty and death.

Jeffrey Bernard obviously took the lead role at first. I spent more days in his company than Boswell did with Samuel Johnson. But Jeffrey was his own Boswell, recounting a version of his life week by week in his Low Life column in the *Spectator*. I used to bring him a copy at Thursday lunchtime when I worked for the magazine. He'd have already been in the pub a couple of hours, since opening time at 11 a.m. By the eighties, his dedication to drink was having an effect.

A bare line sometimes appeared in the *Spectator* in place of his column: 'Jeffrey Bernard is unwell' (which was to give the title to Keith Waterhouse's play about him), and some readers thought that it meant he had been too drunk to write. It didn't. It meant that diabetes, pancreatitis and gradually worse afflictions had interrupted his routine. As Michael Heath the cartoonist perceptively remarked, Jeffrey's hobby was to observe his own physical dissolution.

He usually came into the pub by the door from Greek Street at the far end, the shallow end, where the Italians and shoplifters drank. Sometimes he'd take a paper napkin from a bunch in a glass on the counter put out folded by the landlord Norman's mother, ready for the lunch trade, and blow his nose, which dripped with the exertion in the fresh air of getting to the pub.

His hand shook. It was, he remembered having been told by a medic, a *benign* tremor. His muscles were also beginning to waste. And this was a man who'd fancied himself a boxer and had once got a licence. 'I'm as weak as a kitten,' he'd say, as he climbed onto the high stool at the bar. By the end of the decade, when he was in his late fifties, his knees were thicker than his thighs. On the seat of the chair at his desk in his lodgings was a ring air cushion.

Fings Ain't Wot They Used T'Be

Part of Jeffrey's devotion to being a bohemian – a layabout, he'd call it sometimes – was having no fixed abode. For a few years he'd been a lodger in the Great Portland Street flat belonging to Geraldine Norman, the widow of Frank Norman. Frank Norman was best known for writing the musical *Fings Ain't Wot They Used T'Be* for Joan Littlewood's Theatre Workshop at Stratford East. Enlivened by Lionel Bart's songs, the play was a hit in 1959 and transferred to the West End, running for 886 performances.

Frank Norman also wrote a fictionalized memoir of Soho in the fifties, *Stand On Me*, which explored the lowest of low life. 'She hadn't been around all that long, but she was already a gaffless slag doing skippers in the karzay,' one line read. (*Skippers in the karzay* – or *khazi* as the more usual form has it – means kipping at night in a public lavatory, an alternative to *going case*: going home with a man or woman as much for a bed for the night as anything else.)

Frank Norman was taller than Jeffrey, and the most striking thing about his appearance was a great scar down one side of his face, a *chiv mark* he'd have called it.

Jeffrey and he had together produced a book called *Soho Night and Day* (1966). It's a good book, but Jeffrey's photographs are more remarkable than Frank Norman's text. There's one captioned 'Retired chorus girl' of an old woman, in a wide-brimmed hat with a rosette, drinking from a cocktail glass in the French pub. Another shows a butcher standing in Hammett's ornately tiled shop in Rupert Street slicing with a cleaver down through the carcase of a pig suspended by hooks in its rear hocks, all the way from the tail to the ear. Jeffrey must have had in mind John Deakin's photograph from 1952 of Francis Bacon, stripped to the waist, holding two halves of a carcase hanging vertically from hooks, with the inside, the ribs, on show, facing the viewer.

Anyway, Frank and Geraldine Norman had married in 1970, and he died in 1980. Jeffrey moved in as a lodger the next year. He sat at the desk that had been Frank's and between his typewriter and the window stood a bust of Nelson. 'About twenty years ago,' Jeffrey told Ena Kendall of the *Sunday Times Magazine*, 'Frank and I were walking through Hampstead and we saw that bust in an antique shop window. It was £5. Frank had some money on him and I had only five bob, so he got it and I was angry with him for years about it. I just think: what an awful way to get it, by him dying.'

'I envisaged giving him a comfortable room which he could pay for or not, according to his means,' Geraldine remembered of Jeffrey's arrival, 'and I imagined myself cooking him nourishing meals to cushion the antagonism between alcohol and diabetes.' Like many people in the early eighties, she thought he was dying, but five years later he was still going, sleeping at Great Portland Street, waking early and drinking tea and squeezed orange juice and vodka before making his way to the Coach for opening time.

London's Rudest Landlord

The landlord of the Coach and Horses, Norman Balon, might not be there when Jeffrey arrived. Norman liked to keep the regulars guessing about his appearances. In the morning he would get his hair cut or play the Italian card game briscola somewhere else in Soho before returning to the pub.

If not quite in the way he imagined, Norman Balon was a very unusual pub landlord. Tall and a little stooped, with a beaky nose, he resembled a heron. He was five years older than Jeffrey, uncouth in speech, barely educated, warm-hearted, shy but good with people, adventurous in commerce and at last successful in running a pub in Soho just at the time Soho was coming to a rolling boil.

He called himself 'London's Rudest Landlord'. Even by Soho standards he was often rude, it is true. If someone complained about a drink or the service, he might say: 'Here's your money. Now fuck off.' But awkwardness was the keynote of his character. It was like the furniture in the pub: the chairs were just a tiny bit too wide to draw under the little tables.

The high stool on which Jeffrey perched, at the deep end of the long bar, had to its left the wooden half-partition which marked off this third of the pub. To his right was the end of the bar that curved round to accommodate a gap through which the staff could make a sally when the hatch in the counter was open, as it usually was, secured upright by a well-made brass catch like some ship's fitting from the glory days of steam.

The geography of the Coach and Horses was a vital aspect of the daily power struggle that took place there. As with life in a small ship, every inch was familiar. The wooden rail running round the edge of the bar (useful to hang onto in crowded conditions) had a wobbly end where the bracket holding it had come unscrewed. Below the rail at floor level ran a ceramic gutter, like a step with a trough in it; perhaps the idea of it had been to catch any spilt beer and cigarette ends, but it seemed of little use. The niche behind the bar flap did provide shelter for a book to be stowed out of harm from spillage. Anyone sitting at lunchtime at the table near the dumbwaiter hatch, between the cigarette machine and the door, ran the risk of having a shoulder smeared with gravy whenever a pile of dirty plates was carried from the bar to be sent upstairs with a pull of the rope. There was room for five or six stools at this section of the bar counter. Sooner or later in the day, that arrangement of stools regularly caused trouble.

Jeffrey drank vodka, ice and soda. Norman provided soda siphons, heavy things of polygonal thick glass with shiny fittings and a cream Bakelite nozzle, standing, rather stylishly, on the bar, near the small half-barrel where bottles of white wine wallowed in an icy bath. Soda was free. The soda could be used as a weapon (more often verbal than physical) in the combat of pub life. 'Don't drown it,' Jeffrey might say if the barman added too much. 'Any chance of some soda?' he could call out if the siphon was empty or out of reach.

A hostile act, of which Jeffrey was sometimes guilty, if a barman was in some way deemed unsatisfactory, would be to push the coins for payment over the counter into a pool of spilt beer. In any case, Jeffrey would ordinarily leave his change from a round on the dry part of the red linoleum counter of the bar.

The coins sat there happily when he popped to the lavatory. They said: 'Dare you to steal us.' No one did.

In the Coach, doubles were cheaper pro rata than singles. It was a verbal crime to call a drink *double* rather than *large*, but not so grave a crime as to specify a large size if someone else was doing the buying and had asked what you'd like.

The man in black

From eleven o'clock in the morning the pub remained pretty empty for an hour, weekdays or Saturdays. Perhaps an early arrival, apart from Jeffrey, would be Bill Mitchell, a large man in black clothes and a big-brimmed black hat. He would wear dark glasses, too.

'A pint of Burton ale,' he said in a strangely familiar, gravelly voice. His voice was familiar because he earned a living making voice-overs for advertisements, such as: 'Carlsberg – probably the best lager in the world'. It was bad luck on him that his chosen clothing – black – should in those years have been chosen too by every young person in the pub. They were mostly students from St Martin's School of Art round the corner in Charing Cross Road – or their emulators. Everyone, girls and boys, wore black, every day.

In the morning, Bill would hardly speak a word to Jeffrey but stand on his own on a patch of carpet between the door and the bar, resting his pint of draught bitter on one of the small tables. The gap of cheek between his dark glasses and the edge of his beer glass, as he raised it to drink, looked pale and clammy.

That Saturday lunchtime, 20 September 1986, there were five regulars with whom I was sitting on the tall stools along the bar at the deep end. Since the rationale of the group of regulars who drank in the Coach was to drive off strangers and bores, it might have seemed surprising to find among them, every lunchtime and evening that he could make it,

6

Gordon Smith, a stage-door keeper in his sixties. He wasn't clever, didn't say witty things, had no great store of anecdote. The best he could manage were preposterous stories about wangling a drink at a country pub by ordering a pint and then being interrupted by an accomplice pretending to be a policeman arresting him.

Gordon looked battered by life. He was fat-bellied and had a soft double chin often framed in a roll-neck sweater. His thinning grey hair was parted and combed flat. He'd lost a lower front tooth and his tongue would appear thoughtfully through the gap as he listened to the conversation.

Gordon declared that, in case of trouble, 'I'm a runner.' But he couldn't run. He walked with a limp, from a bad ankle. He feared crossing busy roads. Sitting at the bar, he would grasp the attached wooden rail with two hands, crossed at the wrists – an old naval trick, we were to understand: 'One hand for your drink and one for the barky.' Another relic of navy days was the odd snatch from the *Sod's Opera*, the name for a more or less extempore entertainment at sea. 'Arseholes are cheap today,' he would begin, to the tune of '*La donna è mobile*'. 'Cheaper than yesterday. / They're only half a crown, / Standing up or lying down.' The opera didn't get much further. Gordon drank whisky and lived in the YMCA in Tottenham Court Road. I'd never heard of anyone else living there.

Yet, for all his shortcomings, he wasn't rejected. If anything, he repelled verbal attack by being so obviously wide open to it. He was deferential without being obsequious. Graham Mason, the drunkest man in the Coach, who had a way with nicknames, singled out his anxious fussing in an old-ladylike manner, and called him Granny Smith.

'See you next Thursday'

Someone else who was free most mornings to arrive in the pub early was Diana Lambert. She was an actress. I thought she'd been in *Genevieve*, but it seems she hadn't. She had, though, been in *The Nun's Story* (1959) with Audrey Hepburn, Peter Finch and Edith Evans. In it she played a member of the Resistance called Lisa. She had been 25 then, and so in the mid-eighties was in her early fifties. By then she was not getting work.

She had a flat in Shaftesbury Avenue with an exhilarating view straight down Frith Street. How pleased she must have been when as a young actress she had moved into a flat of her own in the heart of theatrical London. Now she was selling her furniture to buy whisky.

Someone once gave her a pheasant, and she asked three of us to dinner to share it. She was 5ft 3in and wore, as well as could be expected, clothes that looked second-hand. She often seemed to be dirty, her fingernails blackened with mud from her mother's garden, and her hands or even her face smeared a little. She was cheerful and her laugh would turn into a smoker's cough. Since she had no money, she travelled about on an old black bicycle with a basket. This, and her fondness for gossip, prompted the nickname that Graham Mason gave her of the Village Postmistress.

Diana Lambert was methodically tougher than she at first seemed. She had a catalogue of absurd turns of phrase: 'What ho!' 'I vow, you are a wag.' She'd refer to an enemy as a 'See you next Thursday' (a genteelism for *cunt*). She was not easily squashed, and she put up with the squalor and squabbles of Soho. I think she enjoyed it all.

So Jeffrey and Gordon Smith were sitting on stools at the bar that Saturday morning, with the black-clad Bill Mitchell hovering. The other early bird, Diana Lambert, sat at the bar, too, perhaps saying deprecatingly, 'I'm on my own today' when a drink was offered her, to avoid being drawn into buying a round that she couldn't afford.

When the door from Romilly Street opened, the door closer attached to the top always made a clacking noise, and people tended to turn round, when it was quiet enough to hear, to see who had come in. This time it was Mick Tobin.

Stoker Tobin

Mick Tobin had been a stage carpenter, a job which meant more than sawing and hammering, for, as well as having a hand in building sets, he had to take responsibility for the scenery on tour. He had given Jeffrey his first backstage job behind the scenes in 1958 on *Expresso Bongo* when it went on tour (a chance that Jeffrey took for switching his drink from bitter to whisky). The stage musical was, everyone remembered, a bit sharper than the film version with Cliff Richard that came out the following year.

Mick had been brought up as one of several children of an Irish tailor, sharing with other families a single house in Whitfield Street, near Tottenham Court Road. He was a handy boxer. 'I once saw him land a hook on an electrician backstage who had been asking for it,' Jeffrey Bernard remembered. 'The silly man's feet actually left the floor before he became parallel to it prior to hitting it.' When he was serving as a stoker in destroyers in the Royal Navy during the war, Mick fought Randolph Turpin for the navy's middleweight title. He went the distance with him.

Now, in his mid-sixties, Mick did what odd jobs he could find: a bit of carpentry, selling newspapers. He had grave doubts about Gordon Smith's tales of naval life, even declaring that he had never served in the navy.

Although Mick Tobin, as a tailor's son, valued smart clothes, he always appeared in the pub in a worn boxer's sweat-top, with a hood and drawstring, and a grubby checked flat hat. In that dress, his old friend Lucian Freud (whom he called 'Lu') was to paint him in 1991 as *Man in a Check Cap*.

Bruce Bernard once remarked, fairly, that Mick had a talent for making friends. Mick liked to come out with familiar jocular phrases, such as the metaphorical standard of comparison, 'Same meat, different gravy', or the ironical, 'The only sin is to be skint.' Then he'd laugh. He spoke with an old-fashioned Cockney accent, in a fairly deep voice. By the eighties he seldom wore his teeth.

'If you had to eat someone here'

That Saturday, Mick was taking an intelligent interest in the form on the racing pages of the *Sun*, which was widely regarded the best for racing. He borrowed Diana Lambert's reading glasses to study the small print. When the door opened again, it was Sandy Fawkes.

For quite a bit of the long time that they both spent in the pub, Mick Tobin was annoyed by Sandy Fawkes. He didn't like her asking for drinks and he didn't like her demanding a stool.

'Is any of you gentlemen going to give a lady a seat?' she would ask when all the tall stools by the bar at the deep end were already taken. Gordon Smith might have given up his stool, but really his ankle wouldn't let him stand for too long. Jeffrey would in the ordinary way of things stand up every now and then, to ease the pressure on his fleshless bones and stretch his legs, and take the rail at the edge of the bar in both hands and put his head down and draw breath and flick his greying hair back and throw out a remark like: 'If you had to eat someone here, like those people in the air crash in the Andes, who would you start with? Not Richard Ingrams. He'd be like a bit of burnt toast.' But Jeffrey couldn't stand up for a whole session.

Another solid regular, Bill Moore, who'd been a guardsman and drank scarcely credible quantities of whisky, hated Sandy Fawkes and always sat tight. Mick Tobin would respond mildly enough to her request for a stool by saying: 'Nah. Leave it out.' So it was fortunate that on this Saturday there was still a stool free, and Sandy became the sixth of the row of regulars along the bar.

She looked rather unusual that morning, wearing a low-cut evening dress, with a long fur-collared cloak over it. She'd had a row with her boyfriend the previous night, before tasting even a mouthful of their romantic dinner, and had punished him by sleeping alone at the Ritz and, she said, sending him the bill. When she told me, I wasn't quite sure how the practicalities of that would work. She sat down and lodged a high heel behind the low crossbar of the stool, tucking her still shapely legs under the overhang of the bar counter. 'Large Bell's, darling,' she said to the barman.

She was in her mid-fifties. The clothes that fitted her in 1970, when she had ended up as fashion editor of the *Daily Sketch*, fitted her still. Her nails were painted and she wore bright lipstick, which, by its traces, distinguished the remnants of the Gauloises that she had consumed. The other cigarette ends lay unadorned in the common pile in the ashtray on the counter.

Sandy had a way of sometimes keeping the cigarette in her mouth when she was busy with her hands, and the smoke would wreathe upward, past her fair-dyed fringe, and nestle among the hairs of her habitual fur hat (which looked as though a cat had curled up and fallen asleep on her head), giving it a more ginger tinge.

Death in the Afternoon

It was Sandy who had introduced me to the Kismet. The Kismet, underground in Great Newport Street, was an afternoon drinking club, bridging the hours from 3 to 5.30 p.m. when pubs were closed, until the Licensing Act of 1988 changed things. The Kismet had two nicknames: Death in the Afternoon and the Iron Lung. Someone once asked: 'What's the smell in here.' The reply was: 'Failure.'

The Kismet, being damp, also had a more literal smell. Entry was by a passageway beyond the open white-painted front door, and down very steep stairs, with stained carpet and brown semi-detached wallpaper on the walls. Downstairs, it was like drinking in a badly run public lavatory.

Indeed, the lavatories opened out directly from the bar, ladies' on the left, gents' on the right, with no intervening closed door. The arched wall inside the gents' had the gloss paint peeling away, with rough eruptions of calcified wetness forcing it off. On the top of the urinal, I noticed on that first afternoon, someone had left an empty half-bottle of the roughest brandy. The Kismet was reputed to be a cheaper drinking joint than Le Caveau, closer to the heart of Soho, in Frith Street.

Barney Bates, the jazz pianist, had been with us that day, a tall, grey-haired man who looked a bit like Peter Cook. He bought two rounds, costing him £10 in all. He was drinking half-pints of white wine, since they had no red. I was introduced to the barmaid, but not signed in. She remembered my name. I didn't remember hers.

An actor I recognized from television was drinking there, and a balding man in his fifties with a gold chain round his neck and a blue T-shirt on his paunchy body. He wore a chunky gold ring with a diamond in it. Sandy had a violent row with him. 'I never did like you, you fat queen,' she said. 'Just because you've got money …'

Barney talked on the subject of drunken comportment – the conventional way that people behave when in drink. 'It's all right when I'm here,' he said, 'but when I get back to Chelsea, they'll say: "Barney, you're pissed again."'

By comparison with the Kismet, the Coach and Horses was cosy. That Saturday morning Sandy had already been in the French pub, two streets westward, drinking with Daniel Farson. It was there that in the 1940s she had had her first drink in Soho: a gin and orange cordial. It had been bought her by John Minton, who introduced her to Soho when she was a student at Camberwell School of Arts. Minton, talented, good-looking, popular, was homosexual and unhappy about it. He liked Sandy for herself. He killed himself at the age of 39.

'Perhaps I should have signed the pledge that day,' she remarked, years later, of her first visit to Soho. Perhaps. She did sometimes moderate her drinking; in 1987 she spent a month dry. She even wrote a book called *Health for Hooligans* which was supposed to help boozers limit the damage. Drink certainly brought out her unhappiness. She had come a long way. As a baby she had actually been found in the Grand Union Canal. It was not the last time she was to evade a premature death.

The Great Coach and Horses Betting Raid

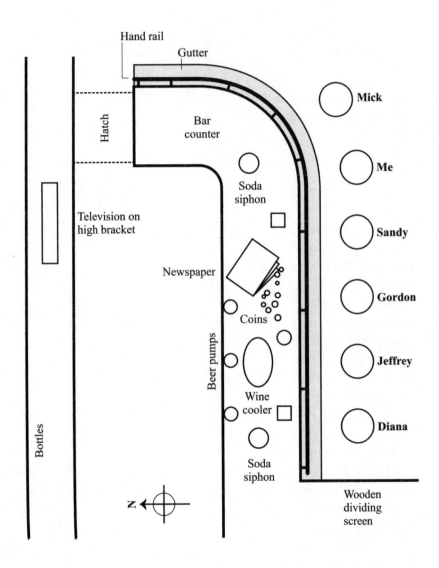

2

The Trap

The inventor of cat-racing – Bookie's clerk – A slew of pound coins – 'He's stitched me up for life' – On bail – Robertson QC – 'Frail and tipsy scribe'

The inventor of cat-racing

So that Saturday lunchtime in September, Sandy Fawkes was happy enough for the moment, rummaging in her handbag and talking of Soho trivialities to Gordon Smith. The line-up of tall stools at the bar went, from left to right: Diana, Jeffrey, Gordon, Sandy, me, Mick.

There were other people around, some sitting at tables, some standing. The place was full of smoke. Stagehands came in for a quick pint or two and left. Italians from the other end passed by on the way to the lavatory. Strangers attempted to get served. Norman Balon had gone out. High on its bracket above the bottles behind the bar, the television was showing *Channel 4 Racing*.

The one regular who was expected but absent was Conan Nicholas. Conan was one of those people whom everyone talks about in an amused way when they aren't there. He was the man who invented cat-racing, as audiences of the play *Jeffrey Bernard is Unwell* were to learn. He was at this time in his vigorous early seventies. He didn't seem to age and was seldom overtly drunk.

Sparely built, of medium height, he stared owlishly from a round head. He had been described as looking like a petrol pump – meaning one of the tall pre-war pieces of apparatus with a white glass globe on top bearing the name of the petrol company.

Conan made a living from copy editing and was capable of proof-reading mathematical textbooks. He also wrote pornography for money and had worked in the press department of the Turkish embassy.

He was a declared socialist, which is why the cats used for racing were called Keir Hardie and George Lansbury. He claimed that he had once been in bed with a woman and asked her if she was a Conservative. When she said she was, he gave her the cab fare and told her to get out. Conan had, he said, spent two years in prison as a conscientious objector during the Second World War.

He was the strangest bundle of prejudices. I once heard him ringing for a minicab after a heavy session in the Coach. 'The driver must be a black man,' he insisted. 'Not an Iranian or Maltese.' He liked to denounce, in punchy, uncompromising terms, anything he opposed – poor spelling, racialism, eating in public. When I called him a doctrinaire elitist he broke into a smile and exclaimed: 'Yes, man, you're right.'

Conan used to gate-crash the annual *Spectator* party, as many people did in those days. The guests were mostly crushed into the little garden behind the Georgian house in Doughty Street. One year he followed Enoch Powell round the garden saying: 'Once you could have saved this country, but you've turned into a complete SHIT!' The next year, when he saw him approaching, Powell simply said: 'Will you please leave me alone.'

It was not easy to place Conan in any pigeonhole in English society. He would tell a story of how, when he was a boy between the wars, his father had won £2,000 on a race (an amount then equal to four years' salary for a professional man). He bought a car and toured with his family, staying at hotels until all the money was spent.

Conan generally drank halves of bitter, having given up whisky, he said, after Frank Norman and Jeffrey Bernard and he had a great go at it in the sixties.

Bookie's clerk

And when Jeffrey was making a book on the television racing at the Coach, Conan liked to act as bookie's clerk. He'd sit on the settle behind the *Private Eye* lunch table (not the table upstairs where the celebrated fortnightly *Private Eye* lunches were held, but the two small square tables put side by side, near the lavatory, where the magazine's staff had their daily lunch). There, on a Saturday, Conan would note down wagers. In theory he'd keep an eye on the odds and the stakes to ensure that the bookie wasn't too exposed to risk.

But that Saturday, Jeffrey thought that Conan was avoiding him because he couldn't pay back some money he'd borrowed. 'In the 1950s he was living in one of those nice mansion blocks in Prince of Wales Drive, opposite Battersea Park,' Jeffrey reminisced, 'and a bookie's man called at the flats and said: "I'm looking for Conan Nicholas." And Conan, with very quick thinking, I must admit, said: "That shit. I've been looking for him for three months." He asked the bookie's man in for tea and toast and went on for a quarter of an hour about what a shit Conan Nicholas was.'

The week before, Jeffrey had made a book on the St Leger, the last of the five annual classics to be run. Conan hadn't been in the pub that day either. He'd phoned up to tell Jeffrey that he was 'under pressure' and couldn't come in. 'He does go into the most extraordinary detail on the phone,' Jeffrey said. 'He'll say: "I've still got my pyjamas on, which is *quite exceptional*. I've just put on a cup of coffee. Then I'll go out to buy *The Times* ..."'

During the racing on St Leger Day, Conan rang up twice, once to put on a pound bet, and the second time to put £11 on

Niswas in the St Leger itself. He lost. That St Leger Day lunchtime, Gordon Smith won £10 from Jeffrey. I lost £5, and then won £10 in the big race on the Dowager Duchess of Norfolk's horse Moon Madness. It was a fluke. I just liked the name.

A slew of pound coins

This Saturday, a week after the St Leger, then, Jeffrey had the *Times* racing pages folded on the counter next to a scattering of pound coins. Another pound was added to the slew when I backed a horse called Print at 7-1 for the five-furlong sprint at three o'clock at Newbury. The odds shortened before the off to 7-4. Just before I was going to collect my winnings from Jeffrey, shortly after the serving of drinks stopped at 3 p.m., when Norman's octogenarian mother was fussing around, ineffectually saying, 'Now, gentlemen, I really must have your glasses', the forces of the law sprung the trap.

All was confusion. Uniformed police were at the doors and plainclothes men at the bar. It was later established that, in addition to three Customs officers, no fewer than nine policemen secured the two exits and surrounded the suspected criminal.

Sandy, with great presence of mind, as the Customs men pounced, swept a pile of Jeffrey's takings under a newspaper on the counter and thence into her handbag. But enough remained to be used in evidence. A tall, fair-haired man emptied the coins from the counter into a plastic bag. He had appeared with a Burberry's carrier bag an hour before and had seemed oddly unattached and unhurried to be served, unlike everyone else.

'He's stitched me up for life'

A plainclothes man came up to a fat regular in a red jersey and said he was from Customs and Excise. He asked the regular his name and address, which eventually he gave. The regular said how long he'd been sitting in the pub, but declared he had no knowledge of betting there. As it happened, I'd noticed that he had been winning on a few races.

Another officer questioned Granny Smith, who was sitting next to Jeffrey, and asked him if he realized the gravity of what he had been doing. Gordon said he had just been sitting there having a drink. He said, 'The only bet I've had is this one,' holding up a Mecca betting-shop slip.

Norman Balon had returned to the pub some time earlier and now, as the fracas subsided, he said to me: 'Jeffrey Bernard's a cunt. He's stitched me up for life.'

The police took Jeffrey to Vine Street nick. The regulars had left quietly, except for Sandy. She had been getting in whiskies steadily and the barman had had to give her a bigger glass to accommodate them. Now she sat there dazed. She kept repeating: 'What have they done with Jeff? What are they going to do to Norman?' I persuaded her to go home and in the street she left me, still able to walk.

I wandered round to Vine Street, hardly knowing how I might help. All I could think of was to warn the desk sergeant that Jeffrey was diabetic and shouldn't be left in a coma. His diabetes might mean he was confused, I said. 'We'll take good care of him,' the sergeant said.

A few minutes later an inspector came out and assured me a doctor was on his way. Some time later, Norman came out of the police station. He said: 'He'll be out in an hour or so, there's not much point staying.'

I thought, rather inanely, that it might be useful in some way if Conan knew. In those days before mobiles, I found a telephone at the Royal Academy and asked directory enquiries for the number of Conan Nicholas. 'I don't know the address,' I said, 'but I know the number ends in 1819, the year of Peterloo.' They found it, but there was no reply. Perhaps that was all to the good.

Back at Vine Street, at about five o'clock, Finola Morgan arrived, a schoolteacher who lived in Islington and had become a long-suffering friend of Jeffrey's. In his column he called her

She Who Would Iron Fourteen Shirts. After some desultory sympathetic exchanges, I left her to it, to hang about until Jeffrey had been interviewed and perhaps charged.

On bail

Back at the Coach at 5.30 opening time, Norman was running the pub, which he did not usually do on Saturday evenings. We went outside into Romilly Street to talk while he leaned against a parked car.

'Did you see any betting? Norman demanded.

'I didn't see any going on,' I replied. I hadn't seen money actually being passed into Jeffrey's hand, though anyone who was not an infant would have understood what was happening. But I was worried about Norman's licence. He thought at that moment that the police would let him off with a warning, and that Jeffrey would get a fine.

Jeffrey himself came in, with Finola, at half past six. He gave some account of events. 'The desk sergeant said: "Sit down, Guv." I said: "My name is Bernard, not Guv." They didn't like that.'

I said that the thing I wouldn't have liked would have been wanting to go to the lavatory.

'Oh, I asked to go, and they wouldn't let me for about twenty minutes. I was bursting,' he said, crossing his legs and grasping his thighs. 'And then they won't let you go on your own. They put a constable there to watch you. The idea is to humiliate you.'

The last thing the police had said before releasing him at the station was: 'Don't write about this, sir.'

Norman loomed round from behind the bar in better humour and ended up buying a round of drinks, not just for Jeffrey and Finola but for all the ten or a dozen regulars in that division of the pub. Norman stalked off and Jeffrey grinned.

He was charged sure enough, under Section 2 of the Betting, Gaming and Lotteries Act 1962, with acting as a bookmaker without holding a bookmaker's licence, and evading betting duty. Having been released on bail, he appeared at Bow Street magistrates' court two days later and a trial was set for a month's time.

In the following week, I found him complaining one lunchtime about a solicitor who had arranged to see him about the case at two o'clock. 'I hate solicitors who make appointments during licensed hours,' he complained to Bookshop Billy, a man who ran some porn shops. Billy rang the solicitor's office, and a few minutes later the solicitor arrived at the Coach to take statements from volunteers. Laurie Doyle, Sandy Fawkes's boyfriend at the time, had already written a letter that said: 'My name is Laurie Doyle. This summer I had a bet with Jeffrey Bernard that India wouldn't win the Test. The stake was a leg of lamb.'

Robertson QC

Extraordinarily, an already famous barrister, Geoffrey Robertson, offered to act as Jeffrey's defence counsel, pro bono. Aged 30, he was known as a brilliant practitioner and was appointed QC a couple of years later.

When the case came to trial, the magistrate showed no signs of pleasure at being lectured by a high-powered barrister who cited rulings by Lord Goddard at him. It didn't help that some of the regulars, who, like me, had come to watch and give moral support, laughed too much and in the wrong places.

The court heard that at 1.40 p.m. on 20 September, Jeffrey had accepted a £2 bet from a Customs and Excise officer on a horse called Irish Passage for the race at Ayr. It won, and the officer recouped £12. Strangely enough, the same officer, on a winning streak, put £2 on Print, the horse that was to come in first in the three o'clock, but, like me, before he could collect his winnings Jeffrey was arrested. Jeffrey had, by the evidence of the Customs men, taken £59 that day, making a profit up to the moment of the raid of £35.

Jeffrey acknowledged that he had annoyed 'the VAT people and the local bookmakers' but insisted that he only 'took bets off friends and acquaintances'. How come, then, the police had asked him during questioning at Vine Street, he had taken bets from Excise men? 'If I have, I must have been pissed at the time. It is quite likely. I hope they got it back on expenses if they lost.'

The Customs surveillance had, it emerged, been going on for three months. They had read in Jeffrey's own column (which was syndicated in *Midweek* magazine) that he took bets in the Coach and Horses. On four separate Saturdays their men had placed bets and had calculated that Jeffrey took total stakes in that time of £389.

Geoffrey Robertson announced in court that Jeffrey had, the evening before, paid the £31.12 betting duty that Customs and Excise said was due to them. The Customs officers had, over three months, attempted to entrap him, the barrister suggested. To add insult to injury, they had won more than they had lost. If he'd been taken outside and cautioned, he'd never have gone on. But it gave the officers rather a pleasant time to go on acting in this way, he said.

Other regulars enjoyed pitting their wits against the defendant, he suggested. The defendant had assumed that the Customs officers were also regulars, and indeed the officers had become regulars themselves by the time the charges were brought. The stakes were coins, not notes. There had been no real profits and no loss to the Revenue, for, as the defendant had said, 'They're really too lazy to walk to the betting shop and desert their drinks.' If they didn't bet with him they wouldn't have gone to the Mecca betting shop. The last horse the officers had backed was called Aid and Abet, and in truth they had been aiding and abetting the defendant.

'Frail and tipsy scribe'

That was the best, perhaps, that could be said by way of mitigation. The maximum fine on summary conviction would have been £2,000. The magistrate said that although the matter was regarded with some levity, the law had to be obeyed. He fined Jeffrey £100 on each of the two charges and ordered him to pay £75 costs within 14 days.

Outside the court Jeffrey told a reporter: 'I expect next March, for the Cheltenham Gold Cup, that the SAS will arrive at the Coach and Horses with stun grenades.' To James Hughes-Onslow from the *Evening Standard*, he said: 'I will now be going to the Coach and Horses to acquire a hangover and to receive bets on England winning the Ashes this winter.'

In the next day's *Daily Telegraph*, Geoffrey Wheatcroft (who had been present in court along with Charles Moore, the editor of the *Spectator*, and Taki Theodoracopulos, its High Life columnist) wrote an entertaining piece next to the leading articles. It concluded with the thought that some sense of proportion should be observed by the police, nine of whom were engaged feeling the collar of a 'frail and tipsy scribe' at a time when 'violent street crime is epidemic'. But two months later, the police who had arrested him invited Jeffrey to the CID Christmas party. Everyone had a good time.

3

Low Life

Five on a bed

It was a cold January evening when Stephen Pickles, a brilliant editor at the publisher Quartet, Diana Lambert the actress and I set off by taxi to Jeffrey Bernard's lodgings in Great Portland Street. Snow had been lying the week before. Jeffrey had asked some people over, to see a programme called *Night and Day* about him in the BBC2 Arena arts series. I think he had an idea that this marked another step in public awareness of him. He had been writing his Low Life column in the *Spectator* for a decade. Unknown, two years ahead, would be the success of the play by Keith Waterhouse, *Jeffrey Bernard is Unwell*, a hit in the West End in 1989.

When we arrived that Friday evening Geraldine Norman wasn't at home in the flat where Jeffrey had a room. He was having a drink there with his friend Finola Morgan and a producer from the programme called Deborah. In truth only half the documentary was devoted to Jeffrey. The *Night* half of it was about Celia Fremlin, a 71-year-old thriller writer, who stalked the streets of London from 11 p.m. to 5 a.m. to lose herself in what she saw as a kingdom magically produced by darkness. Jeffrey's quotidian life represented *Day*.

Finola, with typical generosity, had brought a bottle of champagne, but neither Jeffrey nor Deborah drank it. The rest of us did, with Diana finishing off a spare glass, as well as knocking back whisky. In Jeffrey's room there was only one chair, so to watch the programme Deborah sat on a kitchen chair, Jeffrey and Finola lay on the bed, leaning back on the headboard, Diana and I sat at the foot and Stephen rested sideways between us and Finola.

Taxonomy of queens

Stephen Pickles was in those years the most regular of regulars. He often featured in Michael Heath's cartoon strip by that name in *Private Eye*, identifiable by his shoulder-length hair, not worn in any suggestion of a seventies mullet, but longer than Tennyson's and straighter. Most people called him Pickles, which is what he called himself. Mick Tobin called him Pick. I called him Stephen because I'd known him a little at Oxford. Since then he had published a book called *Queens by Pickles*, a sort of novel, but much more an observational taxonomy of the homosexual scene in the early eighties.

In the years since he had taken up his hyper-regular position, standing at the end of the sweep of the bar in the deep end of the Coach and Horses, Pickles had declared that he was celibate, or 'halibut' as he put it in an unvarying joke. For most of the year he wore a plain dark overcoat when drinking, which hid the thinness of his frame. He stowed his umbrella behind the flap of the counter. His conversation was informed by wide reading and a deep knowledge of music.

If his view of professed gays had been sharply satirical in *Queens*, as the years passed his patience grew thinner and thinner with the young, silly homosexuals that he monitored from his observation post in the Coach. 'They *disgust* me,' he would say to no one in particular. 'Twinks.' As the evening wore on, his impatience with them increased. He only drank bitter beer in the evenings in the Coach – Burton ale – if in great quantities, and he never seemed drunk. Sometimes he was driven to put a curse on more tiresome enemies, a procedure in which a ring that he wore, with an unusual stone on it, played a part. Anyway, Jeffrey liked Pickles, as we all did. Neither of them ever showed fear.

Only three dead

The television film depicted Jeffrey working at home early in the morning with a tumbler of vodka and fresh orange juice. The orange juice came from the fridge by his bed where his phials of insulin were kept. A couple of weeks earlier, Jeffrey and I had been in Dave Potton's pub, the Duke of York, opposite the *Spectator*. Jeffrey said to Dave: 'No, I don't want lime in it. When I was in hospital last year they told me not to drink, but, if I did, to cut out the lime. It's *true*. There's too much sugar in it.'

One television scene showed Jeffrey standing at the bar in the Colony Room Club, calling for two large vodkas and holding up a £50 note. Graham Mason was seen to turn round with his eyes flaming and demand: 'Where the fuck did you get that from?' The documentary was a fair enough representation of everyday life in the Coach. On the rushes of the film, Jeffrey was shown asking the landlord Norman Balon one morning if anything special had happened the night before. 'Nothing special, Sandy was pissed again.'

Walk-on parts were supplied by the stagehands Alan and Jim. They tried to avoid the camera, since they were meant to be working at the time. Tom Baker, still best known from playing the lead in *Doctor Who* from 1974 to 1981, was to be seen at the bar. Francis Bacon was heard saying that he was not the sort of queen to wear make-up. Barney Bates was shown playing the piano at Kettner's. Mrs Balon was seen pottering about at the Coach and Horses.

The least characteristic performance on the screen probably came from Norman himself, who was reserved and nervous. 'Oh, a two-bob bet's about as far as I'm prepared to go,' he was heard to say. That was true of him in those years. His wild days of betting, about which few knew, were over.

Since filming for *Night and Day* had begun, three of the people shown in it had died. One was Bill Simpson, the actor best known for his title role for a decade in *Dr Finlay's Casebook* on television, who appeared in the film slumped drunk in a chair in the Coach and Horses. He had died aged 55. Frank Blake, shown being annoyed by Alfredo the singing doorman at Kettner's, had lasted till 74, despite smoking 60 a day. The third was George Proffer, who had once been trainer of the Olympic wrestling team. It was an average fatal attrition rate for Soho.

At 11 p.m. the programme ended. The phone rang. It was a woman who said she had known Jeffrey 30 years before. She started to abuse him. Then came a telephone call from an admirer. After that, Jeffrey rang the Coach and Horses and put on a pretty convincing villainous voice, like Alec Guinness in *The Horse's Mouth*. 'I want to speak to the guv'nor. Look, you're supposed to be the rudest fucking landlord in London, and I've just seen this programme and you're not fucking rude at all.' At the other end, Norman told him to mind his language. I think he'd twigged.

Radical poverty

At that time I supposed, without thinking about it much, that the Coach and Horses did not suffer the effects of time. In reality, it had reached a frenetic pitch in the later eighties, in which its most famous regular Jeffrey Bernard benefited from a conjunction of favourable influences.

His column in the *Spectator* was called Low Life partly in contrast to the High Life column next to it written by Taki Theodoracopulos, yet they shared interests: women, a drink or

two, even single combat, since Taki held a black belt in karate and
Jeffrey had passed through a phase as a boxer. If anything, Jeffrey
enjoyed more intensely rubbing shoulders with heroes. He
rejoiced in the admiration that Graham Greene had expressed
for his writing, and delighted once in meeting him for lunch in
Antibes.

In a way Jeffrey had come down in the world, hobnobbing
with ne'er-do-wells. His father, Oliver P. Bernard, had succeeded
as a theatrical and opera designer whose foyer for the Strand
Palace Hotel was acquired by the Victoria and Albert Museum
(and stored rather carelessly until its reconstruction for the Art
Deco exhibition of 2003). Having survived the torpedoing of
the *Lusitania* in 1915, Bernard even turned his talents to devising
'dazzle' camouflage for shipping.

What turned Jeffrey to low life was his father's untimely death
when he was seven, and the decision of his mother, née Dora
Hodges, stage name Fedora Roselli, a thwarted opera singer, to
send him to a naval college, against which he rebelled, only to
find Soho waiting with open arms. Jeffrey's mother received
much blame from her sons, but her life descended into tragedy as
they grew up and her alienated daughter fell into mental illness.

Though Jeffrey always declared that 'booze is the main artery
that runs through the low life', there were other characteristics
of it which Jeffrey embraced and Taki could never achieve.
One was homelessness. If Geraldine Norman had not put up
Jeffrey in her flat, he would have had nowhere to go. While
he was there he still sometimes managed to cook for people.
On Grand National Day in 1987, when Geraldine was abroad,
he cooked chicken in a lemon sauce with saffron rice for six
(Jill, his third wife, Finola, Conan, Gordon Smith and me). 'It's
the first time for ages I haven't been pissed by half past two,'
Jeffrey said. He took bets on the racing. Gordon won £35 on
the Grand National, but Jeffrey had won about £280 on it from
his account bookmaker, Victor Chandler.

I got to know regulars who had far fewer than Jeffrey's
precarious resources. This radical poverty formed part of

Soho's radical democracy: no one could buy their way in. The most that was needed was the money for a half of bitter, one's 'entrance ticket'. This democracy was invisible to many outsiders who experienced only the strong forces of exclusion that the place exerted: the carapace of violent verbal resistance of bores.

'This beer's not quite right'

No boundary markers distinguished safety from danger, sleaze from honesty, foe from friend when I had first set my eyes on the Coach and Horses on a Saturday evening after dark. Soho had seemed the City of Dreadful Night then. It was crowded, lit up, bustling and drunken.

But during my next visit, on a weekday, shortly after opening time at half past five, the Coach was quiet enough. I'd come as a stranger in the door in the long side of the pub round the corner of Greek Street in Romilly Street. Next door was the open staircase of a brothel, as the law sternly called any house where more than one prostitute operated.

In the pub the barman pulled me a pint of Burton bitter ale from a brass-mounted pump. The glass was thin, as I liked it, not a chunky dimpled jug with a handle. I sat at a table near the windows of the narrow bar and found that, when I pulled the chair in, it wouldn't quite fit between the table legs, but jogged against them, spilling a little foamy wave of beer on to the black Formica.

I was happy enough with my back to the windows, in a chair with a fold-down red leatherette seat and a curved wooden back that swept down to the floor in a clean line popular between the wars. I took out my book and began to read. *Herself Surprised* it was – the novel by Joyce Carey. A few sips down, the beer tasted unsatisfactory. Held up to the light it looked cloudy. 'Excuse me,' I said to an older man standing behind the counter, hunched over the *Evening Standard*, 'this beer's not quite right.'

'If you don't like it, you can fuck off,' he said, reaching for some change from the pocket of his suit jacket. 'Here's your 73p.'

Like a rush-hour train

That was how I got to know Norman Balon, the landlord of the Coach and Horses. Or, rather, I had got to know who he was. I did fuck off that day, but came back another. The beer wasn't so bad then. I sat down and read and observed the regular but strange comings and goings of the customers.

In came a stocky man who took a bar stool and ordered a large whisky. He was in his sixties, with a weathered face and thick, wavy grey hair. He wore a grey sweater but no shirt under it.

This, I learned later, was Bill Moore, a driver by trade. Most of the time he didn't say much, seeming happy on his own, drinking whisky fairly fast. When he did speak, it wasn't always addressed to anyone in particular. 'A clean bar is a happy bar,' he would say in a rather hoarse Cockney voice that sounded as though he couldn't breathe easily through his nose. He seemed the most amiable of men. On occasion, that was not the case.

Then a woman in her fifties came in through the door from Romilly Street. She, too, took a tall stool at the bar counter, quite close to Bill Moore's, though she neither spoke to him nor caught his eye. She, too, drank whisky. Sandy Fawkes. People were coming in all the time, from Romilly Street behind my back or walking down the length of the bar from the Greek Street entrance.

Quite soon that evening I almost lost sight of Bill Moore, Sandy Fawkes, Bill Mitchell and the other regulars taking up their places at the bar. In a couple of hours it was astonishingly crowded, not just standing-room only, but jammed like a rush-hour Underground train. The air was full of cigarette smoke and voices.

There was no music in the Coach. The people standing had a hard time getting served over the shoulders of the regulars sitting at the bar. To get to the lavatory was an obstacle course of squeezing through gaps, stepping over limbs and nudging, but not nudging an arm holding a drink – or there'd be bellows of anger or worse. As I neared the door of the gents', which opened awkwardly into the room, a thin figure sprawled towards me, grasping like a lobster at the wood panelling. 'Fucking bore,' he spat, glaring at me. It was Graham Mason, a bit drunk.

'I kicked my mother'

One evening not long afterwards, Bill Moore was drinking in the Coach as usual. It was crowded with unknown young people and he left, as I did some time later, going down Romilly Street, where the sound of Chinese people shuffling mah-jong pieces could be heard from open upper windows. By going straight on, crossing Frith Street, then turning right at the end I was brought to the French pub. Same smoke, same crowd of voices, different people. Except that there was Bill Moore, being bought more Scotch by two middle-aged men. I stood at the same end of the pub as he, the one near the stairs. Sandy Fawkes came in.

'I hate her,' Bill Moore said. 'She reminds me of my mother. I hated her.'

He kicked out at Sandy and said: 'Fuck off, you cunt.' She wasn't visibly hurt.

'When I was five,' Bill said, 'I kicked my mother. She was a prostitute.'

Later he began to sing 'The Horst Wessel Song' with the men. Joe the barman told them to be quiet. One of the men said to me: 'You're too nice for Soho. It's hard and cynical. Hard and rough.'

At the end of the counter in his accustomed place stood Sonny, an old black man with white stubble on his chin and long, grey, crinkly hair. Though it wasn't cold, he wore a mac and layers of clothing underneath.

'I've been signing on at Victoria for three months and they still haven't given me any money,' he said. 'How can they expect a man to go straight like that?'

I bought him a half of bitter, Antler, the cheapest. The French only sold beer in half-pint glasses – it was part of the landlord Gaston Berlemont's strategy. Sonny talked about having been born the other side of Oxford Street and of how he now had to go to the dole office in Chadwick Street, near the George V Hostel. He'd make half a pint last until he was bought another. He'd had a row with Norman Balon. 'Norman's been spoilt. I won't go back there. If I want to see my mates, they'll come here. Will you lend me £5 till we meet again?'

'No,' I said.

Bill Moore was standing, unmoving. Sonny asked him for a cigarette. Bill picked up a packet, almost full, and pressed it into his hand.

I realized later it wasn't his but belonged to one of the two strangers.

4

The Office

The Raft of the Medusa — Nightmares of maggots — A drink, a phone and a fag — Private consultation — Photos of the artist — The worst Christmas — Room with a view

The Raft of the Medusa

Was I too nice for Soho? What was I to make of it all? Bill Moore, I discovered, slept each night in the office of the man he worked for as a driver. It was said that his unhappy side was connected to his escape from a prisoner-of-war camp, which involved having to kill a man. Where Sonny slept, who knew? They remained in Soho by dogged perseverance. Certainly niceness was no term of approval round here.

One lunchtime by way of conversation, Alan Holmes, a thin, dark-haired man with a slight hesitancy of speech who worked as a stagehand, said: 'My landlady's changing the locks today, as I haven't paid the rent.'

'Where will you live, then?'

'I have nowhere to go. I'm working at the English National Opera today and tomorrow, and I might be able to sleep there. It's driving me to drink.' He laughed, as he'd long said that he was an alcoholic.

Sometimes the Coach and Horses seemed like the Raft of the Medusa, crowded with survivors clinging on.

Nightmares of maggots

One Saturday afternoon, after opening at 5.30, the bar was quite full by five to six. The matinee had just come out of the musical *Chess*, which was just beginning its three-year run at the Prince Edward Theatre. One of the orders for the harassed barman from the matinee crowd was for nine halves of bitter.

Jeffrey, who had disappeared before the end of the morning session, was there again. Michael Heath, the cartoonist who worked in the same room as I did at the *Spectator*, and drew cartoons every day of his life, had concluded he wasn't going to do much more work that evening and was there, too, standing near the flap of the bar, drinking a strong kind of bottled Löwenbräu that was generally referred to as Blue, from its label. Norman served it in round-bowled, stemmed glasses. Bill Moore was there, too, Stephen Pickles and Alan Holmes, who'd been doing a shift at the Coliseum. We sat at the table near the lavatory.

'Drink, Jeff?' I asked.

'No, I'm going home to make some smoked herring soup. Shona Crawford Poole had the recipe in her column in *The Times* this morning. Actually, I don't approve of Shona Crawford Poole. I rang her once with an idea for an article, and do you know what she said? "Send me something you've written." Can you believe it? I mean, I don't trust anyone who doesn't read the *Spectator*.'

'I don't even trust a lot of people who do,' I said. He smiled one of those engaging smiles that he had when he was amused and wanted to show it.

Jenny Mulherin came in. She was a publisher, then in her forties, small, sharp and Antipodean. She lived in Soho and had saved from homelessness the permanent fixture Ian Dunlop. Dunlop was tall, thin, silver-haired, hook-nosed and distinguished-looking, speaking with a public school accent. He had been a friend of Charles da Silva, the con man, and spoke well of Peter Rachman, the property racketeer who became a byword in the fifties as a slum landlord. By the eighties, he seemed to have no means of support and spent his days smoking and drinking wine, mostly in the French. He died at the age of 83, outliving Jenny. She was usually to be found in the French, having been barred from the Coach for some reason. With her on this day was Janice, who also lived in Soho. They were both drunk.

Jenny said to Jeffrey: 'Your brothers are better than you. Bruce and Oliver. Both of them.'

Jeffrey said: 'In that case, don't fucking speak to me, then. Do you want me to hit you in the face?'

Jenny turned to me and asked me to buy her a half of Guinness. I said: 'No.' Bill Moore bought her one, and then two more. By then she was singing songs. She spilt her glass of Guinness down her dress and Bill's right leg. Michael the barman asked her to go home. Janice got her to go, protesting, but stayed herself.

Bill went on about how disgusting women were who couldn't hold their drink. Michael asked Janice again to go home. She disappeared into the ladies' lavatory. After a few minutes a search party was sent in. Bertie, a second-hand bookseller, failed to raise her. Stephen Pickles assumed responsibility and returned after a while supporting her. Some regulars, disregarding any temptation to human empathy, broke into applause.

By now the pub was full of strangers. Jeffrey was still quite lucid and still looking forward to his cooking. He must have done the shopping between chucking-out time at 3.20 p.m. (with the twenty minutes drinking-up time) and 5.30, afternoon opening time. At about nine o'clock he left for home.

Heath, Alan Holmes and I discussed how much Jeff was drinking.

'It can't be all that much,' I said, 'because he was drinking at about the same rate as me from twelve to three.'

'Yeah, but he'd have started at home,' Heath said. 'And then from eleven he'd have been getting down to it seriously. I think he gets through quite a bit.'

'I reckon it's one and a half or two bottles of vodka a day,' said Alan.

'It's got to be,' Heath agreed.

'Oh,' I said. 'That is quite a bit. Perhaps that's why he has nightmares of maggots eating him alive. But he said the other day that his greatest fear was going to prison. It's the other prisoners he's frightened of. Beating him up.'

'Jeffrey used not to come into the Coach much,' Heath said. 'He'd drink in the French and the Swiss. I always found the French an unfriendly pub. Now he always drinks in the Coach during licensing hours because he knows the newspapers will find him there.'

A drink, a phone and a fag

It was not always a convenient office. A few months later I found Jeffrey in the Coach just after afternoon opening time. He was with Finola Morgan. He went over to the phone to file his copy for the *Sunday Mirror*. I bought drinks. Jeffrey shouted to Finola for a drink and a cigarette, which she supplied. A couple of minutes later he shouted for a match. Finola said: 'I haven't got any.' Jeffrey broke off from dictating to say: 'Well, fucking *buy* some.'

She did buy some and threw them over to him. As he had the telephone receiver in one hand and a typescript and a glass of vodka in the other, he dropped them. He shouted: 'You are the most fucking annoying woman I've ever met.'

Eileen, the barmaid, went over and lit his cigarette. I said: 'You're giving in to moral blackmail.'

After filing his copy, Jeffrey came over and said to Finola: 'You're so fucking annoying, I don't ever want to speak to you again.' Then they kissed and had another drink.

Private consultation

The Coach was sometimes useful for getting other business done. One lunchtime Jeffrey said: 'Oh, good, there's Neil. I'm going to ask him to go into the lavatory with me and have a look at my cock. I think I've got thrush.'

Neil was a doctor of Antipodean origins and bohemian sympathies. He was a painter on the quiet. When Jeffrey came back from the inspection, he confirmed he'd got an infection. 'You know, Neil's very good. He'll hold consultations in any pub or club. One day Dan Farson was in the Colony. He'd been fucked by the son of some minister in Turkey and thought he might have caught something. So he went into the lavatory with Neil. But then he said: "No, you don't understand. It's not my cock, it's my arse." Neil shot out of there like a greyhound.'

A couple of days later, Jeffrey said: 'I've got a prescription from a very nice lady doctor. When she looked at my cock, she said: "Oh, that's interesting." I felt like saying: "Well, it's been in some interesting places." When Neil looked at it, he showed no interest, or disgust or anything. I suppose when you've seen a few hundred, there's not much in it.'

Diana Lambert came in, and called across the bar: 'How's your cock?'

A man at the bar said: 'Did she say cough?'

'No,' I said.

Photos of the artist

When strangers and admirers met Jeff in the Coach they would sometimes say, 'Are you Jeffrey Bernard?' pronouncing the surname like the St Bernard dog. He would say, with a loud sforzando: 'B'*nard*.' He was proud of a small quiver of facts: that his mother was an opera singer (albeit a thwarted one); that he had first made a betting book at school at Pangbourne when he was 15; that he had been a boxer; that he had 500 books on the shelves of his lodgings. 'They'll be worth a bob or two,' he would say. 'When I die you can sell them and have a party.'

Jeffrey used his own knowledge of history, music, art and literature as part of his verbal armoury. He was aware that after spending a few pleasurable days in the company of a young woman he would find himself 'snapping', as he called it. He'd suddenly exclaim: 'And what the fuck do you know about David Hockney, you stupid bitch.' Sometimes, before the broadside, there would be a warning shot, one of the most ominous of which was the question: 'Do you know what the worst thing about you is?'

He had a cast of heroes: boxers, jockeys, writers and Nelson. Byron was also among the heroes, and Jeffrey made his own life an audition for the role of Byronic hero.

In Jeffrey's room at Geraldine Norman's flat there were framed photographs covering a whole wall: Jeffrey with Graham Greene; Jeffrey with Lester Piggott; a very young Jeffrey; Jeffrey with Peter Arthy; Jeffrey in Red Square; John Deakin's photograph of Jeffrey with his brother Bruce and Terry Jones outside a boxing gym; Jeffrey with Francis Bacon; Jeffrey with his little daughter; Jeffrey with Richard Ingrams and Martin Tomkinson striding down Greek Street; Jeffrey at prep school; Jeffrey with Keith Waterhouse. At a party at the flat once, a woman asked Bruce Bernard whether this was Jeffrey's room. 'Either that,' he replied, 'or someone who likes him very much.'

Homelessness had come to Jeffrey as a counterpart to freedom, when he left his mother's house in 1948 at the age of 16 after his school career had come to an end. He had already been introduced to Soho at the age of 14 by his brothers Oliver and Bruce, and now found that he could not hang around there and also pay the £3 a week rent for his lodgings. He took odd jobs as a labourer, or washing up, or working night shifts at a baker's, but it was John Minton, then aged 30, who rescued him from complete shipwreck.

Minton was teaching painting at the Royal College of Art. With a frivolous energy that failed to hide a sad loneliness, Minton was generous and gregarious and addicted to Soho. He had some family money on top of his salary and he had a place to live, at Hamilton Terrace in St John's Wood. He sought promiscuous pleasure with rough trade, 'sailors mostly', but enjoyed the company of good-looking young men.

Jeffrey went with him to the cinema and ate with him in restaurants. He often found a place to sleep at Hamilton Terrace, as did many others of Minton's circle. Minton gave Jeffrey ten shillings a week, apart from irregular gifts. He took him to Paris and in 1949 they went to Spain, to Granada and Barcelona. Jeffrey Bernard's biographer, Graham Lord, spent some pages speculating on Jeffrey's sexuality.

There is no doubt about his heterosexual drive, and pleasing Minton required little more than being good-looking, intelligent and charming, which Jeffrey was. In later years Jeffrey did mention spanking elderly men for money. But that was not Minton's thing, and Bobby Hunt, who first met Minton at Camberwell aged 14 in 1943 and worked on and off as his assistant till Minton's death in 1957, declared that 'buggery was the one thing he hated'. So, that at least was not expected.

The worst Christmas

For Sohoites, Christmas could be difficult. Norman Balon was one of the few landlords who opened his pub on Christmas Day. Being Jewish, he hardly celebrated the day, but he did feel sympathy for customers who spent money in his pub every day. He gave all the regulars a little present. In the eighties it was generally a mug with a drawing on it by Michael Heath of Norman in the act of barring someone. Naturally it was inscribed 'London's Rudest Landlord'. The mug was a different colour each year.

Jeffrey, if he hadn't wangled a freebie in some sunny spot, would make an appearance. One year he said: 'Do you know what my worst Christmas was?' It was in 1949, after the summer tour of Spain with John Minton. Rather than go back to see his mother, Jeffrey preferred to spend Christmas on his own. He woke on Christmas morning in cubicle No. 1064 at Rowton House in Camden Town.

Rowton House was a dosshouse of an unusual kind. Rather than being under local authority or charitable administration it was run on a loosely commercial footing, an arrangement devised by the first and last Lord Rowton, who died in 1903, having provided lodgings for 5,000 men at 6d a night in a chain of Rowton houses and turning a small profit. The Rowton House in Camden Town was a behemoth, with six floors accommodating 1,163 cubicles, each with a bed, chair, shelf and openable window.

Jeffrey might have enjoyed turning the dosshouse Christmas (with a solitary sprig of mistletoe in the dining room) into an absurdly sentimental tale, but none of the Bernard brothers were strangers to desperate lodgings. Jeffrey's elder brother Bruce had lived at Rowton House when he was working as a labourer and many of the single men living at Camden Town were Irishmen working on building sites or digging holes in the road. Bruce found the hardest thing to get used to at Rowton House was the lavatories. Anyway, 1949 was the last Christmas Jeffrey had to avoid spending with his mother, since she died the next year, aged 54.

Looking back, he would sometimes say that he really fancied his mother. Sometimes he said he couldn't stand her. He said that her death set him free. But when she died he suffered a temporary attack of alopecia. In a *Spectator* column written in the form of his own obituary he wrote: 'Some even said that his life was a never-ending cliché of a search for his mother.'

If Christmas 1949 was a low point, September 1951 must have been a close rival. It was back to Rowton House after his army national service had ended with a discharge that he had engineered by a feigned suicide attempt. 'Then I told them I wanted to be a writer,' he would say as he told the tale sitting at the bar 35 years later. 'Do you know what they put in my pay book? They stamped it: "Mental stability, NIL".' With only labouring jobs, Rowton House was the alternative to kipping during the day at friends and spending all night in Lyons Corner Houses. Suddenly he met Anna Grice again, whom he'd known four years earlier. He was 19; she was 22. They were married a fortnight later.

Room with a view

In 1988 Jeffrey moved into an attic flat in Covent Garden belonging to one of his oldest friends, Pete Arthy, with whom, in 1949, he had worked setting up and taking down dodgems for a travelling funfair.

For months he'd been hopping from one temporary lodgings to another since Geraldine Norman had asked him to leave the room in her flat in Great Portland Street. What spurred her to act was opening his bank statement by mistake while he was away in Tenerife and finding that he had £13,500 in his current account. 'If he wanted, he could afford a suite at the Ritz.'

She wrote a piece for the *Spectator* about why she felt she had to part company with her lodger of six years. It was never published, because Jeffrey did not like it when shown a copy. It wasn't the burning saucepans on the stove when she returned in the evening that she minded, but Jeffrey's unhappiness. 'He pours out abuse when he's drunk. Never at me, but at his girls or his friends,' she wrote. 'I love him and wish him well, but I couldn't live in his black cloud any longer.'

Some friends helped him move. I saw him in the Coach afterwards. By one o'clock he was pretty pissed, and annoyed that he was tired and pissed so soon in the day. We were talking about how to pick a good artichoke in the market. 'The little ones are more tender,' he said.

Ron Lucas (nicknamed by Graham Mason 'Edith Head' after the American costume designer), a theatrical wardrobe master who smoked with a long cigarette holder, was sitting on a tall stool close by and said: 'And of course the little ones are very tender.'

'I've just fucking *said* that,' Jeffrey shouted. He left at five past one.

Jeffrey's new lodgings in Endell Street were at the top of a steep staircase that climbed from the street door to the third floor. It was a daunting ascent for his wasted thighs, and a daily invitation to fall backwards with drunken balance and diabetic light-headedness, down, down, till his head struck a sharp stair-edge. That, by luck, he avoided.

He was still capable of cooking a rare Sunday lunch then. It was remarkable to see him, fairly drunk and very weak, swing the saucepans on and off the gas. It was chicken and rice and a chicory and lettuce salad that day, then apple pie (from Marks & Spencer). 'We were going to have lamb chops,' he said, 'but Pete's cat found how to open the fridge and ate them, and then vomited them up on the drawing-room carpet.' Jeffrey's capable and long-suffering friend Finola had cleaned it up.

From his lofty windows, through the tops of the plane trees, Jeffrey could make out at night the lights of the nearby St Paul's Genito-Urinary Hospital. This was his nightly view for the rest of the eighties.

The French Pub

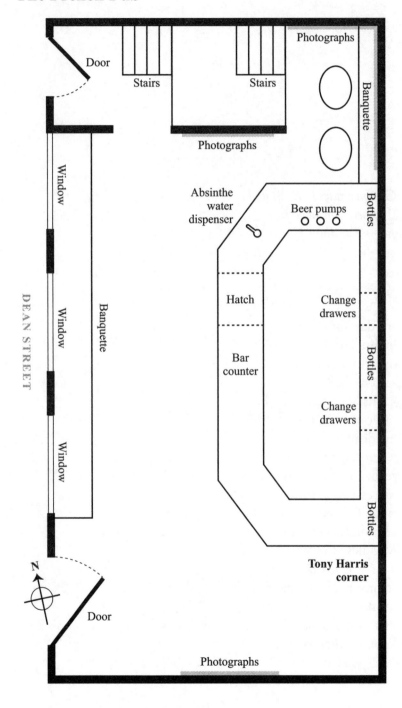

5

The French

Gaston's rules

By day, the French pub in Dean Street seemed genial and well mannered. In the narrow bar, where the sun at lunchtime lit up the clouds of tobacco smoke, Gaston Berlemont, the landlord, kissed the hand of a young woman customer, his handlebar moustache tickling her skin. 'Madame, I should like to see more of you,' he said, pausing for a moment, as if only then aware of his double entendre.

He was sending himself up, no doubt. I was beginning to realize that he was widely liked as a pub landlord for more than his essential role of cashing cheques. He'd been there a long time. Everyone knew that he had been born upstairs in the pub. (Though everyone was wrong, since, in fact, he was born in the Middlesex Hospital, on 26 April 1914.)

It was his father, Victor, who brought in the rule about only selling beer in half-pints. It filtered the clientele and brought in money from the wine that he bottled himself and sold instead. His other rule was to treat everyone with courtesy. Gaston kept to that rule, too. If a woman was too drunk, he would say: 'Madame, I look forward to seeing you again – tomorrow.'

47

Oddities had survived from Victor's day: a glass water-dropper that screwed into the bar, with brass nozzles to dilute absinthe (an apparatus once present on the bar of the Fitzroy, too); a vertical file of little brass drawers to supply change. But there was no one-armed bandit in the pub and no music, of course. Like the Coach it was a conversation pub, even if the conversation, unlike Gaston, was not always polite.

Like the Coach, the French was radically democratic. It took in painters and writers, ex-boxers, failed publishers, working prostitutes, old models, old poofs, stagehands, grocers, pornographers, photographers and a retired lamplighter. To some it seemed a club (because they felt like members); to others it was hostile (because they felt excluded).

The tiny society that ebbed and flowed into Soho daily might ignore some of the laws of the land and most customs of suburban life, but it had plenty of its own unwritten rules. Calling the French by the right name, for example, assumed totemic importance. In 1914, gold letters on the glass fascia had christened it 'Victor Berlemont'. (The new establishment had no connection with Chez Victor, the restaurant on the other side of Shaftesbury Avenue, founded in 1901.) The brewers who later owned the freehold called it the York Minster. That is what long-term Sohoites like Oliver Bernard, who drank there before the Second World War, still called it 70 years later. Then the brewers renamed it the French House. No Soho regular ever called it that. It was the French pub, or just the French.

'Gaston Berlemont was born in Belgium,' Graham Mason would say in his mocking way, picked up from John Deakin, perhaps, the photographer who'd been dead for a decade. That wasn't true, though the Berlemont family was once Belgian. Nor was it true that in 1940 General de Gaulle wrote his broadcast appeal to the French after lunch in the upstairs dining room. By the 1980s, the dining room was closed, but a laminated card bearing twin tricolours and a message headed A TOUS LES FRANÇAIS hung on the wall of the bar. Near it was a jokey plaque giving the average age reached by *buveurs d'eau* compared with *buveurs de vin*, which was naturally far higher.

Behind glass

Far better were the old photographs mounted on the walls in shallow glass display cases. There was Victor Berlemont himself in 1923 with (it couldn't be denied) more luxuriant and curlier moustaches than Gaston, standing, one leg crossed in front of the other, dressed in a three-piece suit, with a bow tie, to welcome to England, with other gents in hats, the boxer Georges Carpentier, looking shy in a leather overcoat. He had come for his fight with Joe Beckett, whom he knocked out in the first round.

There were signed photographs from Les Perrotys, whoever they were, and dancing girls and acrobats. Other photos were signed by comedians in evening dress and banjo players in black face, by Primo Carnera, the boxer (whose younger brother Secondo was to work in the Caves de France further up Dean Street), and by Lilian Dredge, who in 1938 set the cycling record for the 869 miles from Land's End to John o' Groats of three days, 20 hours and 54 minutes. They seemed unchangeable. When Gaston retired in 1989, his successor acquired copies, which faded. When the stairs were rebuilt some of the display cases went, too.

Cashing cheques

Gaston Berlemont collected customers as his father had collected those photographs. He was a discerning judge of character. He'd known Jeffrey Bernard since, like Bruce, he had put in time labouring on the site in Dean Street on which Kemble House was being built where a bomb had flattened St Anne's church and the adjoining buildings. 'He bore a kind of mystic aura,' Gaston told Graham Lord 40 years later, 'an aura of being important, which of course he was not.'

Gaston knew the psychology of inclusion and exclusion. He knew the quickest way to ensure that you never saw people again was to lend them money. So, when he lent money, as he did, he took care to say: 'Pay it back when you can, but don't stop coming to see me.' He cashed cheques even if you said: 'Don't pay it in too soon, will you?' Soon my chequebook stubs acquired a certain consistency. Jeffrey Bernard despised people who filled in chequebook stubs, because not doing so annoyed the tax people, and the police, he said. But I did fill in mine: '20 July N Balon £50. 24 July J Bernard £50. 25 July N Balon £50. 25 July G Berlemont £50.'

Not acting blind

If King George II really did say 'I hate all bainters and boets', he wouldn't have liked the French pub. They did not need to be sought out; their steady availability was taken for granted.

One lunchtime I popped into the French and John Heath-Stubbs was there drinking with Canadian Jo and her other half, Brendan. They were a remarkable trio: she tall and pale with big hands but a soft face that looked as though she might have been crying; Brendan shorter and ruddy with a thick black beard and bushy eyebrows. John, as tall as Jo, was grey-haired, dressed in a tweed jacket, his bony brow raised as if to listen the better. She was a legal shorthand writer, Brendan a postman, John a poet. He was blind, but he did not act like it. It was his 70th birthday. There had been a piece about him in that morning's *Guardian*.

After a bit we walked over to the Coach, as the French in those years was without a restaurant and John was hungry. He carried a stick, but not a white one. It was more like a cudgel. He walked with us, fearless of street excavations and dogs on leads. It was this courageous refusal to be beaten by blindness that made him do his own shopping in Bayswater, where the local shopkeepers knew him and supplied his regular goods.

From the French we walked down Romilly Street, past La Capannina (where Conan Nicholas had once taken a friend for lunch and, thinking the bill too steep, had stolen a bottle of Calvados as compensation, wrapped in a jersey). Past a wholesale suppliers of restaurant ware that sold extraordinarily cheap plates and glasses and tablecloths by the dozen. Past Kettner's, where Oscar Wilde had often dined, which retained a faded air of high bohemia and in the eighties, under Peter Boizot, provided a refuge on Sunday afternoons, when even the drinking clubs were closed. It did seem a grand setting to eat bacon, egg and chips and share a bottle of wine.

On the way, John sang 'Champagne Charlie' in consideration of the celebratory champagne they had been drinking in the French. It was not unusual to drink champagne in the French, but it was in the Coach, where we switched to still white wine.

John ate toasted cheese sandwiches. He said it reminded him of the rat in John Masefield's *The Midnight Folk*. He recited some of Edith Sitwell's *Façade*. I was able to join in because by chance I had learned this poetry sequence by heart. I was surprised to find anyone who had done the same, especially a well-regarded poet, for Edith Sitwell was in the eighties regarded rather sniffily by poetry-reading types. I didn't realize then that she had encouraged John when he was a young poet, inviting him to lunch at the Sesame Club when she was in London.

John mentioned that he'd first been to the French 54 years before, which would make it 1934 and him 16. It was in 1941, while he was still an undergraduate (on a scholarship offered to someone blind or losing his sight) that Herbert Read, the poetry reader to the publishers Routledge, brought out *Eight Oxford Poets*. John was one of the eight. The editors were Michael Meyer and Sidney Keyes. John remembered it as an enterprise in a dark moment for the world in which the eight shared a feeling that: 'We cannot save ourselves without some form of spiritual readjustment.' Philip Larkin, then at Oxford, was not invited to contribute.

Of the eight, Sidney Keyes was killed in North Africa in 1943 and Drummond Allison was killed in Italy later that year. Keith Douglas was killed in Normandy three days after D-Day. This made a big hole in the romantic Oxford poets (as they were seen) of the forties.

Twenty years on, in his preface to a new edition of *The North Ship*, Larkin remembered looking through a copy of *Cherwell* in Blackwell's bookshop in the forties and reading John's poem 'Leporello'. 'I had never heard of Leporello,' he recalled. 'And what kind of poetry was this – who was he copying?' In the preface to his own *Collected Poems*, published in 1988, John brought up Larkin's remark. When I asked him about it, he said he disliked Larkin as a man and as a poet: 'He's against life.'

'I expect you have heard'

That had been on another day, at Sunday lunch with the same two friends, Jo and Brendan, in their council flat in a lovely house from the 1840s in Percy Circus, near King's Cross. John Heath-Stubbs was at ease. He ate Brendan's roast lamb appreciatively, feeling delicately with his fingertips for the meat, peas and potatoes. His clothes were in a bad state and his tie filthy with food. But he was patient and chatty. When I asked him by chance what he'd put in *Who's Who* as his hobby, he said 'Taxonomy', and laughed. But it was true, and it said something about his poetry.

He signed Jo's copy of his *Collected Poems* and wrote for her a line from one of them, though he had by then no sight at all. Jo put on an LP of the thirties musical *Me and My Girl*, which John had reviewed when it was new. Now he said he liked in particular the solicitor's song: 'Say a little and think a little, / And eat a little and drink a little. / Keep a drop of the ninety-four / For the Family Solicitor.' By the time I left at about five, we'd got through ten bottles of wine between the four of us.

As well as Larkin, Heath-Stubbs was prepared to dislike quite a few people in Soho, too. One was John Deakin. 'To be frank I didn't really like him very much,' he replied in a letter answering an enquiry about Deakin after his death. 'I expect you have heard the tragic story of his death. He went into the Golden Lion and asked for a gin, which he drank at one go, but unfortunately the barman had given him bleach, which had been kept in an old gin bottle. He was taken to hospital.' The story was absolutely untrue and unfounded. Was it a joke by Heath-Stubbs or by someone who helped him with administrative tasks and might have typed it and got him to sign it? Or perhaps it was a story too good to disbelieve.

'Booze and the blowens'

John Heath-Stubbs was coupled in my mind with David Wright (who appears, wearing a college scarf, in a photograph by Daniel Farson, standing next to Deakin and John Davenport). They were both poets and had met at Oxford. As far as Soho went, John refused to be kept away by his blindness, and David Wright courageously ignored the isolating effect of his complete deafness. Looking back 45 years to 1947, in reviewing Graham Lord's biography of Jeffrey Bernard, David remembered: 'I first met him, a wildly charismatic urchin standing outside the Black Horse in Rathbone Place supping halves of bitter smuggled out by one or other of the poets and painters and pederasts there foregathered.'

It was T. S. Eliot who had commissioned John Heath-Stubbs to edit *The Faber Book of Twentieth-Century Verse*, and he then asked David Wright to compile it with him. It came out in 1953. But three years earlier they had published together under John

Lehmann's imprint an anthology of poetry written between 1824 (the death of Byron) and 1909 (the death of both Swinburne and Meredith). This volume was suitably called *The Forsaken Garden*. In 1950, poetry from the reigns of George IV, William IV and Victoria lay undisturbed by readers.

The anthology ends with W. E. Henley's lines about Death as the ruffian on the stair. But another poem by Henley in the anthology, written in 1887, suggests a taste of the Soho that the editors had discovered, transplanted from François Villon's Paris. Inspired by the '*Ballade de bonne doctrine à ceux de mauvaise vie*', Henley, rather than translating it, constructs a bravura battery of sometimes baffling argot. Its verses deploy specimens that would soon find their way into the dictionary *Slang and its Analogues Past and Present*, which he enjoyed compiling with J. S. Farmer in the last decade of his life.

> *Fiddle, or fence, or mace, or mack;*
> *Or moskeneer, or flash the drag;*
> *Dead-lurk a crib, or do a crack;*
> *Pad with a slang, or chuck a fag;*
> *Bonnet, or tout, or mump and gag;*
> *Rattle the tats, or mark the spot;*
> *You can not bank a single stag:*
> *Booze and the blowens cop the lot.*

In this, *mace* is 'to cheat'; *mack* 'to pimp'. *Moskeneer* is 'to pawn an article for more than its true value', though how you accomplish that, I don't know. *Flash the drag* is, for a man, 'to display himself in women's clothing'. *Dead-lurk a crib* is 'to break into a house while the people are at church'. *Crack* is simply 'to housebreak'. *Pad with a slang* is 'to take to the road with a hawker's licence'. *Chuck a fag* is 'to give a beating'; *bonnet* is 'to pull down someone's hat over their eyes'. *Mump* is 'to sponge' and *gag* is 'to deceive'. *Tats* are 'dice', especially loaded ones. *Mark the spot* is something to do with billiards. *Stag* is 'shilling', though I don't know why. And *blowens* are wenches, trulls or brasses. As Villon put it, *Tout aux tavernes et aux filles* – 'Booze and the blowens cop the lot'.

A quiet night out

David Wright persevered in his refusal to let his total deafness stop him swimming in the shark-thick sea of Soho, where he couldn't even hear the warning splash of a fin breaking the surface before the snap of a pair of jaws. He had no illusions about the danger of deafness making his presence boring once the initial helpfulness of interlocutors had worn off. 'It is important not to embarrass people with one's disability,' he wrote, 'or you find yourself a drag on people's enjoyment.'

That realistic judgement comes in his remarkable book *Deafness*. 'Deafness is of course very much a nuisance and its disadvantages are severe,' he acknowledged. 'Yet, after forty years of what we will term silence, I am so accommodated to it (like a hermit-crab to its shell) that were the faculty of hearing restored to me tomorrow it would appear an affliction rather than a benefit.' It would be, he said, like having a hand cut off.

So he would stand at the bar of the Coach or the French pub talking and fairly often making that strangulated kind of laugh that deaf people can be given to. He lipread. He said he wasn't very good at it, and that it often led to slapstick misapprehensions. To a lipreader, the words baby and paper are indistinguishable, so once when his wife asked, 'Where's the baby?' he replied: 'I put it in the dustbin.'

Anyway, no matter how good he was at lipreading, he couldn't lipread me, because of my beard. We therefore spoke by means of conversation books, like Beethoven. They were just gatherings of paper. I wish I'd kept them.

One morning, after a particularly acrimonious shouting match in the pub the night before, he said, 'Well, it seemed very quiet to me.' It was David Wright who persuaded me that Portugal was the place to visit. I'd been cautious because I was unfamiliar with the language. He quailed at no such difficulty.

The Tony Harris Corner

If these two poets represented highbrow bohemia, then the lowbrow flag in the French was planted firmly by Tony Harris. He stood drinking retsina at the end of the bar opposite to the lavatory staircase, which the Soho veteran Stephen Fothergill identified as the shallow end. In the sixties Harris tried to make a book on who would be the next person to die in Soho, and installed Jeffrey Bernard as the 6-4 favourite. Like many favourites, Jeffrey proved slow in coming home.

Eventually someone affixed Harris's photograph to the panelling above the spot where he always stood. It showed him as a major in the Royal Artillery in 1941, seven years after he first set foot in the French. Some amused graphic artist among the pub regulars periodically adorned the glass on it with black felt-tip pen, transforming his likeness into that of a cavalier with curly wig and feathered hat, or Kitchener or Colonel Gaddafi. Below the image was printed in capital letters: TONY HARRIS CORNER.

Harris tried harder than most people to become a Soho character. He brought props. He would actually arrive with cuttings from a distant year in a large brown-paper envelope and proceed to read bits out to the nearest drinker. He seemed oblivious to his own absurdity. In that, he resembled Jay Landesman, the lecherous American publisher. I'm afraid I took it for granted that Landesman should be openly laughed at. Tony Harris just had to be kept at a distance, which was easy as he never budged.

He spoke with an accent one notch beyond the journalist and broadcaster Alan Whicker's. His dark hair was oiled and neatly parted. He would wear blazers with brass buttons and a cravat. On hot days a safari jacket with pockets and a broad belt would be brought out. He wore slacks. There was some stage business with a cigarette, such as the tamping of the tobacco against the bar with a few deft taps. Perhaps he hid a life story of deep human endeavour and feeling, but if so he hid it successfully. He was not what Soho was meant to be about. He was a bore.

The man in the mac

Someone that I associate with the French pub, too, is the photographer Harry Diamond, though he was once barred for throwing a glass with some beer in it at Gaston Berlemont. He is the man in the mac in Lucian Freud's *Interior at Paddington* (painted in 1951), with a cigarette in one hand and the other clenched. That was the year he cropped up in Oliver Bernard's diary on a night of rain as they waited in the Lyons Corner House for the 3.33 a.m. bus.

He was still wearing a mac, if not necessarily the same one, in the eighties, when he was turning 60. The mac had also appeared in a photograph by Herb Greer on the dust jacket of Frank Norman's autobiographical novel *Stand On Me* (1959) with Harry looking up at the author (for he was a short man), with his head turned away from the viewer.

A number of Harry Diamond's photographs were acquired by the National Portrait Gallery – Bacon and Freud together in the middle of the road outside the French, with Gamba's ballet shoe shop behind them on the corner of Old Compton Street, and a forceful self-portrait shot in the reflection of a Soho window.

Another photograph of him in the eighties, also in the NPG, taken by Michael Woods, caught him off guard, tipping his hat in a farewell. He was an East Ender and alarmingly aggressive in attitude. Steve Walsh, who printed his photographs, said that he never spoke but always shouted. He nursed resentments and never had a bank account.

When John Pilgrim gave him work looking after his evening bookstall outside Foyle's, he found he was cashing cheques for dubious characters. Colin MacInnes, the author of *Absolute Beginners*, told everyone how delighted he had been to find the only place you could cash a cheque at midnight.

Bruce Bernard respected Harry Diamond's photography, and, what was harder, his personality. He was not without friends. Rose Boyt, Lucian Freud's daughter, remembered how Harry Diamond used to come for a bath every now and then, since his lodgings at the time in Leman Street had no bathroom: 'He always left my bathroom a bit cleaner than he had found it.' He also gave her a photograph of herself, her father and her brother Alexander.

Although conversation was the *raison d'être* of the French pub, in the crush and noise of chatter it was quite possible to drink companionably without talking. I don't think I ever had a conversation with Harry Diamond, not knowing what to say, but I might well have bought him a half of bitter.

6

Jeffrey's Coat

The extreme − By Grand Central Station − The Sacred Ancestors −
Left on the slab − Elastic glue − Boozer's economics − The noise of snow

The extreme

Jeffrey Bernard did once perform what should be called an act
of kindness. He bought an overcoat as a gift. It was for Graham
Mason. Graham had not sought his reputation as the drunkest
man in the Coach and Horses. Unlike Jeffrey, he did not make
himself the hero of his own tragedy. His speciality was the
extreme.

In one drinking binge he went for nine days without food.
At the height of his consumption, before he was frightened by
epileptic fits into cutting back, he was managing two bottles
of vodka a day. His face became in his own description that
of a 'rotten choirboy'. By 1988 he was in his mid-forties, but
naturally looked older.

Graham was a fearsome sight at his most drunkenly irascible.
Seated at the bar, his thin shanks wrapped round the legs of a
high stool, he would swivel his reptilian stare behind him to
any unfortunate stranger standing there attempting to be served,
and snap: 'Who the fuck are you?' Sometimes this prompted a
reaction, and, on one occasion, a powerful blow to the head sent
him flying, with his stool, across the carpet. Painfully clawing
himself upright, he set the stool in its place, reseated himself,

and, twisting his head round again, growled: 'Don't you ever do that again.'

His irascibility – with other people, the world and himself – must have had more roots than alcohol alone. As a devotee of *Tristram Shandy*, he sometimes attributed his abrasive character to having been conceived on a sand dune. That was in Cape Province in 1941. For the past 25 years he had made his home in Soho. Michael Heath often featured Graham in his strip cartoon The Regulars, in *Private Eye*. In one episode Graham is shown apologising for being so rude the night before: 'You see, I was sober.'

Within a couple of hours one evening in February 1988 he had loud altercations with John Hurt ('You're just a bad actor'); with a law writer nicknamed the Red Baron ('You know I don't like you. Go away and leave me alone'); and with Jeffrey Bernard (who stood up and shook him by the lapels).

By Grand Central Station

It says something about him and about Soho that he made many friends, upon some of whom, from time to time, he relied for his very survival. One was Elizabeth Smart, a Canadian, like him a colonial refugee. In 1945 she had published *By Grand Central Station I Sat Down and Wept*, a book about George Barker, the poet, by whom she had, I think, four children without winning his undivided love, since he ended up fathering 15 children by a succession of women, five of them by his eventual wife, Elspeth, whom he'd met in 1963. I never managed to sort out in my mind where all the Barker children fitted in.

George Barker suffered from emphysema in the 1980s and was not in evidence in Soho, but Elizabeth Smart was. When she started a conversation with me early one evening in the Coach, I had no idea who she was. Her appearance was certainly interesting, her face cragged, her eyes pouched, but her fair hair still thick. Her transatlantic accent and readiness to talk of feelings made me cautious. I thought she might be a tourist and pest. So I missed a chance to know her better. Anyway, she died in 1986.

The Sacred Ancestors

George Barker was to die in 1991. To me he was familiar only from the striking portrait photographs by John Deakin. Graham Mason numbered Deakin among his implicit roll of heroes of Soho, the best of whom were dead: the Sacred Ancestors. Certainly he defended Deakin against the charge of being cruel to everyone. 'The only man John Deakin was unkind to was David Archer,' Graham asserted. David Archer, who encouraged poets and ran a bookshop at a loss, was the man with whom Deakin had a relationship.

John Deakin made his living mostly as a photographer for *Vogue*, but surely his most penetrating pictures were portraits of people in their Soho environment. If Bruce Bernard had not retrieved Deakin's life's work of prints and negatives from beneath his bed in Soho when he died in 1972, they would have been destroyed. It was Bruce who got the Victoria and Albert Museum to put on a small exhibition of those photographs in 1984, 'John Deakin: The Salvage of a Photographer'.

It was Bruce, too, who had gone to see Graham in hospital some years before. Perhaps it was after Graham had been sacked from ITN when he had been found asleep under his desk. It was something of a low point. 'I just couldn't stop crying,' Graham recalled of his hospitalization. 'It had been going on for days. Bruce came and got me out.'

It is true that Bruce Bernard did not much like homosexuality as a way of life. As the journalist and author Ian Jack remembered Oliver Bernard remarking of Francis Bacon: 'Francis's rather swankily bad behaviour wasn't quite Bruce's cup of tea.' That did not stop him being a friend of Bacon's and many other relentless homosexuals, including Graham. Not that Graham's feelings about homosexuality were simple. 'I'm just a rotten old poof,' he would say.

There was no doubt that he found himself at home in the Colony Room Club in the years before homosexuality was decriminalized – there no one minded one way or the other. He resented the suicide of John Minton the painter, motivated partly, it seemed clear, by his deep anguish about his own homosexuality. But that had been in 1957, before ever Graham had come to Soho. He viewed the place partly through the eyes of his friends.

Left on the slab

Graham's alcoholism had developed into a commitment to drink. Nothing could be allowed to interfere with it. 'Jeffrey once asked me to lunch at Great Portland Street,' he told me. 'He gave me a huge veal chop and a pile of potatoes to eat. It was torture ... Then he wanted to go on drinking. I simply can't after a meal. That's why I don't eat at lunchtime ... Oh, yes. I see that would seem funny from your point of view.'

But Graham liked shopping for food, if it was in Soho. Soho, in daylight, out of doors, was another world from the smoky, dim rooms for drinking. The rough surface of the damp road glistened where the bristles of the road-sweeper's broom had left parallel scratches.

Graham would buy olive oil, prosciutto, pasta, parmesan, anchovies, fresh basil from I. Camisa on the south side of Old Compton Street. A narrow shop, it smelled of Italian groceries: herbs and cheese, preserved meats and garlicky olives. Sausages hung above the high glass cabinet dividing the customers (always waiting in at least a small queue) from the busy women shop assistants in their overall coats, darting behind one another in the small space as they fetched cheese to cut or ham to slice, or brought down panettoni dangling from the ceiling on cords, by catching them on long sticks like boathooks.

On the opposite side of the street, the Algerian Coffee Stores supplied the blend and darkness of roasting that Graham thought guests at dinner should have. Marsh Dunbar, the woman Graham lived with, had a stylish way of making coffee, which was to put the grounds into an open-topped earthenware jug, pour on the hot water and, after only a little while, to pour it into the cups. Somehow the grounds stayed behind.

For fish, Graham favoured Richard's, a little further west, at the beginning of Brewer Street. Its front wall was open to the air during business hours, with the wet and icy grey-skinned, dappled or ruddy fish looking up with glazed eyes. Jeffrey Bernard had once said to Graham: 'You know those fish in Brewer Street – haddock particularly – you can tell if they're fresh by the eyes. Well, if you were a haddock, I'd leave you on the slab.'

Elastic glue

If Graham wanted grouse or pheasant he might go to Fenn's, which had a game licence and was close by, at the beginning of Berwick Street. Otherwise, if he could walk that far, he favoured a butcher's at the far end of Brewer Street called Slater & Cooke, Bisney & Jones, a shop where beef with flocculent fat hung above a wooden block where a man dressed in an apron attacked it. This butcher's with the unwieldy name was known to Graham as the Solicitors.

Marsh and I quite liked Randall & Aubin, opposite Richard's. Its zenith was under a butcher who had moved from the meat department of the Army & Navy Stores in Victoria Street. But my regular butcher was R. Portwine in Earlham Street, over the other side of Cambridge Circus, on the way to Seven Dials.

To get to Portwine's meant walking past the enticing window of the ironmonger's in Earlham Street, F. W. Collins. In blue letters with red initials, an enamel sign on the brickwork between the first-floor windows read: 'Established 1835. F. W.

Collins. Elastic Glue Manufacturer (Sole Inventor 1857). Leather, Grindery & General Ironmonger Warehouse'.

That side of Earlham Street was lined with market barrows, except outside Collins', where stood a redoubt of zinc baths, stepladders and rolls of chicken wire. I don't know who in Soho wanted chicken wire. Fred Collins, if not the forebear who solely invented elastic glue, still ran the shop. It closed in 2001, but the enamel sign remains.

Collins' was typical of the independent shops that had resisted the takeover by pornography. In the eighties, Old Compton Street, Frith Street, Dean Street and the area around Walker's Court were full of shops selling what were known as dirty magazines. The retail side was lucrative, evanescent and naturally open to corruption with regard to the police. In later years, property yielded bigger profits than porn, which in any case took to the internet, and Soho's independent traders, having been put to flight by high rents, high rates and developers, were replaced by less interesting outlets.

It would be ridiculous to mourn the decline of Soho prostitution, though. The retired prostitutes that I came to know were not happy people. A quiet drink with one woman who generally presented a cheery face to the world always ended with helpless drunken tears and confused accounts of childhood abuse.

Anyway, the butcher now in sight in Earlham Street was always called by Diana Lambert 'Mr Portwine'. In the eighties the shop was indeed run by Graham Portwine. He thought his family had owned the business for 200 years or more. It was a narrow shop, on the corner of Tower Court. The dim interior was dominated by a thick, thick wooden block, worn down on the business side by several inches where Mr Portwine hacked and sawed and scrubbed. Illness was to force him to close in 2003, but above the second floor it still says 'R. PORTWINE.' in black capitals incised into the parapet. Today there is not a single butcher's in Soho.

Berwick Market was the place to buy fruit and veg, but not just anywhere. The market stalls faced each side of the street in a double line. Each was a barrow with large cast-iron wheels. Their canvas canopies rested on thin wooden struts. When it rained, the canvas would collect water in deepening troughs until a stallholder got a broom and pushed up the canvas from below, sending the water crashing onto the road, or onto some poor idiot passing by who wasn't watching where he was going.

The market extended southwards, beyond Walker's Court, the alley cannibalized by Paul Raymond's porn and property empire, into Rupert Street. Here stood the smartest greengrocer's stall of all. The owner arranged his mushrooms and cabbages, carrots and pea pods into a sort of collage like an abstract Arcimboldo on the artificial grass slope supported by upturned crates on the barrow. It was more expensive than other stalls' produce, but it was good stuff. And he threw in a little bunch of mint, enough to go with a joint of lamb, for nothing.

Boozer's economics

Sometimes, Graham ruefully caught himself performing what he called 'boozer's economics'. To a single-minded degree, money was for buying drinks to the exclusion of other things. (Contrariwise, he excused himself from a drinks party to launch Jeffrey's *Low Life* book in 1986 by saying: 'I don't like drink unless it's paid for.') In the morning he would find his pockets full of change that he had stuffed into them from rounds of drinks bought the night before.

Graham managed the picture library that belonged to the illustrator Bobby Hunt, who was usually either drawing at *The Economist* or at home in Suffolk. The first thing Graham would do, on arriving in the morning at the library, was to send out the office junior to the off-licence to buy a bottle of vodka and some cans of beer. This had been the duty of Daniel Thorold, who later managed El Vino's in Fleet Street and then set up his own wine business.

Daniel's mother Merilyn, who belonged to Jeffrey Bernard's generation, had run her own picture library. There is a photograph of her in the National Portrait Gallery as a ten-week-old baby, with her mother Eleanor Reynolds, a baronet's wife. I associated Merilyn more with the French pub, where the proportion of layabouts was lower, rather than the Coach, though she sometimes appeared at the Colony Room Club. There she liked the company of old-fashioned bohemians such as West de Wend-Fenton, who had escaped from the French Foreign Legion and looked after his eighteenth-century house in Yorkshire, Ebberston Hall. By contrast, Merilyn lived, rather romantically, I thought, on a houseboat moored on the Thames below St Mary's church, Battersea, where, two centuries before, William Blake had got married.

When Daniel Thorold moved on, he was replaced as the assistant in Bobby Hunt's library by Rupert Shrive, a student at St Martin's School of Art, round the corner from the Coach and Horses in Charing Cross Road. He went on to become a successful painter, but in the meantime his primary duty was to restock the vodka and beer supplies.

The beer, strong lager, was no doubt principally for rehydration, but also served as breakfast. There was, for Graham Mason, no nonsense about tea or coffee. After that liquid breakfast he would be able to bark down the telephone to clients who had not sent back the photographs they had requested for some magazine feature or partwork on the Second World War.

For him, boozer's economics encompassed a minicab to the distant Isle of Dogs at night, since that was the only practicable way of getting his weakened body home when drunk. But boozer's economics did not extend to clothing. Many of his clothes had belonged to Marsh Dunbar's late husband Peter. They were in a fashion at least a decade old.

Graham's bony ankle joints were often in evidence below the ends of his trousers and from his sleeves his wrists stuck out, displaying his blotched skin, with the odd little row of scabs. 'Kaposi's sarcoma,' I would say, referring to the adventitious skin lesions often associated, in fact and public consciousness, with Aids – a new and peculiarly fearsome disease in the eighties. Graham would laugh. His laugh seemed to have a South African vocalization, low and throaty, often turning into a racking cough. He liked formulaic references to the pathological aspects of the human condition expressed jocularly. He himself would call his alcoholic amnesia 'Korsakoff's syndrome'.

The noise of snow

On arriving at the Coach and Horses on a cold morning, Graham's face would be blue, his haddock eyes swimming and his nose numb. If it was snowing he would complain of the noise that the flakes made landing on his balding head.

On a hook on the wall opposite the spluttering gas fire he would hang his duffel coat. It had been navy blue, but, as the material had grown thinner through wear, it had taken on a greyer, faded hue. The cuffs were frayed. The arms were worn not exactly at the level of the elbows, but nearer the cuffs, where Graham's own bony elbows, inside sleeves shorter than his arms, rubbed at them from inside. The horn toggles were impervious to wear, but one had been crushed in some forgotten accident. All in all, it was no enviable garment.

One morning it was gone. It wasn't that it had been forgotten in drunken amnesia. It had been hung on its hook but it had disappeared. Some fool, perhaps unrealistically hopeful that its pockets contained valuables, had stolen it.

Jeffrey Bernard said: 'Come with me.' Graham did. They went to Austin Reed at the bottom of Regent Street. Jeffrey bought him a classical dark worsted overcoat.

Graham was grateful. He might not have been, but he was. Sometimes when he wanted to show friendship, he would lean over from his stool and grasp someone's hand. It could be quite disarming in the middle of a heated argument. 'Sign of affection,' he would say.

At the same time, the overcoat acquired a name: Jeffrey's Coat. It was a friendly name but one not without irony, as if it were a hospital named after a public benefactor.

It's the coat that Rupert Shrive painted him wearing in a portrait a few years later. Graham Mason is shown in it standing against a plain background, a folded newspaper sticking from his coat pocket. Graham Mason died in 2002. The painting hangs on a wall in my house.

7

Marsh

*Teenage runaway – Dancing alone – A pub each – The tall ships –
'You are a shit. Have a drink'*

Teenage runaway

Graham Mason's closest friendship was with Marsh Dunbar,
whose one-time husband Peter was an admired art director at
The Economist and liked taking pleasure in a green Bentley and
a string of affairs. It was typical of Graham's habit of inventing
sharp nicknames that he called Marsh the Widow Dunbar. Her
marriage to Peter had ended years before his death.

She had herself fallen into Soho after the war, and certainly
had known John Minton, whom she loved for his looks and his
energy, which overlay his sadness. Brought up in Beckenham, she
ran away to Paris in 1947 aged 16, leaving behind her Christian
name, Yvonne, and using her surname, Marsh, in its place for the
rest of her life. Oliver Bernard, after later falling out with her,
was the only one to say things like: 'You'd better ask Yvonne
Marsh.'

When Marsh had run away to Paris, it was with Bobby Hunt.
Forty years on, this seemed an unlikely adventure, since Bobby
had in the meantime grown bald and dithering in manner. He
came up to Soho at least on *The Economist*'s press day, in case
they wanted him to do a drawing, and would have a drink in
the Coach or the French. He must have known that the cheques

from his picture library's account that Graham cashed with Norman did not all fund business expenses.

He had met John Minton in 1943, before even the painter had introduced Sandy Fawkes to Soho. From about 1949, Bobby acted so regularly as his drawing assistant that he was jokingly introduced as 'my ghost'. Bobby liked to tell stories in which he appeared as an unwitting stooge. He was still only 17 or so when he stayed the night with Minton, sharing the only bed, as Bobby had done sometimes with his own father. When he felt Minton's arm about him, he simply took hold of his hand, gripping it tightly. Minton turned away and could be heard sobbing.

Dancing alone

After he left Camberwell, Bobby and Peter Dunbar, whom Marsh was to marry, had been living in Paris at the Hôtel Select, which served as a brothel. It was only when Minton came out to visit them that, by his own account, Bobby was astonished to discover that the girls he met there and at the Café Ambiance nearby were prostitutes, and not, as he'd believed, secretaries.

Marsh and Bobby, on their return from France, sometimes spent the night at Minton's house in Hamilton Terrace, and then found a place to live in Hampstead. Oliver Bernard, who spent some time digging holes in the road for a living, lodged with them. When Bobby married Sally Ducksbury in 1955, they shared a room at first at the house where Minton was then living in Chelsea, before moving in with Peter and Marsh Dunbar. As always, provisionality was a mark of Soho bohemianism.

Marsh sympathized with Minton, feeling sorry that he was so lonely, laughing at his jokes and enjoying his company. 'Come off it!' she would exclaim at some extravagance, with the note of realism she always retained. In her biography of Minton, Frances Spalding included a vignette by the art historian John Rothenstein of Minton's behaviour in the Colony Room Club, where he felt uninhibited. Minton, 'his long face pale and grave beneath its shock of black hair, would dance by himself, literally by the hour, in the middle of the room, the wildness of the gestures of his long arms and legs contrasting in bizarre fashion with the near-melancholy of his expression. If anything was needed to enhance the strangeness of the performance, it was its acceptance by the habitués as entirely normal: I noticed no one gave Minton a glance.'

I don't suppose Minton danced like that every night, but the acceptance of such behaviour rings true. On another occasion, Minton lay unconscious beneath a banquette in the Colony while everyone carried on drinking cheerfully. Exhausted and drinking heavily, Minton killed himself with sleeping tablets at his house in Chelsea in January 1957.

A pub each

In the fifties, Marsh had been petite, pretty and full of life. In the eighties, she was tiny, with leathery cheeks and thick spectacles. She combed her thin hair into a fringe. She wore ample skirts with a broad belt round her waist and shirts with the collar turned up and wrapped round with a lumpy-bead necklace and a light silk kerchief. At lunchtime on Fridays, on her way to the Coach from *The Economist* in St James's, where she worked, she would drop in at Fortnum's to buy bits of groceries which she carried in a raffia basket. In general she drank in the French and Graham drank in the Coach, so that they did not tread on each other's toes.

Though enthusiastically heterosexual, Marsh lived with Graham Mason until her death. He had lodged with her at first in a fine early nineteenth-century house in Canonbury Square, Islington, where she was bringing up three sons. In 1974 they spent a year trying to run a bar in Nicosia. This happened to coincide with civil war in Cyprus, and he and Marsh were lucky to be evacuated by the RAF.

Then they had lived in a flat in Berwick Street in Soho, above the busy street market with its stalls for fruit and veg, flowers, textiles, fish and nuts. It was a side of Soho that Graham loved. But the enemies of his excellence as a cook were three: finding money to buy supplies, getting them home without drunkenly leaving them in the Coach or the back of a minicab, and timing the sobriety of himself and his guests in order to produce a meal they could eat.

A fire sent Marsh and Graham from Berwick Street, fleeing bills, to a run-down council tower block on the Isle of Dogs. It was called a 'hard to let' flat, not surprisingly, since for years the block was plagued by drug dealers, broken lifts, graffiti and a smell of stale urine. The compensation was a view of a sweep of the Thames towards Wren's Greenwich Hospital.

They had on the wall of their flat a couple of oil panels by Deakin, in a knowing naive style, one showing a sea serpent wrapped round a lighthouse. In the kitchen hung a drawing by Elinor Bellingham-Smith, who, after the collapse of her marriage to Rodrigo Moynihan, had gone to paint in Suffolk, mostly landscapes. There's a canvas by her in the Tate, though it's not usually on show.

The tall ships

Marsh treated with astonishing patience not only Graham's regular drink-born verbal rages but also the accidents brought by his friendships. Jeffrey's Policeman was the nickname of a CID man from the Midlands who had come to Soho in search of Jeffrey Bernard, whose writing he admired. Jeffrey soon grew tired of him, and he developed the habit of putting up at Marsh and Graham's flat when he visited Soho. Out of gratitude he offered to paint the ceiling of the sitting room. Through ineptitude reinforced by strong drink he got quite a bit of white eggshell on the shaggy goat rug. This he sought to remedy by cutting off the affected parts with nail scissors. Marsh noticed, minded and forgave.

Marsh and Graham one Saturday filled their flat with Sohoites to eat and drink while the annual festival sent a succession of tall ships up the Thames past the window. Bruce Bernard brought a small pair of binoculars, with which we took turns to view the death-defying crews in the rigging. I still have those binoculars, because Bruce made a gift of them to me when I told him I was visiting Toledo. It was to see El Greco's *The Burial of the Count of Orgaz*, which is fenced off by an altar rail at a distance of a few feet. With binoculars it is possible to see the details, even the painter's signature on the handkerchief hanging from his son's pocket. As so often, Bruce had thought things out.

But when Graham asked Jennifer Paterson, not yet one of the *Two Fat Ladies* on the television cookery show, to lunch, it was a disaster. They were both in a mood to shout and not listen. 'This is overcooked,' she said of a crab tart, poking at it with a varnish-armoured fingernail. It was. 'Who the fuck cares?' said Graham, who cared very much. 'I'd like to go home now,' said Jennifer, turning to me, as if I had a carriage in my pocket.

'You are a shit. Have a drink'

It took me some time to realize that Marsh came into the Coach to see me. She was lovable partly because she retained a talent for finding the agreeable side of Soho's sacred monsters. She thought Francis Bacon very funny and kind, and took the lead in refusing to write John Deakin off as a well of vituperative bile. There was, for example, a story that Deakin had named Francis Bacon as his next of kin because he knew that the painter would hate seeing his dead body. On inspecting the corpse, Bacon was said to have remarked: 'That's the first time I've seen Deakin with his mouth shut.' Marsh was having none of the myth of Deakin's poisonousness, generated by George Melly and Daniel Farson, and always defended him when the subject came up.

Although she had first met Jeffrey Bernard in 1949, just before his 17th birthday, it was not until 1959 that Marsh had an insane affair with him. She and her husband Peter were living at Pebmarsh in very rural north Essex. Jeffrey came to stay with them. He was in no good state of mind. His ex-wife Anna had killed herself. Jacki, who was to become his next wife, had separated from him, but accepted an invitation to come down to Pebmarsh, too. Jeffrey continued his romance with her while beginning an affair with Marsh. It was all conducted in a cramped cottage.

'I really was insane about Jeffrey,' Marsh told his biographer Graham Lord, 30 years later. 'He was mostly sullen and miserable. It was really like an illness – it wasn't even that he was a very good lover. I think it was because he was such a shit. He was a sod unless you did exactly what he wanted. We used to have rows about absolutely nothing. I don't know why, and it's really awful, but being a shit is irresistible.'

I had no idea about any of this when one Friday lunchtime in the eighties Marsh Dunbar and I were sitting in the Coach, at the table by the dumbwaiter, inside the door from Romilly Street, discussing whether Jeffrey was a shit or not. Jeffrey came down the bar from the Greek Street entrance, with a carrier bag containing a bit of shopping. 'Oh, hello, Jeffrey, we were just discussing whether you are a shit or not.'

'Jeffrey,' said Marsh. 'I love you very dearly. But you are a shit.'

'No,' said Jeffrey, blowing his nose on a paper napkin and smiling. 'I'm not a shit. I might have done some terrible things, but I'm not a shit. Shits do it on purpose.'

'Oh, Jeffrey you are,' said Marsh, raising her snub nose towards him and looking at him slightly crooked through her thick tinted spectacles. 'Have a drink.'

Their affair in 1959 had lasted five months. Marsh had left her husband Peter and parked her three young children on his parents while she pursued Jeffrey to London. Peter took her back (and immediately had an affair with Jeffrey's new wife). But there they were, Marsh and Jeffrey, having gone through quite a lot in the intervening 25 or 30 years, on a quiet Friday morning, he with his vodka, she with her gin. The insanity was a memory, but the history remained. The backstory was something that gave the Soho soap opera such power. Even if not all the spectators were aware of it, at least some of the actors were.

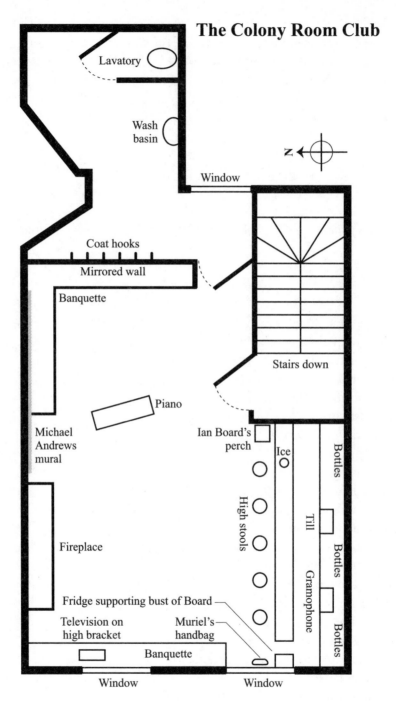

The Colony Room Club

Lavatory

Wash basin

N

Window

Coat hooks

Mirrored wall

Banquette

Stairs down

Piano

Michael Andrews mural

Ian Board's perch

Ice

Bottles

High stools

Till

Bottles

Gramophone

Fireplace

Fridge supporting bust of Board

Television on high bracket

Muriel's handbag

Bottles

Banquette

Window

Window

DEAN STREET

8

The Asphalt Carpet

A smoky afternoon – Regaining consciousness – Theatre of self-destruction

A smoky afternoon

When Ian Board welcomed a visitor to the Colony Room Club with the greeting 'Hello, cunt' he was using the word as an informal abbreviation. Muriel Belcher, the club's founder in 1948, had coined the remarkable hypocoristic form 'cunty' as her habitual term of friendly address, and he, as her successor, was just clipping the coin.

It was on bank holidays, empty Mondays when those who had homes to go to had gone to them, that the Colony Room Club came into its own. The sun, as available, would stream through the two westerly facing Georgian windows and turn the clouds of cigarette smoke into glorious billows. The less glorious stragglers who resorted to the Colony on such a day – a retired press photographer, a failed lawyer, a half-retired tart, a warehouseman – found plenty of room to sit on the high stools facing the bar, where Michael Wojas, behind his tinted spectacles and grim scar, served drinks while the monstrous Ian Board sat on the customers' side, on his stool or 'perch' by the door, stirring the conversation.

When driven by any reluctance on the part of the customers to talk, Board would resort to ready-made prods, acquired perhaps from Muriel. He might pick on someone and ask in his hoarse, breathless way: 'How would you define arch?' It came over as an accusation as much as an enquiry.

But on this sunny spring bank holiday, there was no need for prompts. The most committed regulars trickled in, happily buying vodka, a quiet whisky or, by way of taking things slowly, a glass of wine. Then another round. And another. Michael had put Fats Waller on the gramophone: 'When I come home late at night / I get my favourite dish – fish.'

The door from the stairs opened and shut now and then, and from his perch Board would rasp in greeting, 'Hello, cunt', but there was no crowded throng, just a relaxed chatter in the smoke. 'I want some seafood, mama,' Fats Waller chipped in.

For some reason an idea grew in the head of one regular, known, because of his innocent looks, as Milky, that it would be a good idea to take hold of the edges of the stools on each side of him and throw himself backwards into the void. 'Hold tight, hold tight, a-hold tight, hold tight,' Fats called out, and over went the stools, pulling more stools down in a sideways domino fashion as their occupants instinctively tried to save themselves. Ian Board's stool went with the rest of them, and he, showing no notable sign of saving himself, whizzed backwards through the air till his head came into contact with the lower edge of the piano behind him, sounding a percussive chord that drowned out Fats Waller's piscine pleas. Its echo seemed a death blow.

Lying on the ashy carpet, his legs still entangled in the stool legs, Ian Board opened one eye and said to Milky: 'Don't be a cunt all your life.'

Regaining consciousness

This sound advice was a rare piece of moral counsel from Ian Board, who was a creature of habit, mostly bad habit. His devotion to his chosen life was marked on his body, starting with his great swollen, pitted nose.

His day would often begin when he regained consciousness on some of the green cushions from the banquettes, laid on the asphalt carpet of the club, which was scattered with cigarette ash, dropped fag ends and spilt drink. His first morning sign of life might be a Vera Vomit, the name by which he personified this hangover reflex. It would be set off by an attempt to clean his teeth, or simply by a cough to clear his lungs, grown increasingly wheezy in the smoky air of the club room, where he sat for so many hours, a packet of long menthol cigarettes always to hand.

His morning cough shook his whole frame and would turn into a visceral retching. If he was feeling more than usually queasy, the immediate drink of the day would be a port and brandy, a mixture thought to calm the stomach. In his 60th year he gave up drinking brandy regularly for breakfast.

His hands shook, more particularly when he was raising the glass to his mouth, and they shook when he was lighting the first cigarette. Ian Board did eat, but was seldom seen doing so in his later years. He would go without food for days, then eat a tin of cold ravioli in the small hours of the morning. He drank vodka in the morning at home and from noon to 11 p.m. more vodka and brandy at the club.

His back and limbs ached in the morning, partly through injuries sustained by accidental falls or stumbling into furniture. In the street he carried a stick, since he'd hurt a leg and his back in mishaps. His hips hurt from sitting on his perch at the bar. When the club was not very full, he would stretch out his legs in front of him on the high stool next to his and cross one leg over the other.

Considering his daily sufferings, his temper was surprisingly equable. What appeared like boredom was often an attempt to get a buzz of conversation going so that people might buy more drinks. Of course conversation was not going to be encouraged by remarks like: 'Bored? Yes, I'm Board. Now for fuck's sake say something interesting.' Such a challenge might foreshadow an outburst of verbal hostilities, often provoked by a presumed offence not obvious to everyone present – a reluctance to buy drinks, for example, or a discovered visit to a rival club such as Gerry's in Shaftesbury Avenue.

The rasping torrent of invective that followed would be constructed, like oral epic poetry, from a selection of formulae. Some were designed to undermine the antagonist's confidence: 'Look at y'self. Just look at y'self, you great lump. What do you think you fucking look like? You're a sad and pathetic sight. You've got fuck all to say. You're a dreary, boring id-i-ot. What have you got to offer? Just shut your fucking cakehole. It might do for her with the dyed black hair, but it won't do here.' Her with the dyed black hair was Dee Hammond, who ran Gerry's.

On and on the abuse would go, like a fire catching light when a newspaper is held over the front of the hearth. Late in the afternoon or evening, when he was more combustible, it could sweep Ian Board away and, as his swollen face grew a darker red, he would begin throwing things – a cushion, the signing-in clipboard, his corduroy peaked cap, an ashtray, an empty tonic bottle. A stool would be kicked over. 'Get out! Get out! Don't fucking come back.'

No one was immune. Once he even started on Francis Bacon, though all reason must have suggested his absence would not be beneficial to the club. 'You can't fucking paint!' yelled Ian Board in a voice like a cheese grater as he grabbed an umbrella hanging from the back of his stool and started to belabour the artist about the shoulders as he left by the dark, precipitous, twisting stairway, with a volley of ballpoint pens bouncing off his leather-clad back.

Theatre of self-destruction

If Ian Board had a quiet hobby, it was, as the cartoonist Michael Heath pointed out, to observe the self-destruction of his customers. Some person – it happened from time to time – might enjoy being the centre of attention and buy bottles of champagne. No one really knew what he did for a living. Something to do with computers, it was said. As the weeks went on he would stay longer than he meant, his conversation began to be less interesting than the drinks he bought. His work, whatever it was, would suffer. He'd stay in the club longer and get more obviously drunk. After a few months, he bought no more champagne and he would get sharp words from Ian Board more frequently. His final disappearance would be provoked by a crisis of sickness, debt or the break-up of his love life.

Members who drew something like sympathy from Ian Board would be those who'd already lost a lot and no longer tried to show off. Mumsie, as she was known, was a woman in late middle age, with grey curly hair and an asthmatic wheeze. She drank wine. By profession she was a schoolteacher. Her son had died through a heroin overdose.

Another member who never attracted Board's tantrums was Tom Deas, a graphic designer who drank in the Colony every evening. He was a thin, quiet Scotsman in his fifties with curly black hair and a pleasantly modulated voice. He slowly drank huge amounts of whisky and would buy drinks for the people sitting with him. He didn't try to make everyone laugh, but he chuckled at what other people, said, and if presented with a harsh word would say, 'Och, well …'

Ian Board did not like jokes one bit – not set-piece jokes, that is. It was probably another thing he had learned from Muriel Belcher, that the telling of jokes soon provoked boredom and undermined conversation. 'Don't tell fucking jokes. It's common,' he would say. 'Say something witty.'

Ian Board's judgement was by no means infallible. Gerald McCann had been visiting the Colony Room Club since the fifties, when he was in his twenties. As a fashion designer he was part of the so-called Swinging Sixties, working with Mary Quant and setting up his own clothes production in Soho. Photographs of him in those days, by Norman Parkinson and Francis Goodman, may be seen in the National Portrait Gallery. A photograph by David Bailey shows him in 1965 in sharp suit and tie, resting his cheek on the fleecy collar of a sheepskin coat. 'He's clean looking, and this has gone into the clothes he designs', read the accompanying caption.

Returning to London after two decades in America, Gerald McCann liked to come into the Colony because, perhaps, it felt like home. He'd buy drinks and flick back his now grey or subtly coloured hair, when he laughed showing his expensively American-maintained teeth.

Ian Board niggled him one evening when his feelings were tender. Who could tell why – a death? An anniversary? Over towards him came Board's fire. Dreary. Failure. Fat. Poof. Bore. The usual artillery was aimed at him, though there was no reason to suppose it had found its mark. Suddenly McCann stood up, and his eyes seemed to be full of tears. I never saw him there again.

9

A Cabinet of Curiosities

In Muriel's footsteps – A shy duke – Unity by inclusion – The living museum

In Muriel's footsteps

Ian Board came from a poor family in Exeter. His mother died before he was five. He cared neither for his father nor for his stepmother. Escaping to London as a teenager, he went straight to Speakers' Corner and picked up a man, with whom he lived for some weeks. After a time he became a commis waiter at a restaurant in Greek Street, Soho. 'Friends, I haven't got any friends,' he would say.

His Devon roots were evident in the rustic tinge to his accent, which was dominated by a circular-saw roughness maintained by cigarettes, spirits and shouting. Like a Bristolian, he added an 'l' to words ending in a vowel sound: 'tomorrowl', 'dildol'. Occasionally he addressed people in a Devonian way as 'maid' instead of 'miss'. That was to men, of course.

When in a mellow mood, he would sit on his perch like an ageing brood hen, the paunch inside his green jersey lolling on the worn corduroy surface of his thighs, and sip at another glass of vodka, gargling his habitual: 'Cheer-io!' That, I think came from Francis Bacon. A lot of Soho speech came packaged in quotation marks.

Board relished particular words. He liked to say '*riddled* with cancer'. Any mention of Dusty Springfield would be met with an upbeat cry of 'Dusty!' When looking through the racing pages he would feel obliged to put a wager on any horse with Gay in its name. One strongly fancied creature was the bay gelding Gay Ruffian, which, despite repeated encouragement with small wagers, won a race only at the 14th attempt, and then at the fairly short odds of 9-4. Since Ian Board had 56 years start on it, the horse long outlived him.

Another focus of attention was a television programme called *Prisoner: Cell Block H.* An Australian soap opera, set in a women's prison, it had been renamed *Caged Women* for the Canadian market, but was known to Board only as *Lesbians*. Since he would never watch it in the club, he would chide tardy drinkers late on a Thursday night: 'Fuck off home. It's time for *Lesbians*.' Given his frequent state by the evening, it is not easy to tell what he made of those broadcasts he managed to stay conscious for. Most of the 692 episodes had still not been shown by the time of his death.

Ian Board had a palely spectral existence outside the club. He did go home, to a flat in Judd Street built in the streamlined moderne idiom with touches of Atlantic liner style. He had once been left to die there, tied up by an intruder or treacherous guest. More innocent Sunday lunches there were a thing of the past by the eighties.

But Board did accept an invitation one day to stay for the weekend at the house in Rochdale of Lisa Stansfield, the singer, who had come to value the Colony. By the time he was on the train home, he was quite impatient to be back in Soho. There was a baby in the compartment. and the baby cried. This did not soothe him. Long before King's Cross, he was shouting: 'Chuck the fucking thing out of the window. For fuck's sake shut the thing up.' When the train pulled into the London terminus, some policemen were waiting on the platform to have a word with him.

Some of Board's little ways made sense, though. He always wore black socks. That meant that when he took them out of the dryer there was never any trouble with odd pairs. He inflated some habits of convenience to a level of supreme principle. Lemons, for example. Ian Board never had lemons behind the bar for anyone who liked a slice in a gin and tonic. He couldn't be bothered to go out early in the day and buy some from the market two streets away. So he turned it into a deeply felt hatred of fruit in drinks. 'Fruit, I can't stand it. It's fucking disgusting. Dirty, stinking, rotten fruit bobbing around. What's the point? Get rid of the fucking stuff. I won't have it in the house. Don't ask me for fruit, 'cos you ain't getting any.'

Sometimes the club would present itself more formally than the reality suggested. Each year a little printed card would come through the post saying: 'Your subscription fee of £20 is now due and your cheque by return would oblige.' At the bottom the committee would be listed hierarchically:

Michael Meakin Esq. (Chairman)
Ian Board Esq. (Secretary)
Mrs Merilyn Thorold (Treasurer)
Mrs Jennifer Mortimer (Treasurer)
Michael Dillon Esq.
Allan Hall Esq.
Barry Driscoll Esq.

Another of Ian Board's prejudices no doubt came from Muriel as well. 'Who's wearing cheap fucking scent?' he would ask. 'I can't bear it. It's disgusting.' From her, too, he inherited a phrase, also generally addressed to men, that was intended to encourage the prosperous, hesitant or unpopular to buy a drink: 'Open your bead-bag, Miss.'

Muriel had died in 1979, and I never knew her. She was just history, like the Second World War to anyone born after it. But I liked talking to people who had known her and might still refer to the Colony as 'Muriel's'. Jennifer Paterson, the cook, was one. 'Muriel was never rude to me,' she said, with great certainty.

A shy duke

One afternoon a new perspective on the club opened up. A thin, dark-haired man in his seventies with dark, bright eyes came in and sat to the rear of the room, away from the window. It was the Duke of Sutherland. He lived mostly in Roxburghshire, though he was a member of White's in London as well as the Colony. I'd seen the Poussin *Seven Sacraments* that he'd lent to the National Gallery in Edinburgh, and the Titian lent to the National Gallery in London (which bought it for £50 million after his death).

He'd been a prisoner of war, which was said to have made this shy man shyer. His father, the Earl of Ellesmere, had died in 1944, and when peace came and the son returned to London he sold the family's grand house there, Bridgewater House, overlooking Green Park, built by Charles Barry, the architect of the Houses of Parliament. Death duties were the bane of property owners in those years and in the 1970s, to raise millions of pounds owing, the Duke of Sutherland, as he became in 1963, sold some remarkable Old Masters. There was a row about a Van Dyck leaving the country, but the Fitzwilliam in Cambridge raised £200,000 to buy it.

The Duke never spoke in the Lords, but kept up an interest in owning racehorses. His wife Diana, a daughter of the Duke of Northumberland, died in 1978, to his great grief. So here was this man, dressed in a checked shirt and tweeds, chatting quietly with Ian Board in a place to him less threatening than the House of Lords.

Unity by inclusion

Mick Tobin, the skint retired stage carpenter, found the club welcoming, too. An enlarged photograph of Mick and two other wartime sailors in uniform on some exotic shore hung framed behind the bar. It fitted in with all the rest of the pictures and bric-a-brac that gave the club much of its character. This is what the architect Ninian Comper, in another context, called 'unity by inclusion'.

The Colony was not much more than a single first-floor room, but perhaps because of its limitations the layout assumed a great importance to regulars. Take the lavatory.

There was in theory a gents' lavatory, the door of which opened onto the precipitous stairs up from the street. But it was always locked. Everyone used the lavatory at the back of the first floor, past the wide passage where the coats hung with beside them a cardboard notice issuing a 'Strong warning' to anyone using illegal drugs. Someone had changed 'strong' to 'strange', and so it remained.

The lavatory had a high cistern with an old-fashioned chain dangling, which brought a good, powerful sluice of water when it was pulled. Sometimes Ian Board would leave a shilling or two in the bowl as a test to see which customer might rescue it.

The decor was dominated by gloss racing-green paint. The front door at ground level inside the terrazzo-paved lobby was green, with a puzzling canopy above it of green-painted corrugated iron. The stairs up were green, as were the walls of the club's room. It had not always been the case. When it opened in 1948, the Colony had a vaguely tropical theme, which survived only in a few bits of bamboo trim. Ian Board also had a weakness for green berets and green scarves, which brought out the livid red of his nose.

The best piece of art in the club was a mural 15ft wide by Michael Andrews, on the wall opposite the bar. Painted with household paint on hessian, the colour had sunk so much and been overlaid by smoke that it was hard to make out, beyond the figure of a harlequin in a hat outdoors beside a chinoiserie fence.

It looked a bit brighter in a *Look at Life* cinema documentary from 1965 in which a few seconds' footage showed Bobby Hunt climbing the twisting stair and joining John Deakin by the window opposite Muriel on her perch. After the club closed, the mural sold at auction for £38,400. Spruced up, it was to feature in the impressive Michael Andrews exhibition at the Gagosian Gallery in London in 2017.

The living museum

In the club, a banquette ran in front of half the mural and another ran at right angles, below mirrors lining the wall opposite the windows. The two windows looked out onto Dean Street, opposite the Georgian houses that in the 1990s became Blacks Club. From the window near the bar could be seen a stretch of the narrow Bourchier Street, running directly away from the Colony off Dean Street. Bourchier Street narrowed even more at its far end into what was generally known as Piss Alley. That was historically the very heart of Soho.

Under this window of the club stood the refrigerator with its bottles of cooled white wine, and a freezer from which home-frozen ice could awkwardly be extracted to refill the ice buckets on the bar. Ian Board, of course, put the ice into the glass with his hands.

In front of the other window stood a sort of garden ornament, a cherub bearing a cornucopia, which someone had fitted up with a cascade of Christmas decorations baubles. High in front of that window a tiny television sat on a bracket. It was only ever turned on for Wimbledon tennis in the summer. Muriel's capacious handbag hung from the ceiling, and an old jockstrap decked with some kind of fur tails also dangled nearby.

Behind the banquette against the window was propped a giant Polaroid photograph of Colony members in 1983. Bruce Bernard had arranged for a vast Polaroid camera to be manhandled up the stairs. The group portrait is an uneasy one. Francis Bacon has his arm happily enough round Mike McKenzie, the black pianist who often played in the club. His crutches are propped against the bar. Ian Board sits in the middle with his arm in a sling from some quotidian accident. Tom Baker, who had ended his innings in *Doctor Who* a couple of years before, stands behind Michael

Wojas. Not long afterwards he ended any regular attendance at the Colony. Marella Shearer, then near the beginning of her long career as a make-up artist, was soon too busy to spend afternoon hours upstairs here. Michael Clark is standing beneath a photograph of Muriel Belcher, of whom, sick in bed before her death in 1979, he had made a series of portraits. Next to him, the suave journalist Allan Hall is not looking at the camera, unlike John Edwards in front of him. John McEwen, the art critic, is looking towards Bacon, and Jeffrey Bernard, seated in the foreground, is looking threateningly, it seems, at the photographer Neal Slavin. Bruce himself is formally raising a glass. He is wearing a moustache, something which Jeffrey, too, at one time was tempted into sporting. There must be at least two exposures from that day, as one was given by Slavin to what became the National Media Museum at Bradford.

A handwritten framed poem also stood on the ledge behind the banquette on this side of the room, celebrating Michael Wojas's 30th birthday. It had been written by Chris Potter, a political journalist for the *Sun*, to fit the tune of 'Michael, Row the Boat Ashore', and ended with the couplet: 'Michael's thirty years today / Still insisting he's not gay.' He had to take it in good part, but it was noticeable that, when Potter died, it disappeared.

Quite a good bronze head of Board, in glasses, eventually migrated to the top of the fridge, and wore a succession of straw hats. But it was the wall behind the bar that displayed the thickest collection of pictures and objects. It could have looked a grubby mess, but in fact the effect was like the artistic drawing room of some retired Victorian low theatrical performer.

It was an ensemble greater than its parts promised. Above his perch inside the door, behind Ian Board's left ear, hung a painted wooden or cardboard crown bearing the initials I.D.A.B. He claimed his nickname Ida derived from the initials of his Christian names: Ian David Archibald. That, I suspected, was an invention.

Next to the cardboard crown stood a smoke-yellowed electric fan, in front of a poster for Bacon's exhibition at the Grand

Palais in 1972. Several photographs of Muriel were scattered over the wall: one with her hand on her breast, another of her smoking, one of a detail of a painting by Michael Andrews, and one cheering snapshot of Muriel in a short summer dress arm-in-arm with Ian Board, wearing no trousers, out of doors on some rough grass in the morning, kicking their legs up in dance.

There was a pencil drawing of Ian Board, too, by Michael Clark. A painting of a woman in a straw hat eating a banana had been bought by Ian Board when drunk enough to mistake it for 'a geezer sucking a cock'. Amid the clutter on the wall behind the bar was a cartoon of Princess Margaret lying in a swimsuit being photographed by Tony Armstrong-Jones. The cartoon was by Trog, the pen-name of Wally Fawkes, the former husband of Sandy Fawkes. There was also a cartoon strip of Flook, the series that Wally drew in collaboration with George Melly. Trog drew in a distinctive style unlike any of his contemporaries, and also had the rare advantage of catching likenesses unmistakably.

Sitting on the uncomfortable stools at the bar, sunken in the middle so that their iron circular frames cut into the sitter, it was quite possible to have a quiet conversation, even after dark, when the club was not too crowded. Patrick Caulfield often seemed to turn up when few other people were about. He brought a feeling of quietness with him. Once he spoke about using some unsold canvasses to roof a shed. Could that have been true?

In the middle of the shelf on the wall behind the bar stood the till. This had not been properly converted when money was decimalized in 1971, and the keys had to be crashed down repeatedly to register an equivalent sum. The cover had been lost and the works were dusty. Later, Damien Hirst turned it into a work of art by plating the front of the drawer, inscribed with the word 'cunty' in capital letters, but I'm not sure it wasn't more remarkable before this transformation. From under the till poked out the edge of a drying-up cloth printed with the word: 'Oh, do dry up!' Above the till, clips like giant clothes pegs held very yellowing bundles of bills, the fattest labelled 'Unpaid'.

10

The Parish

Where Soho began — King Charles's exile — Beach with no sea — The
fabulous diamond — The Georgian Coach — Cosmopolitan change —
Unattractive landmark

Where Soho began

Ann Clerke, 'a lewd woman', was bound over to keep the peace
in October 1641 after 'threateninge to burne the houses at Soho'.
A similar threat, with foul language, was made, unwisely enough
to a constable, by Noah Cliffe the following year. Those are
the earliest known references to the place called Soho, a name
supposed to come from a hunting cry popular in the Middle
Ages. So where were these fire-threatened houses of Soho?

The brick-built house that shared its name 'Soho' with a few
tenements around it stood on what is now the north corner
of Bourchier Street and Wardour Street. If, in the eighties,
you looked out of the window of the Colony Room Club,
through the gilded clouds of cigarette smoke into the rays of the
afternoon sun, you could see, across Dean Street, the eastern end
of Bourchier Street. It was a narrow pedestrian alley that grew
narrower as it made its way westward to Wardour Street and
the dark old heart of Soho. In a map of 1585, Bourchier Street
is marked as a hedge. It had anciently marked the boundary
between the land belonging to Abingdon Abbey to the north
and St Giles's Fields to the south.

I don't remember anyone in the Soho of the eighties speculating about the name Bourchier Street. I assumed it was named, for unknown reasons, after the fifteenth-century Cardinal Archbishop of Canterbury who is buried in the cathedral there. But I was wrong. It was a recent name, chosen in 1937 to commemorate the Revd Basil Bourchier, who was rector of St Anne's round the corner from 1930 to 1933. Before that, it was called Little Dean Street, and before 1838, Milk Alley, which was its name in 1692 when French Protestants built a church there. A generation earlier it was Hedge Lane, after that important boundary marker.

Milk and church and hedge and abbey were unknown to us, as Michael Wojas in the Colony put another LP on the record player and served another round. But the notable thing about what we thought of as Soho Proper was how closely it followed the delimitation of the 53 acres of the Parish of St Anne, Soho, that were detached from the older parish of St Martin-in-the-Fields in 1686. Of the parish, the most intense, the most strongly Soho area, was the 22 acres of St Giles's Fields that became known as Soho Fields.

From the 1670s, Soho Fields were developed into streets of houses. The boundaries of those 22 acres were:

to the north Tyburn Road, now known as Oxford Street;
to the east Hog Lane, later called Crown Street and now
     Charing Cross Road;
to the south King Street, rebuilt as Shaftesbury Avenue;
and to the west Colman Hedge Lane, now Wardour Street.

King Charles's exile

The weathered statue of King Charles II in Soho Square, under which the young Jeffrey Bernard had sat down and buried his face in his hands, in Daniel Farson's memorable photograph of a hopeless, hungover dawn, had been there since it was sculpted in 1681 by Caius Gabriel Cibber, the father of the leading dunce in Pope's *Dunciad*. The sculpture's fortunes followed those of the rest of Soho.

It was erected as the high point of a fountain, with a sculpture group representing river gods (Thames and Severn, Humber and Tyne), at a time when houses in the square, at first called King Square and later Soho Square, were occupied by the fashionable gentry and nobility. By 1748, the fencing round the gardens was 'ruinous and decayed', so iron railings were fitted up to replace it. The late eighteenth century, when the titled tenants were moving out, saw hundreds of artists move into Soho, a few celebrated, such as Hogarth and Reynolds, but most not much known now: William Pether and William Beachey, James Baynes and Elias Martin. By 1815 King Charles's statue and its fountain were 'in a most wretched mutilated state'.

In the first half of the nineteenth century the number of inhabitants of the 1,400 houses in the parish increased from 11,637 to 17,335. The Duke of Portland had sold all the houses he owned in Soho Square, but he remained the freeholder of the central gardens there, and refused a request in 1869 to open them to the public. But in 1875, in a period of municipal pride, flowerbeds were laid out in the square, while the statue of King Charles was acquired by Thomas Blackwell, of the food company Crosse & Blackwell. (In 1840 Blackwell, whose company had warehouses nearby, rebuilt No. 21 Soho Square, on the corner of Sutton Row opposite St Patrick's. The house he demolished to do so had survived unscathed since the 1670s. Prosperity proved more of an enemy than impoverishment to the preservation of old buildings.)

Blackwell gave the statue to his friend the artist Frederick Goodall. Goodall was then at the height of his career as a painter. His diploma work for the Royal Academy, *The Song of the Nubian Slave* (1864), was followed up by endless views of Egyptian agriculturalists tending their flocks by the Nile. He even had a flock of Egyptian sheep shipped to the grounds of the imposing timbered and tall-chimneyed house, Grim's Dyke, that he got Norman Shaw to build for him at Harrow Weald.

Goodall erected the statue on its own little island in the lake at Grim's Dyke. In 1911, the sculpted King Charles was to witness a strange accident there. By then, the house had belonged for 20 years to W. S. Gilbert, the librettist of the Savoy operas. He swam every summer day in the lake. On 29 May 1911, Gilbert was due to give a swimming lesson to Winifred Emery, a 21-year-old teacher, and Ruby Preece, her 17-year-old pupil.

They were both in the water, Winifred Emery told Gilbert's biographers, when Ruby 'shrieked out "Oh, Miss Emery, I am drowning!" I called Sir William, who was on the steps, and he called out to her not to be frightened, and that he was coming. He swam out to her very quickly, and I heard him say: "Put your hands on my shoulder and don't struggle." This she did, but almost immediately she called out that he had sunk under her and had not come up.'

The coroner's jury, sitting in the billiard room at Grim's Dyke two days later, hear that Gilbert, rushing to her aid and plunging into the cold water, had suffered a heart attack.

His widow lived until 1936, and her will provided for the return of the statue to Soho Square. It was re-erected in 1938, and it was perhaps then that it acquired a new face, which seems to be attached like a mask onto the front of the head. A cement wash all over the statue was visible in the eighties, but the rain has worn it away, so that the marks of Cibber's chisel can once more be made out on the eroded figure.

Beach with no sea

By the eighties, Soho Square had grown seedy. In the summer it was one place where it was possible to sit down in the sunshine, on one of the benches or on the long-suffering grass. Some men would take their shirts off. Some women would loosen their bra straps. Some sunbathers leaned on a bicycle lying beside them. Some played tinny transistor radios, against the rules.

Who was there? Drunks, drug addicts, resting and retired prostitutes, the mentally disturbed, homosexuals looking out for others, the daytime homeless, the anxious, people waiting for the pubs to open, the sleepy, local people wanting a bit of fresh air, casual thieves. It was as crowded as Ramsgate Sands in the Victorian painting, only there was no sea.

On one side stood the tall brick Italianate tower of St Patrick's, with the door always open. In the eighties, it was a bit smelly in the lobby, near the plaque that recorded the rectors since the days of the French Revolution, when England welcomed more than 5,000 refugee priests. The first rector was an Irishman, though, a Franciscan friar, Father Arthur O'Leary. Many of the successive waves of immigrants were Catholic. By the eighties there was even a Sunday afternoon Mass in Chinese.

One day in July 1986 I was sitting on a bench in Soho Square in the sun at half past five in the afternoon and a woman in her forties, in a brown artificial-fibre dress with flowers on, and wearing sandals and white towelling socks, sat down beside me and said: 'I don't care. I don't want to go over the road and expose my body for money anyway. I've had enough of men. I don't want money. If I can't have my cigarettes, it doesn't matter. I've had enough of that hospital. They hardly give you anything to eat all day. You have to wait till half past seven for a cup of tea. If I can't get money by prostitution, I'll make do without. I don't mind one way or the other if I have cigarettes. They said they'd send my B-100 but they didn't. They said: "Come back on Monday." I don't see why I should. I don't want the money. I'll go back to Warlingham and see that psychologist. I'm sick you know. I don't want to go over the road, anyway. Men don't seem to want me. I don't know why. They just turn away. Scuse me, love, have you got 50p for some chips?'

'No.'

'I'll go and get some chips.'

She got up and walked from the square.

The fabulous diamond

The architectural history around us in the Soho of the eighties was in a way taken for granted. It was shabby, but its beauty had been preserved by neglect. The Colony Room Club might have horrible green gloss paint, but the panelling it covered went with the house in which it nestled, one of six on that side of Dean Street built in 1732.

They were among the 39 built in the 1730s that belonged to the Pitt family, clergymen and MPs (two becoming prime minister), who had been owners of the fabulous Pitt diamond, bought for £20,000 and sold for £135,000 in 1717 to become part of the French crown jewels.

The row of houses that included the future Colony Room Club were four-storey, built of London stock brick, of grey-brown, which turned black with the smoke of domestic fires, with the windows dressed with red rubbers (bricks that could be rubbed smooth as a rounded moulding for the edges of doors and windows). In this part of Dean Street the window openings have slightly arched tops to them, as can be seen at No. 39, two doors north of the Colony, which also preserves the eighteenth-century glazing bars of the sash windows.

At No. 41, the Colony's house, the brick façade was refaced in about 1770, and later painted over, the head of the windows made square and then given slightly projecting brick hoods or labels, in the Gothic idiom, which at least one architectural historian has said look ridiculous on such a house.

The ground-floor beneath the Colony was a restaurant, and the entrance to the club was by a street door next to it, always open. The lobby there was floored with cracked terrazzo across which the neighbouring restaurant would slide dustbins of their sloppy daily refuse. Where the green paintwork began, an uneven staircase rose into gloom and turned upwards, past a landing with a locked door and up again to a closed door ahead. This was not locked and could be pushed open with a bit of effort to free it from the constraints of the warped frame, to propel the visitor in a more or less controlled manner into the one big room on the first floor that the club occupied.

The Georgian Coach

Since the 1720s there had been a Coach and Horses on the corner of Greek Street and Romilly Street. The victualler in 1734 was Peter Rowlandson (or Rawlinson), who was responsible for building No. 28 Romilly Street, now part of Kettner's restaurant.

To the confusion of many a casual visitor, since at least 1731 a Coach and Horses had also existed almost in sight of the Coach in Greek Street, just round the corner at 2 Old Compton Street. Not until the 1990s was that pub renamed Molly Moggs. In the 1980s it was a cramped, dim, smelly pub, only distinguished for being, with its neighbour the 101 sandwich bar, the best preserved of the modest three-storey houses from the 1730s surviving in what was Crown Street before the building of Charing Cross Road.

The real Coach and Horses is now a Grade II listed building. On the top floor, where Rupert Shrive was to have his studio, the wide, bare floorboards with their gaps and mouseholes lent it a Dickensian air. What gave this early nineteenth-century building a visual character like no other in Soho was the ground-floor row of twelve slender, fluted, cast-iron columns 'with enriched necks' as English Heritage puts it, along both the Greek Street and the Romilly Street façades, supporting the three upper floors. Behind this row are set back the almost continuous windowpanes in their wooden glazing bars. One other agreeable feature is that the building turns the corner of the street not with a sharp right angle but with a rounded aspect.

The windowed architecture of the bar of the Coach invited customers to make a sally into the sunny street in summer. In winter after dark it no more felt an extension of the street than the inside of a ship feels like an extension of the sea.

Cosmopolitan change

In 1711, two-fifths of the new parish were French, mostly living as lodgers. The French remained the dominant foreign element until the last quarter of the nineteenth century. In 1903, 60 per cent of the parish was foreign, with two-thirds of them being Polish Jews.

By then, the English had begun their slow discovery of Soho as a place to eat. Until the founding of Kettner's in 1868, an English face in the French restaurants of Soho was a surprise. While Soho became known as a cosmopolitan place to shop and eat, its resident population steadily fell: 16,608 in 1881; 12,317 in 1891; only 2,777 by 1951.

There were other pubs in the eighties apart from the Coach and the French: dozens of them. Before she took over the tiny Seven Stars behind the Law Courts, Roxy Beaujolais ran the Three Greyhounds, just north of the Coach, with its absurd false timber beams on the outside and cramped bar inside. The Helvetia, round the corner from the Coach in Old Compton Street, was often sparsely attended in the evening. It stood on the site of previous pubs from the nineteenth century and was later to become the Soho Brasserie. The Swiss, further west in Old Compton Street, was roomy but chilly. It later became Comptons, pitching for gay drinkers.

In the eighties, the only definitely queer pub, as the terminology still had it, was the Golden Lion, at the bottom of Dean Street, rebuilt in 1930 in a slightly Tyrolean style. The Admiral Duncan in Old Compton Street, named after the hero of Camperdown against the Dutch in 1797, was not exclusively queer in the eighties, but by 1999 was to have become enough of an emblem of gay life to attract the attention of David Copeland, a nasty bit of work who planted a nail bomb there that killed three and wounded dozens of people.

A pub I enjoyed for its interior was the Intrepid Fox, which acquired its name (honouring Charles James Fox) in 1784 and was rebuilt with faience cladding in the nineteenth century. The bar was full of brass, wood and beaten copper round an open fireplace. It was ransacked and ruined when it later became a Goth pub and then an unsuccessful burger joint. Walnut veneer covered the panelled walls of another extraordinary interior, in Newport Place – a pub thronged with Chinese people, who also enthusiastically crowded the betting shop next door.

All these pubs and places like the Café España in Old Compton Street (which once cooked me a *tortilla de patatas* from scratch, no instant task) were there for a quick drink or a bite, but were not to be relied on for conversation with a changing body of regulars.

Cafés, unlike those in the fifties, did not much care for customers ordering a cup of coffee and sitting there for hours. Maison Valerie in Old Compton Street had not yet been spoiled by being turned into a chain enterprise and Maison Bertaux, next door to the Coach in Greek Street, preserved its ramshackle interior, as if recently set up with second-hand furniture. You could buy patisserie there for a dinner party – the plum tart was excellent – or climb the steep and narrow stairs for a cup of coffee before opening time in the pub. It had been founded in 1871, but its survival through the eighties was won by the hard work of Michele Wade, an actress by training. She once assumed the role of Delacroix's *Liberty Leading the People* (on the barricades with breasts exposed) for the annual Soho Festival. There was also a waiter with a marvellously sinister air, a ponytail and a limp.

For people like Norman Balon, who had known the business side of Soho all their lives, the very buildings preserved memories of families who seemed always to have been there. In Frith Street in the eighties an open fire still burned in winter to heat the shop at the Welsh Dairy as it was known, even though it said 'Oxford Express Dairy' in gold letters on the black fascia board. It had been run by Jack Pugh since the twenties. 'Downstairs in the kitchen under the shop,' Norman remembered, 'it was just like a Welsh farmhouse, with an Aga in the fireplace and big scrubbed wooden table.'

Unattractive landmark

Externally the French pub was architecturally undistinguished. Once upon a time its upper floors had been rendered and white-painted and the ground floor ornamented with lacquered woodwork of a Baroque flavour with two arches flanked by stained glass held in leading of geometric and vegetative patterns. The glazed fascia had proclaimed in letters of gold: 'VICTOR BERLEMONT Whisky Bonder, Brandy Shipper'.

Since then it had not helped that the bomb which destroyed St Anne's church had also broken down its façade, which was rebuilt flat and raw, in red brick with metal window frames. At least the wide ground-floor windows let in the sunshine to light up the exuberant clouds of cigarette smoke. The frontage was not plumb north–south, but followed a line that was more like north-north-west to south-south-east, so that by half past eleven, when Gaston decorously opened up, the sun, if visible, was already striking it obliquely.

The time could be checked by the clock of the curiously shaped steeple of St Anne's church, the only part to survive wartime bombing. *The Survey of London* calls this construction of 1801, by S. P. Cockerell, an 'original, powerful, but rather unattractive composition'. From a sphere at the top bulge four blue clock faces, turned to the cardinal points of the compass. This is surmounted by 'an unassertive finial'.

The unattractive composition could be seen from an unlikely perspective: the gents' lavatory down in the cellar basement of the French. As one stood there looking upwards, its disembodied bulge loomed against the sky on the other side of the bars securing the narrow gap for air and light in the pavement of Dean Street above.

Baby Face Scarlatti

The case of the mobile phone – 'I'll get you for this' – The News of the World *– What the black policeman said – 'No worse than you'd see in a film' – 'Not violent and never vindictive' – Waiting for Baby Face*

The case of the mobile phone

For someone so much on edge Ian Board showed a surprising degree of courage. He took a big risk one day by standing up to a gangster of Italian background. Baby Face Scarlatti, for such was his improbable name, had come to the club for a drink and had made the mistake of using his mobile phone.

Board was as punctilious as the secretary of any Pall Mall club in prohibiting their use. In a fury he snatched the machine from the gangster and threw it across the room.

That's what I think happened, though I wasn't there. I was, though, at the comedy-thriller magistrates' court trial that followed the incident.

Though Baby Face had shown violence at the time, tussling with the police and, more worryingly, threatening future violence against Ian Board, it was the proprietor who was on trial, charged with criminal damage to a mobile phone. It must have been a private prosecution.

In the late eighties, mobile phones were thick objects like a pound of lard, the shape of a terrestrial telephone receiver, with a speaker at the top, a microphone at the bottom and an array of buttons in between, with a little aerial sticking up at one corner.

Baby Face didn't look very babyish in court that afternoon. He was 49, grizzle-haired, with a prominent chin and flattened nose. He gave his name as John Allen Haines and took the oath.

The counsels for the prosecution and defence conferred with the magistrate, and after a few minutes permission was given for Scarlatti's criminal record to be read out. Six years earlier he had been convicted of causing death by reckless driving. Before that he had been sentenced to three and a half years in prison for possession of a firearm, actual bodily harm and assault on police. Those were the most notable, but there were plenty of offences such as driving while disqualified, and taking and driving away vehicles. There was no jury, but some people in the public gallery gasped.

In answer to questions, Baby Face said: 'On 7 April 1989 I visited the Colony Room Club with the chief investigative reporter from the *News of the World* and another man. We met beforehand somewhere close by. I had a phone, a mobile phone, in working order. I received a call on it.

'We were let in at 3.30 p.m. by a barman called Michael. I am not a member, or the other two. We were signed in by Mr Board, whom we'd met before.

'All three of us bought drinks. We bought drinks for everyone, and Board and the barman Michael. After an hour and a half or two hours, the mobile phone rang. There was no trouble till then.

'There was hardly anyone there. One of us left before the phone rang. The reporter was still there. The phone rang and it was my wife asking if I was coming home to dinner. I put the phone on the bar.

'I felt a shove in my back, which pushed me off my stool, and the phone hit the wall. Ida – Mr Board – did it. He was using bad language, which he does all the time, but that didn't upset me. He used expletives about the phone. He said: "You fucking cunts are all the same, with your yuppie phones."

'I was angry. I picked up the phone and tested it. The key panel was smashed in and the aerial broken off. I told Mr Board what I thought of him in the same Anglo-Saxon terms. I didn't hit him or anything. He's a friend of the local police.

'He picked up the receiver of the telephone on the bar and rang the police. I had a penknife on my key-ring and cut the cord. The police arrived in seconds. They asked me to leave, and I left.

'I took the phone to a radio shop to be repaired. It cost £225. The receipt gives the cost.'

'I'll get you for this'

Baby Face, in answer to questions (in italics below) from the defence counsel, said:

'I know Ida Board fairly well, and he's a character well known in the West End. I have nothing against him. When he's not drunk, he's quite a nice person.

'On 7 April I was charged by the police with criminal damage, being drunk and disorderly and with threatening behaviour. I pleaded guilty to cutting the cord.'

Then came a series of questions seeking to establish his violent and untrustworthy character.

How long had you been drinking? – Some two hours. I was not the worse for drink.

Slurred in speech? – Totally wrong.

Unsteady on your feet? – Totally wrong.

Drunk? – Outrageous!

Were you aggressive when the police arrived? – No.

Did you shout: 'You'll regret this, you stupid old queen'? – No.

Did you say: 'I'll do as I please. I've spent £50 in the club this afternoon. I'll get him for this'? – No.

Did you say: 'Can you hear me, queeny? I'll get you for this'? No – the police are a good friend of him [sic].

You signed in under the name Baby Face Scarlatti – My mother's name is Scarlatti. I signed in under that name.

Your previous convictions include making a false statement to obtain a driving licence. In 1976 there was possession of firearms. Assault on police. You are a violent and aggressive man? – If someone hits me or offends myself or family physically, I respond.

In 1982 there was actual bodily harm against police. You like throwing your weight around? – I resent that. I never throw my weight around.

The Colony Room Club is a small club? – Not very big. [A plan was handed round, and photographs of the bar, numbered 2a, 2b, 2c, 2d.]

You three were seated at three seats by the bar? – Yes.

There was a narrow distance between the stool and the banquette – four or five feet? – Yes, I had my back to Mr Board. The other two were facing me. One left.

The use of a portable phone in a room as small as this is unpleasant – That's ridiculous. This is no mausoleum, this club.

That afternoon, it was quiet. And you made calls – That is a lie by the defence and you know it.

There were two other phones, one of them a pay phone – I don't know.

You were asked by Mr Board to stop using that machine – A lie.

You went on behaving in an aggressive and ill-mannered fashion. He told you to stop and there was a pay phone. You eventually held up the mobile phone in an aggressive way, and at that point he was standing before the furthest stool in the photograph, within three to five feet of the banquette, to speak to you – He never said anything to me.

You held out the phone to Mr Board? – Oh dear. That's the most unlikely piece of rubbish that I've heard for ages.

He lobbed it a short distance on to the banquette or cushion? – No, he smashed it on the wall.

I suggest that it is totally untrue that Mr Board threw it against the wall – I didn't know he didn't like these phones.

You used it in the presence of people in the club – Friends of Board's.

You shoved a member of the club, Mr Glen Reynolds, a solicitor, off his stool – He wasn't even on a stool.

Did you say anything to the police when they arrived? – There were two policemen, one of them coloured, and a tall Yorkshire one who knew Mr Board by name. I showed them the phone. It was unusable. It was obvious.

Did they arrest you? – I said: 'Look at this phone.' I said: 'This happens twenty times a week. He calls you twenty times a week.' He said: 'I'm nicking you' in as many words.

Did you phone later in a further incident? – Maybe in the car. The car was left on a yellow line. I was arrested again.

You were involved in a struggle? – The police struggled with me. [Laughter in court.] I went to get the car out of the police pound. They'd left it under a leak, which cost £750 to repair.

You were throwing your weight around? – No.

The *News of the World*

The prosecution called Trevor Edward Kempson, chief investigative reporter of the *News of the World*, of Barbican, London EC2.

He said: 'I'd been asked to meet Mr Haines by the news editor because he possibly had a story. Within fifteen minutes of talking to Mr Haines, it was clear that it was absolutely useless.

'I met him in the doorway of the Colony Room Club, of which I was not a member. I didn't know it existed. I was not, to my knowledge, signed in. We had several drinks and quite a lot of conversations.

'We three bought drinks and so did the proprietor. I can't say with accuracy, but there were five or six other people, two ladies. I was talking to the barman at this time. I was leaning on the bar. Mr Haines was talking to Mr Board.

'I suddenly heard a lot of shouting and swearing between Mr Haines and Mr Board. I'd heard a phone ring, and Mr Haines had this portable phone to his ear.

'The next moment, I saw this gentleman snatch the phone and throw it across the table, breaking the glass. Mr Haines fell off his stool.

'No one had complained about the use of the phone. The phone suddenly hurtled across the room, and hit some glasses on the table.'

Asked whether it was lobbed onto some cushions, Kempson said: 'No. If it had, I wouldn't have heard or seen glasses go over.'

'Two people then told me they would throw me out of the club because I'd brought him in. I've had cancer of the spine, so I didn't want to be thrown.'

The defence counsel asked: *Is the* News of the World *generous with its expenses* – Yes, we pay our way.

Everyone was having a fair bit to drink? – It depends.

How many? – I was having singles – six or seven.

A fair bit – Yes, but not by my standards. I was not incapable of remembering. I've a strong capacity for whisky, without it showing any effects.

At this point there was another consultation with the magistrate. The defence said there were two summonses, for criminal damage and common assault. But assault was not on the court register. The clerk of the court said it was a clerical error.

What the black policeman said

The defence called a police constable from West End Central. He was black. He said he'd made notes an hour and five minutes after the incident, while it was fresh in his memory.

He said: 'Police in uniform were called to the Colony Room Club at 5 p.m. I first saw a gentleman who said he was the owner and proprietor. The only other person in the club was Mr Haines. The proprietor said: "He is not a member here, and I want him out. He's got a knife, and has cut the handpiece of the phone."

'I asked: "Do you know him?" Mr Board said: "Yes, but he's not wanted here."

'Mr Board said: "Please go. Don't come back. You're too dangerous."

'Mr Haines said: "You'll regret this, you stupid old queen. You check your records, officer. He must do this twenty times a week."

'I have never met the proprietor. I am not influenced by prejudice, or against Mr Haines. I noticed Mr Haines was unsteady on his feet and his breath smelled of intoxicating liquor.

'Mr Haines said: "I'm out of his shabby little club. I'll do as I please … I'll get him for this." On the pavement he said: "Can you hear me, queeny. I'm coming back. I'll get you for this."

'Mr Haines said: "I could snap that old queen's neck just like that. I'll be back in tomorrow. It's just a domestic." Eventually he was arrested.

'The proprietor came into view and Haines said: "You'll regret this, queeny. They can't be here all the time".'

The defence counsel asked: 'Did he complain about a broken telephone?' The policeman said: 'No. He did have a phone in his possession, on which he made various calls.'

The prosecution counsel asked:

After he was arrested in the street, did he make calls? – He asked the sergeant if he could make a call. He made quite a few in the street and in the station.

I suggest no calls were made – They were.

I suggest you're partial – No.

Are you saying the exact words used, or the gist? – As best as I can remember.

If I asked you to fold away your book, you couldn't remember the conversation – No. But I have a record of Mr Board complaining about the telephone: 'He's cut the handpiece of my telephone.' I had been at the station for a year then. I have never been called to that club. We thought that if we let Haines use his telephone, he wouldn't be violent.

'No worse than you'd see in a film'

Ian Board, the defendant, was declared to be a member of the Church of England and took the oath. He gave his name as I. D. A. Board of 124 Clare Court, Judd Street, London WC1.

'I have been honorary secretary and manager of the Colony Room Club for nearly forty-one years. I have no convictions.

'I was sitting on the stool opposite the window when Mr Haines came into the club. I did not sign him in, the barman did. He and the others had a few drinks and were chatting. He used the phone a couple of times. I can't remember it ringing.

'He was speaking in quite a loud voice. I did ask him not to use it but to use the pay phone [in the cloakroom]. I went up and said: "Please don't use it. It's very annoying."

'He almost gave it me. In fact he did give it me. I threw it on to the banquette, a yard or so away. There was not enough room to hurl it. I don't think it fell on the floor.'

[An exhibit was produced: a banquette cushion. The magistrate felt it.]

'I had to clear the room. The people all left, except for Mr Haines, who had previously got a knife out. He tried to bite the cord of the telephone on the bar, then cut it. He wasn't sitting. A solicitor who was there was knocked off his stool. Mr Haines was waving the knife around.

'When the police arrived I showed them the cut phone flex. I said: Would the police please get rid of him?

'Yes, I am known as a bit of a character. Bad language may have been used, but no worse than you'd see in a book or a film.

'Mr Haines had previously bought a couple of rounds. I didn't have as much to drink as them. They were talking mostly to each other. Mr Haines made three or four phone calls. I didn't hear a phone call coming in.'

'It was annoying because he was speaking in a loud voice. The whole procedure was annoying. It's a very small room, and people talk sense, nine times out of ten. But he was talking rubbish.

'If he had been talking on the phone quietly I would still have objected. I've never allowed it in the club. It was outrageous. It didn't make me see red, I was just being sensible. I just find mobile phones boring. I wasn't aggressive; there was no need to be, as he offered me the thing. I did ask him two or three times not to use it, when he first started.

'The whole incident was over in ten minutes or so. I asked him from the perch. He may have put it down the first time. I think it was the third time he used it, I asked him to leave. I had said: "I've asked you not to use the telephone. Use the pay phone."

'It wasn't a penknife he produced. It was a big knife. It was in his pocket, not on a key-ring.

'I don't think the *News of the World* witness recalls that much, the state he was in. There was no crashing of glasses on any table. I can't recall whether the phone hit the ground. The ground is carpeted.

'Did I look where I threw it and not just throw it over my shoulder? That's a stupid question to ask. I know where the banquette is. It didn't fall to the floor, not that I recall. He cut the cord and looked threatening.'

The counsel for the prosecution said:

You saw red and said it was a boring yuppie thing – I may have said that, though 'common' is a word I use more.

Ian Board said:

'The *News of the World* man was unsteady. He really had gone. I asked him to leave. I didn't see any two other men threaten to throw him out. I said: "I'm closing, will you please leave?"

'I didn't call the police; the phone was out of order. Someone else did. I went to the bottom of the stairs – not two flights but the first one. The officer said: "You'd better not come down." I heard Haines use the telephone before the police arrived and I heard him use it downstairs. He said to the police: "Can I use the phone?" I offered him the taxi fare to the police station. The police asked if I wanted to charge him. I said No.'

'Not violent and never vindictive'

The defence called Michael Meakin, of Warwick Square, London SW1. He was a small man, neatly turned out in a well-made dark suit. His hair was well cut and combed down. He spoke with a received English accent. His limbs were spindly, he had a twisted spine and he rested his weight on a shiny black stick.

He said: 'I have been a member of the Colony Room Club for fourteen or fifteen years, and I have been chairman for two years. I know Mr Board. It is a respectable club, properly conducted. I am also a member of a club in St James's Street, the name of which I am willing to write down.

'Mr Board is trustworthy. I've looked at the accounts quarterly. He is truthful and not violent at all. He deals extremely well with things in a disciplined manner, which is what it needs. Yes, he is a character, and robust rhetoric is used in the club. It is a private club.'

Another witness for the defence, Miss M. Pearmaine of Crewe, the retired head of a school for educationally disruptive teenagers, said: 'I have known Mr Board since 1967, when I became a member of the club. My grandchildren know him, and he often spends Christmas with us. He is quite acceptable to family and friends: kind, responsible and sensitive. He is not violent and is never vindictive. He has worked in the school with me and had a calming effect on the pupils.'

It was time for the verdict. The magistrate said that the evidence for the prosecution had been tenuous, weak and inconsistent. 'It is difficult and dangerous,' he said, referring to a judgement by Mr Justice Turner the previous year, 'to act on the plums and not the duff.' The charges against Mr Board were dismissed. He was granted costs. Case dismissed.

Waiting for Baby Face

It was in a way a vignette of the times, of gangsters and police who knew the local owners of pubs and clubs. Of a policeman who was unusual for being black and needing to state explicitly that he wasn't prejudiced against an old queen, nor chummy enough with the club owner in the parish to give false witness in his favour. Of hard-nosed crime reporters, quite accustomed to six or seven whiskies in the afternoon – on expenses. Of carefully selected character witnesses – a well-spoken St James's clubman and a motherly teacher of needy teenagers.

But there was still Baby Face to contend with. His threat to get Ian Board was not idly made, and, as he said, the police couldn't be there all the time. The next evening that I was in the Colony some unfamiliar figures were there, or, rather, figures familiar from elsewhere. Two or three of the larger Italians from their end of the Coach and Horses were enjoying a quiet drink and keeping an eye on the door. These were not braggarts like Baby Face. I knew that some of them could be difficult when drunk and angry; I would certainly not have made fun of them.

I'm not sure that in the coming days their presence made me feel safer in the Colony. The fact of their being there confirmed that the danger was regarded as real. After a couple of weeks, the club went back to its ordinary daily fare of life and death, free from the violent eruptions of Baby Face Scarlatti.

The Unknown Norman

The midwife – A game of spoof – Handbag full of forks – Bombs and brasses – High life years – Going bust – 'I love you. I love you not' – Jeffrey's angel – Beating Den-Den – The cigarette machine

The midwife

Norman Balon, the landlord of the Coach and Horses, was a sort of midwife for Jeffrey Bernard's Low Life columns in the *Spectator*. But Jeffrey claimed it was he who had invented Norman. In any case, Norman soon got the idea that he was a celebrity. He had already gained a shadowy public profile through the odd reference in various *Private Eye* spoofs to 'Monty Balon, the genial meinhost'.

By the mid-eighties he would cry, 'I'm famous! I'm famous!' with innocent pride as he came into the pub waving a copy of the *Evening Standard* diary column with his name in. Eventually he even painted the wall on the corner outside, above the advertisement for 'Fine ales and wines', with the word 'NORMAN'S' in large capitals. No one ever called it that. It was always the Coach.

Norman never told the staff where he was going, or for how long. His daily routine was quite regular, though. After checking the takings and the till roll, the stock and the staff rota well before opening time, he would go and play briscola at 11 a.m. with Italian friends at the Evaristo Club in Greek Street. 'I abuse the Italians and call them unsuccessful people and they call me a Jewish cunt,' he told Spencer Bright, the ghost writer of his memoirs.

Sometimes he played briscola in the pub, at the table by the gas fire next to the gents' lavatory. It required the Italian pack, of swords, cups, coins and clubs. Most non-Italian regulars never learned the rules. There were two schools of thought: that it was impossible to understand, or that it was not much better than snap. Norman tended to crow when he won and slam down the pack on the table with annoyance if he lost. A frequent opponent at briscola was Gabi Pierotti, the canny Tuscan proprietor of I. Camisa, the delicatessen in Greek Street with its wonderful smell of herbs and preserved meats and a constant queue for its brisk service.

Norman and Gabi were natural friends. Gabi, with his London Italian accent and wry smile, was in his thirties in the eighties. He worked at least a 12-hour day at his shop, opening up at 5.30 a.m., but there was still time for a few hands of briscola. He preserved his humour and manners no matter what tantrum Norman seemed about to throw.

A game of spoof

Norman was a bad loser, too, at chess, to which Conan Nicholas was often eager to issue a challenge, being the stronger player. But even as a chess player, though he swept the pieces off the board when he lost, Norman wasn't utterly despicable.

The law allowed games of pure skill to be played in a pub for moderate stakes. The games included chess, dominoes and cribbage. I did see people playing cribbage once or twice in the Coach, but it could hardly be said to be a common activity. Spoof, however, was. Spoof is a game played throughout Europe. I was delighted one Friday night to find it being played in the obscure Castilian city of Toro, where it is called *chinos*, 'pebbles'.

Spoof is usually played with coins, by two people. They take turns to call the number of coins to be disclosed when both players open their clenched fists. You might think it sounds like a game of chance. As far as I can tell, it is very much a game of skill. In his day Jeffrey could pay for his dinner with a game. Bill Mitchell was no mean player. Michael Heath was deeply suspicious of the skills required.

Handbag full of forks

In the fifties Norman and his mother had grappled for dominance of the pub. By the mid-1980s, Mrs Balon, as old as the century, was still helping out, or so she thought.

She would arrive in the morning with Betty, who seemed the same age as she was, a woman whom they had apparently found one night during an air raid and who had stayed with them in an undefined ancillary role. As Mrs Balon disappeared up the steep stairs behind the bar, Betty would trudge behind her, carrying the shopping, her feet slopping in her stiff shoes on the steps.

Before lunch, Mrs Balon, her face powdered and earrings hanging from her long ears, would sit near the gas fire at the lavatory table folding napkins, polishing cutlery and making remarks like: 'It's terribly cold, isn't it?' Jeffrey swore that she once said, out of the blue: 'My husband had an umbrella shop in Gower Street.' As the years went on she developed a habit of secreting forks in her handbag, and Norman would instigate a search of the bag and the pockets of her fur coat before she went home.

For a large part of her life, the Coach was home. It was an odd, rambling, echoing, dark building to call home, with its steeply turning stairs, windowless passages, random cubby-holes, bare floorboards and an upper floor that was eventually abandoned to mice and the occasional pigeon that somehow got in under the eaves. In a dim corridor on the first floor a notice was pinned to a door: 'This toilet is not to be used by members of staff.'

We assumed that Norman had been born in the Coach. We were wrong. In truth, he had been born in Ilford, Essex, on 13 January 1927. His father was failing to prosper as an insurance assessor in the City, and Norman and his brothers and sister lived for a time in a hotel in Bournemouth that his mother acquired.

Norman hated school and was shy of his weedy, lanky appearance. He later attributed his stooped appearance to having tried in youth not to look so tall. Before he was even 16 he did some work in a pub acquired by his mother's sister and her husband: the Red Lion in Great Windmill Street. It was their success that spurred Balon senior to take a tenancy of the Coach and Horses. The licence was granted at eleven o'clock on 3 February 1943.

Bombs and brasses

For Norman at 16 it was a liberation from hated studies at technical college. He liked to tell of their first night in the pub, which had acquired a reputation for dirtiness. 'We found twenty-two mice in the slop bucket, that night,' he would remember. Another problem was the bombing.

Although they had missed the Blitz, the Balon family ran the same risk of air raids, flying bombs (V1s) and rockets (V2s) that the whole West End suffered. Norman's bedroom was on the top floor, his parents' below on the second floor. The building was exposed to blast on three sides. When bombing came close they would take to the cellar. At Le Petit Savoyard restaurant, diagonally opposite in Greek Street (where the Ming Chinese restaurant was in the 1980s), diners would take their plates down to the basement and eat off trestle tables as the bombs fell.

The third difficulty after mice and bombs was prostitutes. Greek Street was at the lower end of the trade (which was plied in the streets until the Act of 1959). Before the Balons arrived, successive landlords of the Coach had found their licence at risk through trouble with the police over prostitutes picking up customers there.

Mr and Mrs Balon banned any unaccompanied woman from drinking there – all except one, known as Ten Bob Annie, a fat woman with thick spectacles, who would tip Mrs Balon the wink if a brass came in. Brass was the common term for a prostitute. It was rhyming slang, short for *brass nail*, rhyming with *tail*.

Norman's aunt's pub, the Red Lion, had been a place where homosexual men met. Homosexual acts were illegal until 1967 and the police in Soho, as with prostitution (not in itself against the law), could be tolerant or awkward as they saw fit.

One day the Red Lion was raided and Norman's Aunt Cissy was in the dock. 'How am I to know whether a man is homosexual?' she complained to the prosecuting counsel. 'Well, there may be certain signs. Some, for example, may have their hair coloured in two tones.' Cissy pointed her finger at the police inspector who had arrested her: 'What, like him? He's got two-toned hair.' She was found not guilty.

High life years

For the Balons at the Coach, with mice, bombs and brasses dealt with, the pub throve during the war, thanks to the American soldiers who thronged it. They knew young Norman as 'Junior' and would order whiskies, on which there was a good profit.

No one in the eighties would have guessed that Norman had once been a spectacularly heavy drinker. Between the ages of 25 and 30 he sank great quantities of champagne and spirits. He would habitually drink more than a bottle of whisky when he went out on a Saturday night. He simply knocked it on the head one day because he realized that it made him feel ill all the time.

In the Coach in the eighties he would pour himself a Coca-Cola. Occasionally he would order drinks for the round of people sitting with Jeffrey. It was more difficult to buy a drink for Norman. I suppose he wanted to differentiate himself from the customers.

In the fifties and sixties he had made large sums, spent lavishly on theatres, clothes and eating in restaurants, and he had lost a lot of money, too. Most surprisingly, to those who knew Norman's care in the eighties in getting value for money, he had lost £1,000 30 years earlier in a single session at a casino in Cannes. It was a sum equalling a good annual salary at the time. His father simply said: 'Well, it's a very cheap lesson.' He paid the debt, said no word about it again and Norman never placed another bet.

Norman spilled the beans about his drinking and gambling to Spencer Bright for his memoirs at the end of the eighties. I'd offered to act as a ghost myself after Susan Hill at the publishers Sidgwick & Jackson had suggested to him that he should write his memoirs. I hadn't met Susan Hill then. In her obituary in 2004, Simon Brett was to describe her as 'a depressive bundle of neuroses'. In the eighties she was in her thirties and was slipping into working less as a publisher. She had some friends who drank at the Coach and I went to see her at her bookish, untidy, Turkey-carpeted house off the Balls Pond Road. I put my proposal to Norman in writing. I'm very glad he turned me down, ostensibly because I asked for too great a share of the advance. Perhaps he suspected I wouldn't ask him hard enough questions.

Going bust

For Norman a great failure came in 1961, when his restaurant in Baker Street, Balon's Grill, went bust. He had run it according to his own ideal of how a swanky restaurant ought to be. That cost him £50,000 over three years. Bits of crockery and cutlery from the venture turned up in the Coach decades later, among them the forks collected by Norman's mother in her handbag. I still have some at home.

The odds and ends of crockery and cutlery for lunch went with the awkward bits of furniture in the Coach. For lunch the little tables lined up beneath the windows along the bar were spread with white cloths, and local businessmen, publishers or theatre people would eat the rota of roasts and veg that went with the days of the week, Friday always being fish. It felt as though lunches had always been served at the Coach. But hot lunches only began again after the war in 1956.

A cheerful, sympathetic Irish woman called Mary acted as waitress, a person genuinely charitable in her habits. Stephen Pickles, who often dropped in at lunchtime, one day had an accident on his bicycle that left him with a painful but not serious wound in the groin area. Whenever she saw him she would be sure to ask: 'How's your leg, Pickle?' She always called him Pickle.

'I love you. I love you not'

One day regulars came into the pub and found Norman sitting at the lavatory table with a heap of matchboxes, scratching away at the labels. He had had them printed with his name and that of his wife Suzanne. Now he was scraping her name off each one.

They had married in 1962 when he was 35 and she had just turned 18. He hadn't married out of love exactly, but to settle down and have children. It was the thing to do, like going to the best restaurants and West End shows. 'Love, I find, is a very overrated emotion,' he told the ghost. 'One should control it because it leads to jealousy and fighting.' They had two daughters, Lisa and Natasha.

One day, after the scratched matchboxes had run out and Norman was on a more even keel, I was drinking in the Coach with Jeffrey Bernard, Michael Heath, Gordon Smith, the solicitor Glen Reynolds and Nissa, the Maltese builder. Norman asked Michael and Jeffrey home to lunch. Michael said he couldn't. Jeffrey almost said, 'Sorry, I've got to go and eat.' He was going to the Ming for a bowl of won-ton soup and an afternoon drink. He managed to change his reply to, 'Sorry, I've got to go to the *Observer*.' So Norman asked Glen Reynolds and me to lunch instead.

Norman's house, or ground floor of a house, was in Golders Green. The front room had festoon curtains in gold satin. The standard lamp was converted from an oil lamp. A Victorian chamber-pot cupboard stood in a corner. He told us that the plates cost £14 each and that the cut-glass glasses cost £100 each.

There was endless roast beef, not overdone, wine and spirits. Norman wolfed down his food but drank nothing. His wife, almost his wife then, at any rate, Grazia talked continuously, often when Norman was talking, too. At the same time there was music: *Norma* with Maria Callas, *My Fair Lady* and then Nat King Cole.

The two other guests were Peter and Eileen, unknown to me. Peter wore a heavy gold chain and medallion and five heavy gold rings, some set with enamel. They ran the box office at the Barbican. Norman's two daughters arrived one after the other, one joining us in eating, the other sitting in a chair chatting to us. There were no embarrassing silences.

Jeffrey's angel

Norman's hobby of going to theatrical first nights cemented his friendships with impresarios. He would sometimes act as an angel for a new production, or as one of a host of angels. He'd put up money in advance and earn a percentage if the play did well. It was out of kindness that he asked me if I wanted to put some money into the play *Jeffrey Bernard is Unwell* that Keith Waterhouse had written.

In 1989 Michael Redington had decided to try it out in Brighton with Peter O'Toole. The idea was that if it did well it would come to London. Of course I was eager to invest, convinced that it would succeed. What did I know? In any case I hadn't got any money really. Norman carefully kept track of the fortunes of my few hundred, which I recouped several times over, just as Norman did with his lion's share.

Hero-worship is not a principle for investment that I would recommend, but it happened to go with a tremendous script by Waterhouse, only gently adapted from Jeffrey's Low Life columns. The director was the wry, spry Ned Sherrin, who as a young man had directed the television satire show *That Was the Week That Was*, and was determined not to show any signs of slowing down a quarter of a century later. Best of all was O'Toole playing Jeffrey.

They had elements of resemblance: the bony profile and the head of straight hair. They had been born in the same year. O'Toole was much taller, but he embodied part of what Jeffrey would like to be: poetic, amused, eloquent, romantic. From O'Toole's point of view, Jeffrey's life expressed the dangerous side of his own: drunken, devil-may-care, attractive to women. His performance was brilliant. Successors in the role, such as Tom Conti or James Bolam, had less to bring to it, though in a radio production of the play John Hurt was able to achieve what was needed.

Brighton was duly wowed and a triumphant season followed at the Apollo theatre in Shaftesbury Avenue. Jeffrey enjoyed the fame and fantasy very much, though he could still be melancholy alone with a drink at the theatre bar as the second half played beyond the doors of the auditorium. As for Norman, it was to him a piece of good fortune in which he revelled: it was like winning the football pools, not because it enriched him much, but because it was associated with his name, his pub, the West End world that he inhabited daily once he'd come in each morning from Golders Green. That did not mean that he was without fellow feeling for Jeffrey's own success; for by this time, Jeffrey counted to him as one of the family.

Beating Den-Den

One of Norman's accomplishments, which went with his appetite for West End showiness, was to spend good money on well-made clothes, but to very little effect. His shirts were made by Harvie & Hudson, with his initials on the breast. The shirts were usually of a loud stripe. The pockets of his well-cut suits bulged because he stuffed bags of change or a wrapped bread roll into them. His silk ties were somehow tied so that the wide end was too long and flapped about awkwardly. Once a week he had his hair cut.

One day in 1986 he bought a leather jacket, made to measure. It cost £1,180. I said: 'Clothes can change people's characters. I hope you won't have to act tough now.'

'Look you,' he said. 'You were making a nuisance at eleven o'clock last night complaining you couldn't get served.' It was a shrewd debating point.

An unrivalled expertise that Norman boasted was in chocolate creams. He always brought a pound box as a present whenever he and Grazia came to my house for a crowded drinks party. He would hand them out to friends at first nights at the theatre, which could be annoying to some people.

Having fallen out with Floris the patisserie over their sugared almonds, he took his chocolate cream custom to Fortnum's, only to abandon that shop when, he said, they stopped hand-dipping the fondant. When they reverted to the old method (he would tell anyone who'd listen), they rang him and he returned to their fold.

Norman liked coming out on top, and even managed to get the better of Denis Shaw, a man of truly repellent disposition. He played baddies in British films. 'Twenty stone and encrusted in warts' was how Jeffrey Bernard described him. 'Imagine a toad wearing a dinner jacket.' Norman remembered that Denis Shaw got off a charge of exposing himself to a little girl by turning evidence against the confidence trickster Charles da Silva.

Jeffrey used to say that Shaw, or Den-Den as he liked to be called, would stand in the shallow end of Marshall Street swimming baths masturbating. I don't know if he did or not, but the story showed that Jeffrey didn't like him. Nor did a lot of other people, because one of his tricks would be to get out of paying a restaurant bill by starting a row and getting thrown out. When he tried it on Norman, he called the police. Shaw paid with a cheque, which then bounced. He only paid up after Norman rang him and said he'd have him prosecuted for obtaining credit by false pretences.

Norman played straight with the police. He didn't act as an informant, but he expected the police to help if there was trouble. He did not pay gangsters protection money as others did. He knew the police on the beat and he knew the officers at the local police station. He dealt with most trouble on his own, often with considerable courage. Both he and Michael O'Donnell the barman would march a drunken man who was becoming violent out of the pub heedless of threats and broken glasses.

The cigarette machine

A scene characteristic of Norman acting as Norman in his own habitat was played out each time he came from behind the bar and unlocked the cigarette machine on the wall near the lavatories.

The machine was an exercise in awkwardness worthy of the high awkwardness normal to the Coach and Horses. Once it was unlocked, Norman would pull off the whole front section between his outstretched arms, lugging its weight over to a nearby table to let it rest on the black Formica surface.

Inside, the machine was almost entirely of wood. Columns of cigarettes towered above drawers released by the right combination of coins in the slot. Strings and pulleys wove up and down. There was a lot that could go wrong.

Norman would empty the coin drawer onto the lavatory table and sit on the settle to count the money into little plastic bags for the bank. He pulled coins across the table top in pairs with his index and middle finger. Sometimes the phone would ring or the barman announce that a barrel in the cellar needed changing, and he would lose count.

The cigarette machine was naturally more trouble than it was worth. If some customers were glad to stay in the pub and buy a packet of cigarettes to go with another drink, just as many, it seemed, complained that they had lost their money. When the pub was crowded, shoulder to shoulder, it was impossible to take the front off and investigate.

In any case, Jeffrey Bernard didn't like the cigarettes in the machine. Sometimes I popped out to the sandwich shop next to the other Coach and Horses on the corner of Moor Street and Charing Cross Road.

The shop at 101 Charing Cross Road was a cornucopia of sandwiches as well as cigarettes. There were heaps of things stuffed between rolls and baps – omelettes with a macedoine of vegetables sticking out from their surface like stones in an adobe wall; large, round, strikingly pink slices of foreign sausage folded with slack lettuce; cold batter-coated bits of veal hammered into flaps. Like stacks of carcases on a Smithfield trolley, these pressed their sides against the walls of the glass display counter.

A glass case on the counter exhibited large numbers of obscure and beautiful cigarette packets: Passing Cloud, Sweet Afton or the brands Jeffrey smoked, Senior Service, with a ship in full sail on the packet or the Players packet with a bearded sailor on.

Norman out of kindness decided to stock Jeffrey's preferred brands separately. These were kept behind the bar in the narrow cupboard at the side of the stairs where they twisted round steeply for their ascent. When Norman wasn't there, temporary barmen either didn't know where the cigarettes were kept, or how much to charge for them. Or supplies would run out. So the cigarette privilege provided another *casus belli* in the daily battle of layabout life in the Coach.

13

A Farson Attack

The click of drunkenness − Never a Normal Man − The eye of a
photographer − Sausages fried in rancid fat − 'I've lost all my money'

The click of drunkenness

Daniel Farson was one of those drinkers who suddenly went −
click! − at a critical level of intoxication. In the mid-eighties,
he was a fat man in his late fifties, the solid kind rather than
sagging jelly, his corpulence somewhat disguised by his tailored
suit. This was made with the arms too long, so that they would
conceal the fishes tattooed on the backs of his hands, a memento
of his merchant navy days. One was meant to depict a shark,
which Francis Bacon called 'Dan's sardine'. He never lost his
hair, which was fair; by then he presumably dyed it.

The great virtue of his character was the ability to begin life
all over again after a setback that would have sunk most others.
He'd been a most successful television personality, exploring,
a little like Alan Whicker, topics such as nudism, in single
documentaries. Starting again, with an inheritance from his
father, he had then attempted to preside over a pub in the East
End that put on music hall acts. He was taken for all the money
he had.

So he returned to writing: art criticism and biographical
sketches, such as *Soho in the Fifties*, which was published 30 years
after the glory days that he remembered, with Deakin, the two

Roberts and Minton, Lucian Freud and Francis Bacon. It was a romantic view of Soho, a place he loved and regarded as a home. As it seemed to him then, in Soho 'there were no rules to be broken, because there were no rules and none of the conventions regarding, money, age, class or sex which curbed the rest of Britain'.

He was a brave man even when sober and strong enough to make an antagonist think twice. He would go off at night to such places as a pub nicknamed the Elephants' Graveyard, or further afield to haunts in Istanbul.

A different kind of courage kept him going till his death in 1997. When he told me in the French pub one day that he had cancer which looked certain to end his life, he said it with such an unwavering tone that I didn't believe it. It was true he was dying, though. The death certificate gave an underlying cause of fatal pneumonia as Aids. That was in the decade after the wild eighties.

In the eighties he lived quietly at Appledore in Devon (where he was said to be barred from all the pubs except one) and made raids, as it were, on Soho. He'd drop in at the Coach and the French in the morning for a gin and tonic, always scolding the barman if he poured too much of the bottle of tonic into the glass.

The little bottle would last a double, then another, another and another. At this stage, Daniel would be all affability. He would buy huge rounds, sometimes for ten people. His chubby cheeks and well-moistened mouth made his smiling remarks all the more buttery. 'I do like the things you write. It's such a change to find a little intelligence and wit in the papers,' he might say as we bought rounds.

The turn – click! – would come suddenly. He would swing round and yelp: 'I loathe you. I can't bear you. You're so clever, aren't you? I can't stand the way you write. It's a little bit of *this*, and a little bit of *that*. It makes me sick. Don't talk to me. Of course you wouldn't want to buy a drink, would you? Oh no. It's no good offering now, I wouldn't take it from you. So

The stage carpenter Mick Tobin portrayed in *Man in a Check Cap* by Lucian Freud, whom he knew as 'Lu', just as he addressed Maria Callas as 'Cally'. He had a talent for friendship.

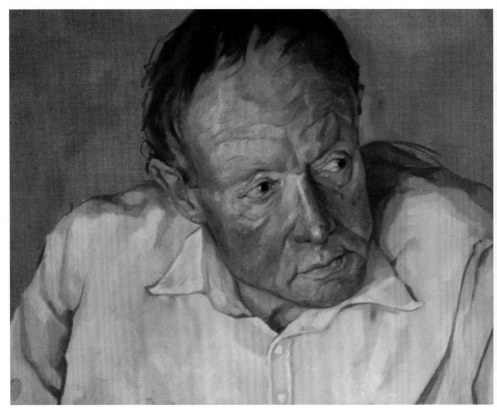

Graham Mason, the drunkest man in the Coach and Horses, portrayed by Rupert Shrive.

Jeffrey Bernard, not too unwell in 1986, enjoying a cigarette in a photograph by Phil Nicholls.

Oliver Bernard photographed by John Deakin in the fifties, showing a remarkable likeness to Rimbaud, whose *Une saison en enfer* he translated and later performed.

Bruce Bernard spent weeks in the same clothes to sit, or stand, for Lucian Freud's portrait with a shadow over his brow. It became the Whitechapel Freud exhibition poster in 1993.

Michael Heath's catch-phrase for his *Private Eye* strip The Regulars was: 'Jeff bin in?' Here, police ask for him as Bill Mitchell (left) plays spoof, Ian Board delivers a rare joke, Norman bars someone and the monocled Red Baron walks past my frown, beard and beer.

'Francis Bacon on the Piccadilly Line' by Johnny Stiletto (1983). Bruce Bernard learned that it was Bacon's favourite photograph of him and arranged for the two to meet.

On Derby day 1988, just as the big-wheel car came down, with the fairground hand standing by, Bruce Bernard's camera clicked to catch Ann Robson chatting and my knuckles petrified.

Christopher Battye's *Friday Night in the French* shows eighties men and women drinking like monstrous fledglings.

End of the eighties: the Colony Room Club on the day Francis Bacon died, 28 April 1992, in Craig Easton's photograph.

patronising. Don't speak to me. Ever.' On and on he would go, in strangulated periods, short of breath, gargling gin, spitting froth, his cheeks blotched like some scarlet aurora borealis.

When he had become as drunk as this, he would ping like a ball in a pinball machine, from bar to bar, sometimes leaving his glass of gin and its guardian yellow-labelled bottle of Schweppes tonic on the counter until an unpredictable return.

In the Colony Room Club it caused no harm if he launched into a shouting fit at one of the members. That was not out of the ordinary on any afternoon. If his bayings were directed at Ian Board when Board, too, was overtaken by drink and rage against the world, the shouting would depart from the conventions of antiphony and coalesce into a melee of cries, as though two pigs had got stuck in a narrow metal gateway.

Ian Board would rasp out childish insults: 'Fatty Farson, yeah.' Farson would yell: 'No one likes coming here any more. It's so dull. I despise you.' *Look at yerself, you 'orrible blob ... Tedious ... Fucking idiot ... No wonder Muriel hated you ... Detestable ... Dyed hair ... Failure ... Dreary old cunt ... I don't care tuppence ... Get out, get out!* Then the door would slam and Daniel would ricochet down the steep zigzag stairs into the night and some other encounter.

Never a Normal Man

Often, the morning after, he would appear with a cut face, from a fall, a fight with a rent boy or some forgotten tussle with a policeman. But he would return immediately to the alcoholic fray and the never-ending job of seeking work from newspapers or publishers.

At the beginning of 1987, Daniel turned 60. He wasn't finished. He had, it turned out, another ten years of life, and his future enterprises would include a thick autobiography which told many truths. One of his earlier books had been called *Sacred*

Monsters. He was a notable monster among the menagerie of monsters of Soho.

His autobiography he called *Never a Normal Man*. It was a remark that a doctor had made, not about him, but about his father, Negley Farson, a renowned American-born journalist. Daniel lived with his late father at his shoulder. 'He was a stronger man than I am,' he was to write, 'free from the taint of homosexuality.' He was an alcoholic, though, as Daniel knew himself to be.

He recalled how he set off with his parents in 1935, aged eight, as they drove across Europe: 'I crouched underneath a blanket on the floor at the back, pretending to be asleep – impossible with the arguments raging in the front, my father constantly wanting to stop, seizing any excuse for a drink, while my mother implored him not to. Occasionally he lost his temper, sometimes violently, followed by angry silence and the utter desolation of my mother's sobs, when I did not dare to move. Then there were whispers as they remembered I was there.'

Accompanying Negley, little Dan was patted on the head by Hitler as a 'good Aryan boy'. Later in life Daniel had an annoying way of claiming intimacy with famous people and writing about them on the strength of it. It was not that he did not know them, but that he wrote, often inaccurately, about private conversations from past years. His book about Bacon was called *The Gilded Gutter Life of Francis Bacon* – a title which sounded silly, even though it was a quotation from a joking telegram that Bacon had once sent him.

Bacon had taken to Daniel in the fifties, despite occasional differences. One night in the Gargoyle Club, a male friend with whom Daniel was infatuated butted in on Bacon's conversation. Daniel apologized to Bacon, only to be met with the reply: 'It's too bad that we should be bored to death by your friend and have to pay for his drinks, but now you have the nerve to come over as well, when you're not invited.' But next day, Bacon bought Farson champagne in the Colony Room Club.

He got into worse trouble by trading on his acquaintance with Lucian Freud. He had become muddled over names, using the name of Freud's daughter by mistake for that of a lover. As the libel lawyer Peter Carter Ruck told the High Court, Farson's article in the *Telegraph* 'included the statement that Lucian Freud publicly acknowledges five children by Rose Boyt. As the defendants now readily acknowledge, Rose Boyt is Lucian Freud's daughter, and has no children by her father.' The defence counsel said that, unfortunately, the 'very serious error in the manuscript was not noticed before publication'.

The eye of a photographer

Daniel Farson had fallen into early success in journalism in an odd way. In 1942, aged 15, he returned to wartime England from North America, to which his school had been evacuated. He then went to Wellington College, a ridiculous misjudgement on his parents' part, but after a year they were persuaded to let him leave.

He soon landed a job at the Central Press Agency. This decrepit organization was staffed by an aged skeleton staff during the war, but it had the privilege of sending a lobby correspondent to Westminster. The head of the agency, Guy L'Estrange, had not been to the Commons since the end of the nineteenth century, and Farson, aged 17, was sent to cover parliament. This blond-haired youth was a strange sight in the corridors of Westminster, down which he was pursued without success by the predatory MP Tom Driberg.

For a while, though, his career almost progressed backwards. He went with the US Army to Germany, where he discovered the possibilities of photography in the ruins of Munich. Then, aged 21, he went up to Pembroke College, Cambridge, with a grant under the GI Bill of Rights. Though he took a degree, he thought he had wasted his time academically. He did learn about the realities of sexual relations, but never found a satisfactory way of accommodating his own preferences.

In 1951 Daniel joined *Picture Post* as a staff photographer. In this period he made such friends as the impossible, drunken photographer John Deakin, who had broken with his Liverpudlian background on coming to London. Deakin, arrested for indecency when a nightclub was raided, was asked in court if he had not thought it odd to see men dancing together. 'How could I possibly know how people in London behave?' he replied; he was acquitted. Farson was sacked from *Picture Post* at about the same time Deakin was sacked from *Vogue*.

Farson took good photographs. He caught the changing moment and his pictures were often of interest for their subjects – knots of people and a handcart outside the Café Torino on the corner of Old Compton Street and Dean Street in the fifties, or the smoky French pub, with Gaston Berlemont opening another half-bottle of champagne for a crowd of overcoated and hatted men and women. Others had poignancy, such as the little boy with a dirty face and a dart in one hand at Barnstaple Fair or the handsome beggar with two peg legs in Barcelona.

At an exhibition at Birch & Conran's little gallery in Dean Street I bought an old print, signed by him on the mount, of a photograph of the one-time artist's model Nina Hamnett sitting on a banquette near the stairs in the French pub, with Gaston's intelligent Jack Russell, Peter, sitting protectively next to her. Nina Hamnett, once one of Picasso's muses, used to boast: 'Modigliani said I had the best tits in Europe.' In the photograph she wore an old wool suit with a limp rose in the lapel, her hair straggling and her face leathery, her mouth opened in a stained-tooth smile. She had been barred from the Colony Room Club because she would wet herself while sitting on one of the bar stools. But Farson's portrait at least made her an individual, a dignified human being, soiled as her immortal diamond might be.

Sausages fried in rancid fat

I once made the mistake of telling Daniel that photography was his real gift, not writing. It was probably the wrong time of day, too, for the explosion of wrath went on as long as a thunderstorm in the Pyrenees, with continuous lightning, and detonation following detonation.

The fact is that he had been a star journalist. When Colin Wilson made a name for himself with his weird book *The Outsider* (1956), Daniel wrote a double-page spread interview in the *Daily Mail* beginning: 'I have just met my first genius. His name is Colin Wilson.' Daniel visited him in his Notting Hill flat reeking of sausages fried in rancid fat.

It was to Daniel's father's house in Devon that Wilson escaped after being pursued by his girlfriend's father bearing a horsewhip and shouting incoherently: 'Wilson, the game is up! You're a homosexual with six mistresses.' But Daniel played a part that he was to regret in bringing down Wilson's reputation as a genius. He egged him on to speak unguardedly and published an interview in *Books and Art*, from which, Daniel insisted, all his favourable comment was cut out. The remaining farrago of self-conceit was picked up by the popular press and Wilson became a laughing stock.

But it was on the strength of his original piece in the *Daily Mail* that Daniel was commissioned to interview Cecil Beaton for *This Week* on television, and a new chapter opened. Daniel might have been made for television of that period. He was quick-thinking, still handsome in a chubby way, with enough charm to beguile interviewees. He spurred Dylan Thomas's widow to talk excitedly in a live broadcast which had to be faded out when he provoked her to fury.

On television, he went from strength to strength. He caused outrage with a programme, *Living for Kicks*, about coffee-bar teenagers, dubbed 'Sexpresso Kids' by the *Daily Sketch*. He embarked on a series: *Farson's Guide to the British*. He was fascinated by misfits. A series called *People in Trouble* focused on meths drinkers, midgets, illiterates, spinsters, discharged prisoners and people with disfigured faces. The production crew nicknamed it *Cripples' Cavalcade*. But it proved popular and was written of with respect for its apparent honesty. Another series, *Out of Step*, dealt with people who believed in such things as witchcraft or extra-terrestrial life.

Daniel was in the middle of filming a programme about lonely old people at Christmas when he was called to the phone and heard that his mother had died after falling downstairs at the end of a lunch with Lady d'Avigdor-Goldsmid. A man in a pub told him he had just heard the news on television: 'Daniel Farson's mother dies in fall.'

'I've lost all my money'

He knew it was time to move on. It was out of the frying pan into the fire. The rapid failure of his music-hall pub, the Watermans Arms, lost him perhaps £30,000, enough in 1963 to buy a row of houses. That was why in the eighties he was living in Devon, having moved to his parents' house near the sea.

Over a decade or so, everything movable that could be sold had to be sold: the best of the furniture, a signed lithograph by Sutherland of Somerset Maugham's head, a surgeon's head by Bacon, two Auerbachs and a Freud portrait of John Deakin. He missed most of all a Gaudier-Brzeska sketch of a tiger, which he remembered gazing at as a child in his grandmother's house.

At last the house, too, had to be sold and, though still in Devon, he was living in a smaller cottage in narrow Irsha Street, Appledore, with a dilapidated boathouse next to it at the water's edge. He lived with the younger Peter Bradshaw, whom I remember in London as silent and greasy-haired. Peter's girlfriend ran off with a fisherman, but he found another who stayed true to him till he died just after the eighties ended.

Even though money was draining away, Daniel refused to attenuate his generosity. In 1987 he launched his book of

reminiscences and photographs, *Soho in the Fifties*, with a party at
Kettner's for about a hundred people – many of them old Soho
hands with a vast capacity for the wine and spirits freely available.
Francis Bacon had come, and Bruce Bernard. Tweedy, pony-
tailed Garech Browne, the co-founder of Claddagh Records,
was over from Ireland. Graham Mason had kept sober enough to
climb the stairs. Ian Board had clambered down from the Colony
and Norman Balon had beetled over from the Coach. Sandy
Fawkes and Laurie Doyle came together. I spotted Auberon
Waugh, Geoffrey Wheatcroft, Christopher Silvester, Candida
Crewe and Fred Ingrams all shouting to make themselves heard
in the crowd. Barney Bates played the piano. The next day I met
Daniel in the Colony and told him how much I had enjoyed his
party. He replied: 'Oh, were you there?'

Daniel Farson hated the two motive forces of his life most
obviously on show in Soho: alcoholism and homosexuality. 'I
have always been a lousy drunk,' he admitted, 'wild, euphoric
and abusive after that beautiful preamble.' His reference to the
'taint' of homosexuality did not keep him closeted in shame.
One day in 1987, he came into the Coach and Horses, followed
by a brown young man who looked like a rent boy. That is what
he turned out to be.

Daniel said: 'What would you like to drink?'

He replied: 'A gin and tonic – just a small one 'cos I'm driving.'

'But I thought you were staying with me.'

'Oh, I am.'

'I'll have to get some money, because I've lost all my money.'
Daniel's voice was thick. He was very drunk. He took out his
change and put it on the counter. After the barmaid had taken
the money for the drinks, there was £15.75 left. The rent boy
picked it up, bit by bit, and put it in his pocket. One pound coin
was lodged behind an ashtray and he got at it only when the
barman emptied the cigarette ends.

'What would you like to eat?'

After much consultation he decided on steak.

'You are staying, aren't you?'

'I get as much pleasure from it as you.'

They went out into the night.

Sandy Fawkes shuddered theatrically.

I said: 'He'll lose all his money.'

'We'll find out in the morning.'

I think Sandy had a fear that Daniel might be murdered, not only because of its inherent likelihood, but also because of an incident in her own life when she narrowly escaped such a death. In the United States in November 1974, after an unsuccessful trial period with the *National Enquirer*, she met a man in his late twenties in a bar in Atlanta, Georgia. He looked like 'a cross between Robert Redford and Ryan O'Neal', she thought. They began an affair, and she joined him on a leisurely drive down the coast to Florida. She knew him as Daryl Golden. In reality he was Paul Knowles, who killed at least 18 people. The day before Sandy met him, Knowles had killed two people, one of them a 15-year-old girl he had raped.

The car they drove in had been stolen from a man missing for four months. Even the smart clothes Knowles wore were those of a murdered man. 'He told me he was going to be killed soon, but had made some tapes which would make a world news story,' she recalled. 'After a week, I just had a feeling I wanted to get away from him.'

Knowles had set off on his trail of killings only that May. It ended with his arrest within days of their parting. A month later, in a scuffle in a police car, he was shot dead. Sandy wondered ever after what it was that had prevented Knowles from murdering her, too. She wrote about it all in a book called *Killing Time*. This dangerous liaison did nothing to alleviate her underlying anxiety.

Daniel's own more trivial offences, such as being found with his trousers round his ankles in the corridor of a hotel, led to his being barred from several establishments. In Devon he often found himself in the trap of being too broke to go up to London to find freelance work. But during his attacks on Soho, he would get drunk earlier and earlier in the day. He would miss his train back to Devon more than once, and perhaps return to the country two or three days late.

The people of Appledore never quite got used to him. As he staggered down the cobbled alley leading to the boathouse which had become the narrow space where he laid his head, he heard one of the village children say: 'There's poor Mr Farson, going to his shed.'

14

Bank Holiday Bacon

'I can't paint' − *The colander* − *On the Piccadilly line* − *'If it's a monster'*

'I can't paint'

Francis Bacon in his late seventies appeared much younger. It was partly because he retained his hair, which he would sweep back with one hand. He no longer dyed it with boot polish as he once had. It was artificially coloured more subtly. He often wore an expensive leather jacket, fastened at hip level, which concealed his paunch. Daniel Farson said that Bacon looked at the camera with the 'slack-jowled vacancy of an idiot child'. He certainly had a funny-shaped head, like a pear with the stalk upmost; his piercing eyes were deeply set in it.

He often bought a bottle of champagne. 'Champagne for your real friends; real pain for your sham friends' was the old joke he invoked until it went beyond a cliché. John Edwards, his steady friend in those years and eventually his heir, wasn't always with him. When he was, Edwards, notable for wearing terrible Pringle sweaters, would often sit on a stool by the bar while Bacon stood with a knot of people to one side.

Despite his harrowing pictorial interpretation of the world, Bacon always declared that he was temperamentally cheerful. He liked to talk, and laughed easily. Marsh Dunbar remembered him as the funniest person around in the Soho of the fifties.

He would visit Soho in the afternoon after a hard morning's work when he 'felt like showing himself off while buying as many drinks all round as he possibly could'. That was Bruce Bernard's summary of his behaviour in a benign mood.

'I can't paint' was one of Bacon's more surprising declarations. It was just what Ian Board had shouted at him in a drunken tirade. Perhaps I agreed with him too readily when he said that to me one bank holiday afternoon (when he would more often than not drop in to the Colony), for he looked at me sharply as though I was being drawn into an ambush. But what he said about his painting seemed to have some validity. After all, his *Painting*, from 1946 – showing a grimacing figure under an umbrella with an opened beef carcase hanging behind it – had earlier been intended to depict a bird standing in a field.

Bacon liked to refer to Aeschylus, remembering one line in particular in translation: 'The reek of human blood smiles out at me.' I wondered how deep his knowledge of the *Oresteia* was, but, not having an accurate acquaintance with it myself, I had no chance to probe.

The colander

I'm not sure how much was generally known about Bacon's life in the 1980s. In recent years there has been an excellent stream of biographical material and documentary film, but in the eighties not much of this was familiar to me at least. Soho regulars could take people as they came with a strange lack of curiosity about their past. I'd heard that in his London studio in earlier days his nanny, Nanny Lightfoot, who lived with him, slept on the kitchen table. Ian Board said they had to shit in a colander, though I couldn't quite follow the plumbing necessity for this.

I could see from photographs of Henrietta Moraes, Isabel Rawsthorne and Muriel Belcher that Bacon's portraits of them were of great interest. But I'd never met those women, though

Henrietta had once phoned up the *Spectator* and recounted a dream in which she had seen Jeffrey Bernard dead. (He lived another few years, though she outlived him.)

After she started it in 1948, Muriel Belcher had given Bacon free drinks at the Colony for bringing in customers who spent freely and produced a lively atmosphere. He was said to have gone through the coat pockets hanging in the passage for money. Above all, in the eighties, he was reputed to be deadly in the art of conversation.

He never attacked me verbally. I was lucky. He did, though, use some of the exaggerated Mayfair cockney that he deployed to such comic effect. Once when he was picked up by the police very drunk in Old Compton Street he had said in a ridiculous camp accent: 'I'll have you know I'm a very fime-ous pine-ter.'

Michael Heath would tremble if he opened the door to the Colony and found that Bacon was there. Ian Board would always make a point of introducing the cartoonist to the painter, saying: 'This is Heath. He's an artist, too.'

'Oh, really, what kind of art do you do?'

After a few torturous minutes, Heath would finish his drink and make a beeline for the door. Before it closed on his heels he would hear Bacon saying to Board: 'Who was that cunt?'

On the Piccadilly line

In 1984 Bruce Bernard took two series of photographs of Bacon, which 15 years later were put on show in San Diego along with the exhibition of Bacon's papal portraits from 1953. The Arts Council published them as *Twelve Photographs of Francis Bacon*. 'The only distinction the pictures have,' Bruce wrote then, 'is that he felt no need to look friendly, tragic or anything else, as he knew they weren't for a magazine or any purpose at all and might well never be seen.'

In taking them, Bruce had in mind John Deakin's directness in photographing Bacon in 1950. As it turned out, 'anyone could be forgiven for thinking Francis indifferent, bored and even hostile towards me, but although he was perfectly friendly before and after each session (cups of tea and small talk to begin with), he became preoccupied and a little depressed when faced by the camera or even to be harbouring hostile thoughts about someone.'

It was not that Bacon resented the possibility of being instrumentalized by his old friend. 'He always liked helping friends make some money out of his privilege,' Bruce wrote emphatically, with regard to this photographic exercise, 'and would have put on an act for me had it been necessary.'

One evening in 1988, during a chance meeting in Jimmy the Greek's cellar restaurant, Bruce gave me a postcard of a photograph of Bacon on the Piccadilly line. It showed the painter in a full-length suede coat with the belt knotted, standing in an Underground train, holding the stainless-steel pole and staring at the presumptuous man behind the camera. I later found out that Bruce had discovered the phone number of the photographer, Philip Thomas, who went by the pseudonym Johnny Stiletto.

As Johnny Stiletto explained it to the writer on photography Lucy Davies: 'This guy came on the Tube, and he had a fantastic suede overcoat. It was a suede trench coat, and there was this sort of half-pounder Rolex, and I thought "Wow! This is great!" And the way the cuff was falling over the Rolex was just exquisite.

'So I thought "Maybe this is Francis Bacon. Shall I take a photograph? Suppose it's not. Suppose it is." So I took about five or six photographs, and he gave me a fantastic eyeline, straight into the camera.' The next thing Johnny Stiletto knew, *Ritz* had run the photograph as a centre spread.

'I got a call from somebody on the *Independent*, Bruce Bernard, who was a fixer for Francis Bacon, and he said Francis has seen this photograph and it's his favourite and he'd absolutely love one. So I said that's fine. So he arranged this thing that I went to, at the Michelin restaurant [Bibendum], on Francis Bacon's birthday, hosted by Bruce Bernard. I took two prints along and he signed one for me and I signed one for him. I've still got it.'

Bruce wasn't quite a fixer, as he might have seemed, just a friend, but he did like to arrange pleasurable occasions for people he liked. It was absolutely true that the snap on the Piccadilly line train was one of Bacon's favourite photographs of himself.

'If it's a monster'

Bruce Bernard detected a change in Bacon in the mid-eighties. 'His marvellous good humour of past decades had greatly diminished, and he felt defiantly defensive about his work,' he wrote. 'He had also alienated his few good painter friends and kept on asking me (and certainly others) what I thought of Lucian Freud's latest pictures – and didn't I think that Frank Auerbach had lost his way a very long time ago. It was sad.'

This fits with some of the evidence that the art historian Michael Peppiatt gives in his memoir *Francis Bacon in Your Blood*. In 1985, the year after Bruce's photography sessions for *Twelve Photographs*, Bacon had a retrospective at the Tate. Peppiatt had the opportunity to talk to him away from the champagne that Bacon had paid for and the celebratory crowd (Gaston had been invited, and even Maltese Mary, who ran the Kismet Club.) He recorded that 'the moment Freud's name comes up I sense him go aggressively tense, as if the hair at the back of his neck was suddenly bristling like a dog's – just as it did, I remembered, years ago when a hapless hostess in Paris introduced him to Jasper Johns'.

At that time Peppiatt was in love, and his own changed demeanour had made Bacon ask if he was becoming religious. Bacon deployed his weapon of verbal aggression when Peppiatt introduced Bacon over dinner to the woman he was to marry. 'And what do you like in modern art?' he asked her, with dangerous intentness. She explained that she had specialized in German Expressionism. 'Well, I simply detest German Expressionism,' he replied. 'I can't think of anything I loathe more than German Expressionism.'

In this I can smell the cordite of the classic Soho verbal bombardment. I'd heard such aggressive barrages from Daniel Farson, from Ian Board, from Graham Mason, even from Bruce Bernard. All of them were influenced in conversational style by Bacon, even if they possessed plenty of home-manufactured munitions.

It was the same with a phrase that Peppiatt records Bacon using of Matisse and his 'squalid little forms'. It's absurd to dismiss Matisse in such terms, as Bacon must have been aware. But there was a delight in a striking phrase, as when, about this time, Bacon took pleasure in refining a remark he made to the surrealist writer Michel Leiris, then in his eighties. '*C'est horrible la vieillesse, n'est-ce pas?*' Bacon had suddenly asked him, as Peppiatt records. '*Oui,*' was his reply, '*C'est horrible et c'est sans remède.*' This delighted Bacon: '*Voilà! C'est horrible et c'est sans remède.* Ghastly and irremediable.'

But the most memorable and terrible example that Peppiatt gives from this period is Bacon's reaction to the news that Peppiatt was to become a father. He grew agitated and tugged at his shirt collar (as he did when excited and feeling the effects of his chronic asthma). 'I just hope that if it's a monster or something, or even if the thing doesn't have what's called its five fingers and all its five toes you'll just do it in and get rid of it. Do you see? Do you see what I mean? Just do it in and get rid of it altogether.'

In this pathological outburst, I can hear the voice of Ian Board screaming at the mother of the crying baby on the train: 'Chuck the fucking thing out of the window. For fuck's sake shut the thing up.' As an anecdote this behaviour of Bacon is so monstrous as to be comical, like the behaviour of Quilp in *The Old Curiosity Shop*. But to an old friend, the father of a real child, it must have sounded altogether more alarming.

Peppiatt persevered in his friendship till Bacon's death. For Bruce Bernard, things were to turn out even more painfully.

15

Hard Words

'Who can you be rude to?' – 'You're just a bad actor' – The biter bit – Insult Handicap Hurdles – Counterblast to misogyny – Cold steel

'Who can you be rude to?'

On the last day of March 1987 I found myself on a tall stool at the bar of the Coach and Horses, sandwiched between Sandy Fawkes and Graham Mason, also on tall stools. Sandy was weeping on my shoulder: 'Tomorrow's the anniversary of the death of my baby.' Graham was leaning over from my other shoulder, saying to Sandy: 'You're an ugly, horribly drunk old woman.'

Drink disinhibited the regulars. They knew each other so well that unresolved tensions and undercurrents of animosity could easily turn into verbal combat. 'If you can't be rude to your friends, who can you be rude to?' Francis Bacon had often asked.

The answer, though none was intended, was strangers. The point of being rude to strangers was to stop them turning into bores, the great enemy. When the public houses of Soho became so very crowded in the late eighties, there was a feeling among many regulars that their territory was being invaded, that uninvited guests were arriving in their sitting rooms.

'You're just a bad actor'

One crowded Friday night in the Coach, the thunderclouds soon began rumbling and setting off bolts of lightning. Jeffrey Bernard seldom ventured out in the evening in the late eighties to fight through the tightly packed scrummage of smoking, drinking, shouting strangers. When he had smartened himself up for the evening not long before, by shaving before making an appearance, it had been counter-productive. He had cut his chin, which was dripping blood. Every now and then he'd wipe it and lick his smeary fingers. His shirt had islands of bloodstains down the front, and somehow it had got onto the back of his collar. It could have happened to anybody, but it was the sort of thing that was happening more and more often to Jeffrey.

Just this week he was trying to beat his early morning insomnia by staying up. It wasn't he who caused the trouble at first but Graham Mason, who had been drinking in the Colony all afternoon and now lurched with crustacean movements of his limbs to secure a tall stool by the bar.

First Graham had a row with Adrian Searle, the writer on art. The *casus belli* was not anything Adrian had said, but something he had been reported as saying. 'You fucking arsehole,' Graham shouted. 'I used to have some regard for you. I don't want to have anything more to do with you.' Adrian simply replied he hadn't said whatever he was reported to have said.

A few minutes later it was Graham's turn. He said something to annoy Jeffrey, who slid off his stool, stood up, grabbed his jacket and shook him. 'Don't ever say anything like that to me again.' Graham was a bit rattled. After a period of silence between the two, he stretched out his hand, palm down – his usual sign of affection when pissed. 'Oi, Jeffrey,' he said, 'I'm sorry.'

When Graham had been in the Colony that afternoon, John Hurt the actor was there, and now he was drinking Guinness in the Coach. Graham turned his attention to him. 'You're just a bad actor. All you want is fame.'

Jeffrey said: 'Well, I want to be rich and famous – though I'd settle for the former.'

The Red Baron, wearing a monocle and a hat, was standing a little way off, obviously quite drunk. Now he came over and talked to Jeffrey, who was amused for a time. But when the Red Baron moved on to Graham, he rebuffed him immediately: 'You know I don't like you. Go away and leave me alone.' So then the Red Baron tried John Hurt, who was interested at first, but after a while said: 'I'm getting bored with your funny voice. Either you're spastic or you're boring.'

Having repelled the Red Baron, John Hurt got bored with Graham, too, and left. Jeffrey was woozy, drunk and tired of the noise and crowd, and left as well. Graham then got into a row with a bewhiskered man of about 30, who had been hanging around recently, and now threatened to hit him. Norman came from behind the bar and stood between them. The bewhiskered man sat down and Graham staggered out, hauling himself into the night by the door frame, to get a taxi. By then it seemed as though we'd been through a hard night of it. In reality it was only seven o'clock.

The biter bit

The degree of verbal abuse was remarkable enough, but more remarkable was that for the most part the combatants spoke to one another the next day and maintained a drinking relationship, even friendship, sometimes for years.

In reacting to a bombardment of obscenities, both regulars and strangers were sometimes surprised by the others' attitudes. One evening Eddie Linden, the garrulous editor of *Aquarius*, the poetry magazine, came into the Coach and introduced me in his high-pitched Glaswegian voice to a man who he said was Professor John Jordan from Dublin. It must have been the poet, who died the year after. I'd never met him before. They had both been drinking all day. The professor had to sit down.

We had a drink. 'He's one of the best critics in Ireland, but he's been ruined,' said Eddie mysteriously, 'not necessarily by what we have before us.'

Eddie went over to Graham Mason and offered him a copy of *Aquarius*. Graham waved it away dismissively and said: 'Elizabeth Smart thought you a boring nuisance and a pest.' Elizabeth Smart stood high in the cult of the Sacred Ancestors, especially for Eddie. She'd died the year before.

Eddie (among whose impressive achievements was to navigate to any part for the country by public transport for the funeral of any notable poet) was often sent packing in public houses because of his wheedling manner after a pint or two. The world should have been grateful to him for the poetic benefits that *Aquarius* had brought it since he founded it in 1969. But this part of the world, at least, was less magnanimous. Eddie went away, then came back again. This time Graham said: 'You're a boring cunt. Leave me alone. You're a bloody stupid old poof.'

At this, Nick, the mild-mannered cinema manager, said: 'You shouldn't say things like that.'

Graham turned on him and said: 'How many poofs do you know? They're just ordinary chaps. But Eddie makes a big fuss about it.'

A group of earnest-looking women were sitting at a table. One young woman detached herself from them and came over to Graham, saying in a Dutch accent: 'I must ask you to leave.'

Graham replied: 'You want *me* to leave?' He was outraged. 'Why don't you fuck off? That's English, by the way. Leave me alone, you boring cunt. What are you trying to say to me?'

Norman Balon came into the pub at that moment, not at all apprised of what had passed. But he could see something was up and said to Graham: 'It's time for you to go home. You're not getting served any more tonight.' Norman went over to the table by the settle to play chess. After a little while he realized that the woman was still expostulating. So this time he stood up and said to her: 'Will you please leave this pub?'

'Why?'

'Never mind why. Just fucking leave.'

Norman was aware that publicans could refuse service without having to give a reason – a provision of the licensing laws intended to avoid arguments with drunks. Now, finding that she was with a group, Norman relented and let her stay, as long as she left Graham alone. He then said to Graham: 'You've had enough.'

'Don't you talk to me like that, Norman Balon, or I'll report you to your mother.'

That made the regulars laugh, and the bar staff, too. So Norman played chess, and Graham bought another drink.

Insult Handicap Hurdles

The year 1987 proved a rich vintage for shouting matches in the Coach. One day Heath said: 'If you come into this pub at eleven a.m., Norman abuses you. If you come in at two o'clock, Jeffrey abuses you. If you come in at seven o'clock, Graham Mason shouts at you. If you come in at nine thirty, Pickles is rude to you.'

To mark the publication of his book *Talking Horses*, one of the races at Lingfield on 2 November that year was named the Jeffrey Bernard Handicap Hurdles. At the Coach, as the evening of that day went on, the racegoers came in. Charlie Clarke, a market trader with good connections in the criminal world, entered, wearing an overcoat, and bought drinks. He had once been jailed for four years in connection with the murder of a gangland figure whose head was later found in an Islington public lavatory (disproving the prosecution's theory that he had been shot, and setting Charlie free). Gordon Smith, the stage-door keeper, sat to one side. Conan Nicholas ordered a half. The Red Baron was incoherent. Glen Reynolds joined Fred Ingrams. Bruce Bernard drank a bottle of strong Löwenbräu and didn't say much. Jeffrey had not been sighted since half past three.

Michael Heath had been at Lingfield station waiting for a train back with Norman Balon and Val Hennessy, the journalist. Heath had said: 'Did you enjoy the day?'

Norman had said: 'No, it was fucking miserable.'

Val Hennessy said: 'Oh, I thought it was lovely.'

Norman said: 'What do you fucking know about it?'

Val was upset and insisted on sitting at another bench. 'You are the most horrible man I've ever ...'

This was the day that earned Jeffrey £10,000 after he brought a libel suit against the *Evening Standard*. The paper had suggested he was too drunk to present the owners' award after the race, but had been 'snoring peacefully' when it ended, 'a skinny hand clutching the glass bowl trophy that he was meant to present'. If he wasn't drunk, it was a rare day, but it is true that he had succeeded in presenting the bowl without dropping it. I remember 1987 as a period when newspapers were settling libel cases out of court with generous payments. Jeffrey had struck lucky again.

Counterblast to misogyny

A few days later, Conan Nicholas received more than he gave in an outburst of misogynist insult. The last time I'd seen him, he said he'd had a headache for three days, 'unprecedented' for him. Now he came over to where I was sitting in the Coach and said loudly, for no reason that I ever knew: 'That man' – pointing to Robert Bridges, a fat actor who'd played Mr Bumble in the revival of *Oliver!* and was now in the last year of his life – 'is loathsome, and he's sitting between the two vilest women in Soho.' One of these was Diana Lambert and the other Jilly, who had worked sometimes as a barmaid in clubs, and even in the Coach occasionally.

Conan was drinking brandy, slurring his words. He leaned on me heavily.

Suddenly Jilly turned on him, speaking in a very loud voice, like a Cockney barrow boy. The whole noisy pub could hear her and fell quiet. 'Just leave me alone,' she yelled. 'I may not be clever, but I've worked bloody hard. Leave me alone. I'm not Shakespeare. I don't earn £40,000. I get £50 a week. But I know what Soho is. You don't know what it is to want things. Leave me alone.' So she went on, perfectly clearly, till she brought herself to tears. Stephen Pickles comforted her. A few minutes later, I found that Diana had gone.

No one could say anything. Jilly bade a tearful goodbye and kissed everyone, including me. Conan was reduced to talking drunkenly to a young stranger with safety pins in his denim jacket. Then Conan played chess with Norman. That was how I left them at 9 p.m.

Cold steel

I didn't know what had got into Conan. I found out later that he had had a big row with Jeffrey Bernard, an old friend and one he had come to rely upon emotionally. The occasion for their bust-up was money. Jeffrey had lent him £50 perhaps and wanted it back at an awkward time.

Early in January 1988, Michael Heath and Jeffrey were playing the gambling game spoof in the Coach. Conan said that he wouldn't play, on the grounds that he'd given Norman Balon his word. 'I had a game of spoof with Frank Norman once,' Conan said, 'and I won £1,000 off him. I said: "Forget it, you can buy me lunch."'

Jeffrey leaned over and said: 'The true story is that Frank won the £1,000 and then dismissed you *with contempt*. He said: "Fuck off. Forget it."'

'Honestly, Jeff,' said Conan, 'I can't remember which way round it was.'

'I should drop that word "honestly",' said Jeffrey.

It was a chilling example of how Jeffrey could drive people away by ruthlessly withdrawing affection and challenging them to rebuff him.

16

Heath

The loudness hypothesis – A liking for monsters – Soho in the USA –
Mrs Balon Bebop – The Regulars – Accidental craziness

The loudness hypothesis

Michael Heath had a hypothesis that if, instead of half whispering,
you talked loudly enough about someone in the same room,
they wouldn't notice. From experimental evidence I would say
that the hypothesis is false.

One day in the Coach and Horses he tried out the loudness
hypothesis on Frank Dickens, the cartoonist who drew the
immensely popular Bristow strip in the *Evening Standard*, all about
bowler-hatted office workers and pigeons on the windowsill.
When not drawing, which was most of the time, Dickens spent
lengthy periods in what seemed to be a drunken fugue.

He had recently won £170,000 on the football pools. At the
same time he had been served with a bankruptcy order over a
debt of £180,000. So when he got his pools cheque he tried to
cash it at the *Express*, which owned the *Standard*. They agreed to
let him have £800 a day. He had been spending it and dropping
some on the floor. Since this account of things came from
Dickens, it was probably not all true.

That morning in 1987, Dickens came in and said he had
bought a castle. As he tucked into one of Norman's round-
bowled stemmed glasses (which held half a pint of wine or

spirits and ice), Heath, standing at the bar just next to him, started to do an imitation of one of Dickens's endless drunken monologues: 'Oh, Miriam Karlin, I can tell you a funny thing about her. I was on this volcanic island and Bernard Levin said to me: "Here, I've got this wonderful Picasso and I'd like you to have it." And do you know what I did? I took it from him and tore it in pieces. The problem was that we were marooned and there was this smashing bird, and her father had to have his leg amputated, and I was the only one who could do it, and he said: "Look, here's a million pounds. No, take it." It reminded me of the time I met the Queen Mother. No listen. And I said to her ...' By this time even Frank Dickens had had enough and left, saying that he had a date with Freddie Jones's sister-in-law.

A liking for monsters

Heath saw the point of Soho, or some of its points. He liked monsters – Ian Board at the Colony or Daniel Farson in his cups or Jeffrey Bernard most of the time – partly because of their ability to *épater les bourgeois* by refusing to play by the rules imposed by men in suits who had ruined so much, including *Punch* magazine, from which he had jumped after many years, to take refuge at the *Spectator*, where I shared a tiny office with him at the back of the building looking out on the little garden.

He'd been drawing cartoons both for *Punch* and the *Spectator* since 1958, when he was 23. Now he was in his fifties but looked much younger – because he dressed young, wearing things like horizontally striped T-shirts and shoes that seemed to have been cut in pieces and sewn up again with binder twine. His face was unlined and he had kept his hair. Its brown hue owed something to the hair preparation with which he rinsed it.

He never ran to fat but had a thick neck, something he attributed, with what foundation it is hard to say, to the potion he took before appearing at an army medical, in order to avoid national service. Iodine came into it and palpitations. It seemed to do the trick, because he was classified as unfit to serve, but he did not die.

Michael Heath was the finest observational cartoonist of his day. He noticed things that were pretty awful and turned them into humour – commuters from Brighton lining up the miniatures of spirits on the early morning train to work; a crackhead crazily mugging someone with a shovel. It was the stuff of desperate humour, of satire at its harshest.

Before Soho it was Brighton that he observed. He lived there for decades, astonished by its racecourse razor gangs and spivs and billiard-hall sharps and smoky, shabby pubs. In Brighton, he ran into Gilbert Harding, who in the fifties was universally known as an irascible personality on television panel shows. Long before John Freeman made Harding cry on television, Heath found that this outwardly successful media celebrity was a tangled mess of drink, anger and homosexuality. He would take the whole range of his pills prescribed for the day, pour them out into a saucer and knock them all back at once, washed down with brandy.

In his drawings, Heath did not fall back on out-of-date conventions but always depicted people with the clothes, hair, demeanour and mannerisms of the moment. He was immensely pleased when Lucian Freud once complimented him on the economy with which he depicted a nipple, with a little spiral stroke of the pen.

Line was the essence of his work. As we sat in the small garden room at the *Spectator*, he would spend hours moving his dip pen across A3 pieces of paper, hatching in parallel lines, then constructing blocks of cross-hatching with lines at 90 degrees. I could hear the scratch of the nib on the paper, scratch, scratch for hours as another deadline approached and a bike messenger arrived to take a finished drawing to the *Sunday Times*, the *Independent*, the *Mail on Sunday*.

He always feared growing into his father, who drew endless frames for children's comics – cowboys and air aces – and worried about getting the fighter plane right, and worried about getting the next commission. Heath never stopped as the decades wore away, but kept on scratching,

He would buy nibs at a shop at the top of Drury Lane and was furious when it closed down to become yet another coffee bar. He often left ink bottle tops off, so that the Indian ink solidified to a shellac crust. Scalpels would lie around splashed with Tipp-Ex correcting fluid. I would sometimes tidy up his finished artwork when it had been returned for him from newspapers and stack it in drawers to preserve it, but he would lose it, tread on it, scrunch it up.

Heath's humour grew out of adversity. He was a hard-done-by only child. His parents, of a socialist outlook, did not believe in Christmas presents, or, it seemed, birthday presents. If he did receive any presents they were given away. With the war, he was evacuated to Devon, but it was to a spot on which the Luftwaffe dropped their bombs if they couldn't find Plymouth. So he was sent back to London in the Blitz.

Staying with an aged relation near the British Museum, he was thrilled to be given a present. On the box was a lovely picture of a battleship with an intricate superstructure. When he opened it, he found nothing but a block of balsa wood and a diagram of how to carve it.

Soho in the USA

Since Heath was often rewarded with bottles of vodka or whisky by delighted customers for whom he had done drawings, the shelves of our office soon acquired the appearance of an amateur speakeasy. What surprised me was that Heath did not become an alcoholic. He could certainly drink, though he never displayed notably drunken behaviour. He recounted dark periods of his life – usually to do with women, with whom he was forever in trouble – that he had methodically drunk through.

One of those times was 1985. The publishers Heinemann sent him to America, to which he had never been. He started off by going to the wrong London airport, and fevered anxiety followed him round the New World, from New York to California via the Deep South, from the baggage carousel to the spot with the feeblest grasp on reality – Las Vegas – where he drew a circus trapeze act staged above rows of one-armed bandits before which huge-bottomed men and women sat in a trance.

Elsewhere in America he drew subway passengers scowling at graffiti; flocks of cloned gays in T-shirts and peaked caps, all sporting moustaches; huge cops festooned with handcuffs and equipment; newspaper readers consuming stories such as 'Gang roasts poodle', 'Housewife commits suicide in her dishwasher', 'Teen delivers Bigfoot baby'.

A full-page cartoon, captioned 'Drinking across the US', showed, under a big sun, a spaghetti tangle of freeways turned into continuous bars before which, on fixed, round high stools, men (mostly) in hats or baseball caps nursed their beers or exchanged words with the bar-keeper while above them televisions displayed unattended talking heads. It was recognisably drinking, if not quite as we knew it.

Mrs Balon Bebop

That book was dedicated to the jazzman Thelonious Monk. Heath wanted to draw as Monk played: accurately, inventively, with blue-note knight's moves. He said he had listened to Monk every day of his life since he discovered him as a teenager. I listened with him to 'Straight, No Chaser' or 'Crepuscule With Nellie' on his record player at a flat he had above an antique scientific instrument shop on the corner of Bedfordbury on the edge of Covent Garden, or another flat on the edge of Bloomsbury. Flats came and went like women, accompanied by puzzlement and private anger.

Perhaps an element of jazz improvisation came into his conversation, which also reflected the absurdities of daily life by way of imitation. It was catching. One desperate bank holiday when the normal rhythms had been upset, we were both in the Coach and began swapping the stock phrases endlessly repeated by Norman's aged mother.

'I got this ring at Harrods.'

'Always get the best.'

'Do you know how old I am? Well, I'm ninety.' (She was then in her eighties.)

'I went for a holiday in Kiev last year. We went on a liner. It was simply fantastic.'

'Betty has been with me forty years. I found her in the gutter. Isn't that wonderful?'

'Every day she takes cabbage for the orphans. They don't like it.'

'She's got terrible arthritis, but she does all the shopping. She's simply fantastic.'

'Of course we have our little rows.'

'I always say to Norman. If you want to tell a girl off, take her up to the office, like my husband did.'

'Do you know what he was? He worked in an insurance office in Queen Victoria Street.'

'I've got three sons. One's a lawyer, one's a chemist, and one of my grand-daughters is a judge in chambers.'

The Regulars

At the end of the eighties a collection of cartoons was published by John Murray under the misleading title *The Complete Heath*. Along with single-column items from the *Sunday Times* in the series Style Victims, and the square-format, finished drawings for Great Bores of Today (with words by Richard Ingrams and Barry Fantoni), the book included 32 strips from the series The Regulars, which appeared in *Private Eye*. The strip succeeded another called The Gays, which was very funny in an observational way, but had, Heath felt, become impossible to continue when people began to die in numbers from Aids.

The pub interior of The Regulars was recognizably the Coach and Horses, with the stools before a bar with a rail running along it and a television on a high bracket. The cast was recognizable, too, with Heath's version of the lanky Norman yelling 'You're barred!' or simply 'Out!' at the jostling, swearing, shouting regulars, among them black-hatted, black-clothed Bill Mitchell, rotund Daniel Farson, angry-faced Graham Mason, long-haired Stephen Pickles, the dresser Ron Lucas with a long cigarette holder, Sandy Fawkes with a cigarette unattended between her lips, high-browed Bruce Bernard, bearded me and a strawberry-nosed visiting Ian Board. The funny thing was how many readers wrote in swearing that it was their pub and their regulars from which Heath must have got his inspiration.

The running gag was the query 'Jeff bin in?' in a speech bubble attached to a head round the door, a telephone receiver, a cricketer on television, a ventriloquist's dummy, printed on a T-shirt, written as graffiti on the bar or sprayed on the window.

The Regulars ran each fortnight for 15 months from August 1986. The last strip depicted Norman pushing down the plunger of an explosives detonator, crying: 'Time, gentlemen, please!' It was to have appeared on 11 November 1987, but, the Sunday before, the IRA set off a bomb at Enniskillen, killing 12 people. So that Regulars strip was pulled and only appeared in a frame on the wall of the Coach. Although they were screwed onto the wooden panelling, many of the Regulars strips were stolen.

Accidental craziness

The sorrows of cartooning formed a subject to which Heath often returned. They didn't all happen to him. David Austin, whom I knew and liked, was for a while drawing a pocket cartoon for the tabloid *Today*, which sometimes suffered production difficulties. '*Today*'s gone and put the same caption on David Austin's cartoon as it did on last Saturday's,' Heath reported one day in the Coach. 'He did a cartoon of a placard reading "Baker for Education" and a teacher saying: "At least we'll get more dough." Today he drew some runners for Geldof's famine aid. It has the same caption: "At least we'll get more dough." It looks crazy.'

One Boxing Day, between wives, Heath was at a loose end in Soho and we had a drink in the Coach and then wandered round to Dean Street, and somehow we were asked in for a drink in the beautiful Georgian house opposite the Colony where Blacks Club was soon to be set up.

On the first floor, in an unimproved panelled room before an open fire, a very new baby was lying unclothed on a quilt in the warmth of the firelight. There seemed to be no one else much about. Since it was Christmas this was a strangely memorable scene – certainly not of the regular Soho kind.

17

Soho Sickness

Crashing out – John Hurt's jump – 'Oh, sleep's lovely' – Non-speaking parts – Irma's agony advice – Michael Elphick's vodka – Mysterious Tom Baker – Overseas members

Crashing out

Closing time in Soho arrived earlier and earlier. Chronologically, time continued to be called at eleven o'clock, and the law allowed an extra 20 minutes' drinking-up time. But by half past ten it was already borrowed time, as though only the tired muscles of a drunken stagehand were preventing the curtain falling on the night's entertainment.

Never mind the clock, the feeling of it being half past ten – with friends shouting at each other, the heat and smoke and noise blurring out any focus, and then at least one person in the company becoming drunk enough for their legs or speech or short-term memory to pack up, so that they staggered, or slurred or went round and round in constant repetition – that half past ten feeling could strike before *The Magic Roundabout* came on the television at teatime.

Towards the end of the lunchtime session one Friday at the Coach, Daniel Farson, jowls flushed, was complaining. 'Jeffrey says that I'm envious of him,' he said. 'It's so unfair.'

'I couldn't give a fuck,' said Graham Mason. Hunched over the bar with a cigarette between his fingers he turned his pickled-onion eyes towards me. 'Let's go to Muriel's,' he suggested.

On my other side, Conan Nicholas was having a drink with his son Julian, a young jazz musician. That day Julian, who had recently become a father, was wearing a spangle earring, eye make-up and a bright red polo neck with braces over the top.

'We're going to Le Caveau,' Conan said, the dark, smelly drinking club in Frith Street, little better than the Kismet.

'I'll join you later,' I said.

In the Colony Room Club, Ian Board was sitting on the tall barstool in the corner and the lank-haired barman Michael Wojas was dispensing drinks. Graham drank vodka, ice and soda. I drank vodka and water, which I was stuck with at the Colony since it was the first drink I'd ordered there and remained my usual, there and only there. Following Ian Board's practice I did sometimes have a port and brandy if I felt queasy. It was easy to drink, though there was no evidence it did any good.

Tibbs turned up with Mandana. Mandana Khaki was a great beauty, clever, nervy, amusing and shrewd. She even smoked attractively. She later made a great success of the Academy Club in Lexington Street. Tibbs was now staying with her in Maida Vale, while in his flat in Brixton was living an American girl he'd picked up the year before. I found her pretty awful. Tibbs had apparently married her, to help her secure right of residence.

Tibbs's official name was Andrew Tiffen. He was a young cartoonist who had a strip in the *Sunday Times*, but he worked for a living in the Vintage Magazine Shop in Brewer Street, heaving packages of film posters around. Although he sometimes sat at the bar looking at himself in the mirrored wall behind it, he was even fonder of women. He enjoyed their company as well as one-night stands.

A few months later he took up with a girl from Sweden. She must have gained a funny idea of England, since all she saw of it was the Coach, the French and the Colony, with perhaps some pasta at the Pollo on the north side of Old Compton Street. The only change of scene came when they went to see a production of *Waiting for Godot*. It must have seemed the most rational thing since her arrival. It was Tibbs who once gave me a drawing for a birthday present showing me with a pint of beer and a blotchy nose, looking at my watch and saying: 'Hmm, half past ten already.' He was still young when he died, of hepatitis.

At the bar of the Colony, Graham was being rude to Jay Landesman, the tiresome American publisher, who was wearing a straw hat and smoking a cheroot. Maurice, a tall, curly-haired man who wore a coloured handkerchief round his neck and seldom seemed to say much coherent in the afternoon, was quietly drinking and smoking a roll-up.

Barney Bates came in. He was a quizzical man with a laugh that dismissed the absurdities inherent in daily life. Wine was his drink, and lots of it. When he played the piano in the Colony, people would buy him a glass of red wine, and the glasses would line up on top of the piano. He might not be able to speak, but he could play the piano apparently unaffected. His undoing was his bicycle, on which he was to collide with a vehicle in Chelsea Old Street, making him walk and talk as though he were drunk all the time.

Graham Mason said: 'It's fucking boring in here. I might as well go back to the office.'

I went on to Le Caveau. Conan was there with Julian and Bookshop Billy, whom Westminster Council charged many thousands a year for a sex shop licence. That meant he could sell magazines, principally. I think a proviso was that, as with betting shops, nothing enticing was on display in the window.

John Hurt was in the corner arguing. He seemed manically drunk. He grabbed Conan by the lapels and then scrabbled at the wall with his hands.

'I should go,' Billy said to him. 'You're out of order.'

'Yes, man. You're totally out of order,' said Conan.

'He's just drunk and unhappy,' I said.

'That's fair,' said Conan, and bought me a whisky.

I confessed I hadn't got enough money to buy a round, which came to more than £4. Billy bought me a pint.

No daylight reached Le Caveau. It was fuggy and noisy. It seemed like half past ten. I looked at my watch. It was 5 p.m.

John Hurt's jump

John Hurt was generally so volatile that it often seemed unwise to light the blue touch-paper. He enjoyed conversation in pubs, pushing it along with his expressive voice, an undercurrent of emotion always available. I once told him that I thought his performance – as Stephen Ward in *Scandal*, I think – was 'quite good'. Perhaps that was naive, but I didn't mean to be provoking. He went off like a skyrocket, with a full range of tone and volume, to show up the shallowness, the moral self-betrayal, the immaturity, the inexcusable crassness of my patronising verdict.

Then there was drink. The death of Hurt's long-standing girlfriend in a riding accident in 1983 and his marriage in 1984 to a beautiful American, with whom he could start a new life in Kenya, did not seem to me circumstances which, combined with the great strains of his acting roles, were likely to abolish the explosive episodes of public drunkenness for which he was known. At difficult times, his eyes became more hooded and his jowls ruddier.

Not that I knew anything of his psyche. I just saw him standing on the counter of the Coach and Horses one afternoon poised to jump with outstretched arms into the array of bottles and glasses on stands and glass shelves attached to the rear wall of the bar. A couple of people grabbed him by the shins and eased him back down to earth.

'Oh, sleep's lovely'

In the Coach in the mornings you could hear and breathe. On Sunday mornings at noon the only person in the pub might be a small, shy, thin old man called Ted, sitting alone with a flat hat on, drinking barley wine. But people came and went.

It was always cheering to find Michael Nelson in the pub. He felt it a duty to amuse. He was in his sixties in the eighties, a round-faced, balding, slightly baffled-looking man in a check overcoat.

He was best known for a novel he had at first published anonymously, in 1958, *A Room in Chelsea Square*. The book, whose hero is called Nicholas Milestone, was based on his own experiences as a young man finding his way in London. It wasn't reckoned obscene, indeed it was happily reviewed in the *Daily Telegraph* (by John Betjeman) and even in *Punch*, where Julian MacLaren-Ross, the old Soho hand, had opined, with more optimism than foresight: 'This may be the novel about homosexuality to end all novels on the subject.'

One Friday lunchtime in January 1987 Michael Nelson was chatting to Graham Mason near the sputtering gas fire. 'When I was at Anzio,' he was reminiscing, 'I told my troops: "Look, this is very serious. If you are in trouble, put your hands up like this, and say *Kamerad*." Well, they were trying this out when the Colonel came past, and put his hand on his revolver. So I said: "Just joking, Sir." And the men said: "No he fucking wasn't."'

It was neatly told, not for the first time, doubtless. Another day, in the Coach, Michael was talking with Jeffrey Bernard, and mentioned that his war wound was feeling better.

'You notice how his wounds are all in the back,' Jeffrey said.

'I don't know why you find that funny,' said Michael.

Micky Nelson, like so many Soho characters, seemed to exist in a parallel universe which occasionally overlapped with the French or the Coach. There was little thought given to what he did between appearances. Gone were the days when he earned a good living with a regular slot in the *Daily Express* called Nelson's Column.

The next time I saw him I was having a drink with Michael Heath, whom I showed something amusing I'd read in a magazine. Heath leaned over to Micky to share it with him, too, but he waved it away.

'Can't you see it without your glasses?' asked Heath

'I can't see anything at all. I'm pissed. I always think you should be pissed by midday.'

'But don't you mind sleeping all afternoon?'

'Oh, sleep's lovely.'

That was how talk got round to Lucian Freud, with whom he had been in bed one afternoon and thought to himself what a nasty thin cock he had. Was that true? It wasn't a kind thing to say. On the other hand it was not easy to forget.

Non-speaking parts

The periodic entrances of witty Micky Nelson into the Soho soap opera contrasted with the daily presence of people who were undoubtedly Soho characters but scarcely had a speaking role.

Some barely spoke at all. Danny Kirwan, who had played with Fleetwood Mac in their 'Albatross' days, liked to sit for hours with his back to the window just inside the door at the deep end with a pint on the table. He had seen years of bad health and homelessness. He kept himself to himself, and that was fine.

Chirpier was Harry Kitto. He had a home to go to, in the suburbs, towards closing time. Sometimes he had breakfast in the Court Café in St Anne's Court, a cheap and friendly place which later became a Thai restaurant. A retired man with wispy white hair and a weak chin, a raincoat and a sort of squashed trilby, he resembled the television comedian Harry Worth in his habitual look of surprise.

The thing that he most often said was 'Shostakovich!' There was little else that was coherent beyond exclamations, 'Oh, I say!' and a hand clamped over an astonished open mouth. He was universally liked. There was sympathy when he was mugged one night in the leafy suburbs, and reappeared bruised and frailer than ever.

Another affable figure who seemed to join the conversation while hardly saying anything comprehensible was the picture editor Tom Hawkyard. He seemed to make remarks in a friendly way, but though I often met him by chance in the Colony and drank with him, he never put two intelligible sentences together. He showed no other signs of drunkenness, indeed he was always sprucely turned out in a well-pressed grey suit, his hair neatly combed and his moustache trimmed.

His face was hardly lined and he seemed much younger than his years, for he had started work with *Vogue* during the war and was credited with having introduced John Deakin to the French pub. He probably had a hand in a photograph of Deakin that is in the National Portrait Gallery. Taken in 1952, it shows him leaning on a marble pillar supporting a baroque figure; the backdrop is of black hangings. Anyway, although Tom amiably raised his glass and said, 'Your good health, sir', that was about it.

A rarer bird of passage who did talk, and very amusingly, was Charlie Riddell. He looked extremely unusual for 1987, wearing his hair cropped and a long beard on his beefy face. His long coat was made out of upholstery fabric and his trousers were rolled up over high boots. The ends of his moustaches were twisted into rings. He bought the wax at Trumper's. He was beginning to work again as a designer after a year with nothing. After a while he was no longer around. I wonder what became of him

No one who set out to become a Soho character had much chance of success. The ecology was so dense that few niches became vacant. Nicknames, and not just those invented by Graham Mason, could have an unwelcome power to pin down established denizens like moths in a display case. I never became a friend of Brian the Burglar, but one could see that his nickname was a professional disadvantage.

Then there was the Russian Spy, who was Russian, but not a spy, unless his taste for drink and frequent physical injuries were brilliant cover. At one party he tried to cut his wrists with a broken glass while his girlfriend was banging her head against the wall in the corridor, saying: 'He doesn't love me anymore.' The Spy survived, with bandages for a few days acting as a reminder of the high emotions punctuating his life.

Stuttering Sarah, a clever woman who often said sharp things, frequented the French and the Colony. She did stutter but could hardly have wanted that to become her label.

Certainly anyone who called Eddi McPherson 'Big Eddi' to her face would answer for it. She was a jazz singer who first arrived in London to make her fortune in 1959. In the eighties her son Graham had become famous as Suggs in the group Madness. In the Colony she generally drank white wine and seemed a comforting presence. I was going through a low moment one day. Who knows what it was – insomnia, a touch of anxiety – and found myself shedding a tear. Eddi gave me a hug and said reproachfully: 'You're trouble is that you're full of shit.' It was a memorable diagnosis, but I didn't understand quite what she was getting at until years later when someone explained that she disapproved of my being a practising Catholic. Most people seemed not to mind.

The most generous compliment I ever received was from Susie Bardolph. She had a quiet voice, a trim figure and an affectionate manner. I was much younger than she, but no oil painting even then. Sitting at one side of the Colony with an arm about me, she ran a hand over my spine and said: 'Oh, haven't you got a lovely back.' Kindness could stretch no further.

Irma's agony advice

One sunny morning I found Jeffrey and Irma Kurtz talking at the bar. Irma, a tough but sweet-natured American, then in her early fifties, had made her home in a tiny flat in Compton Street. She had known Jeffrey since the sixties and I got the impression that she dealt with him with the attitude of a grown-up, even if that implies an element of childishness on his part.

That year she had accompanied him on a trip to Kenya, which was hard work at times; when Jeffrey had been bad-tempered, she had given as good as she got. When they dined out with some fossilized colonials, their hostess said: 'Are you sure you're not married?' Irma remained a friend all his life.

Irma had since 1970 written an agony column in *Cosmopolitan*, the progressive women's magazine (which eventually, decades later, she told me had turned into nothing but soft porn). She gave an agony aunt analysis of Jeffrey to his biographer Graham Lord, if only as a hypothesis. 'On the one hand he lacks self-confidence,' she said. 'On the other he thinks he's pretty damned great. I think it's got to do with being the baby son of a doting mother, or something.'

That morning she talked cheerily of an attempt by the feminist Dale Spender to have him barred from the Groucho Club on account of his language. Jeffrey asked: 'Is it really true that she tells her students that they should be rude to a man three times a day?'

'Man or men, Jeff,' Irma replied. 'It doesn't have to be little old you.'

'Oh God, it sounds like war. I'd been thinking it was all a bit of banter. That's the last time I lay my Crombie overcoat down in a puddle in Dean Street for a woman to step on. They can just drown in that. The days of drowning in my eyes are over.'

'She Who Would Drown in My Eyes' was the label that Jeffrey pinned on Deirdre Redgrave, the former wife of Corin Redgrave, the actor, after an unguarded remarked she was supposed to have made. I must say she took it very well. Perhaps she knew that he only said it to annoy because he knew it teased.

Michael Elphick's vodka

A few minutes after Irma had gone, the actor Michael Elphick came in. He was then about 40 but looked older, with his stocky body and weather-beaten face. He was just beginning to attract a large following in the television series *Boon*. Jeffrey saw him as a bit of a hero, for succeeding as an actor without losing his common touch or his appetite for alcohol.

'I went to Fortnum's this morning', Jeffrey said, 'and had a huge ice-cream sundae. All the waitresses were staring at me gobbling it up like a little boy, and making noises with the straw at the bottom. Then I bought a lemon ice cream from an Italian at Piccadilly Circus.'

Thinking of his diabetes, I said: 'It sounds like you should have a hotline to the Westminster Hospital.'

'That's funny,' said Elphick, 'I'm opening a fête there this afternoon. Well, my wife's in there. She had a breast off a few years ago, and now they've found something else. It's not fair. She doesn't smoke and drink, and sleep around. And here's me, doing all sorts of things and there's nothing wrong with me.'

While Elphick was in the lavatory, Frank Dickens came in, with a stranger. His first words were: 'I've got a cheque so big that no one can cash it.' Jeffrey was getting impatient. Dickens was trying to tell the whole bar about having just lost the dressing on his back where a girl had poured a kettle of water over him in the bath. Then, in his confusion, he started to drink Elphick's drink. Jeffrey restrained him.

Elphick had downed four or five large vodkas. Jeffrey had been drinking since eleven. At about a quarter to two he had to go and get something to eat.

Mysterious Tom Baker

In the mornings Jeffrey and Tom Baker usually seemed equally glad to see one another, I think. Tom, a couple of years younger than Jeffrey, was recognizably famous as the Doctor from *Doctor Who* on television, but in the eighties he often did work on voice-overs early in the day and dropped in at the Coach for a Guinness. He certainly did not present himself as a celebrity, and I suspected he liked to ally himself with Jeffrey as a tearaway.

I was surprised not that, in his later teens, he had been a monk, in Jersey, but that he had since so utterly changed as to have dropped everything that went with it. He did not like conventional morality or anything to do with God. He had not retained a love for Gregorian chant or, so far as I could tell, any part of the culture he had once embraced. He talked about women and drink. He enjoyed talk, and Jeffrey and he bounced well off one another. He would stand with a scarf round his neck, his protuberant eyes glinting and his excellent set of teeth smiling. I spent a lot of time with him but didn't penetrate his mind.

The expectation was that there would be someone in the Coach worth talking to, if one turned up before lunch. Yet there were persevering regulars who depressed the atmosphere whenever they came in. One was Eddie Judd. He had been in *The Day the Earth Caught Fire* in 1961, playing an alcoholic reporter caught up in a global catastrophe when the Earth is pushed out of orbit by nuclear explosions. The film ended with the presses about to roll on one of two front-page stories set up in type: 'World Saved', or 'World Doomed'. Eddie, now in in his fifties, had begun to find work mostly in voice-overs. His beard sprang grey from his leathery face. He seemed always to be resentful, and spoke mostly to Bill Mitchell.

One morning in the mid-eighties the actor Freddie Jones came in, no doubt expecting cheering conversation. He'd recently been in Fellini's *And the Ship Sails On*. He was grey-bearded and red-faced and his nose looked like a pimple with the top taken off. He was wearing a black jacket embroidered with flowery patterns. He tried to have a conversation with Jeffrey, but Jeffrey was pretty pissed and a bit slow in recall and response. Jeffrey was at least aware that pub conversations meant more than set-piece stories. He liked quoting a remark by George Barker: 'Anecdote is not a form of conversation.' But today, alcohol and diabetic imbalance had robbed him of his main talent. For Freddie Jones, it was an occasion when a visitor brought more to the bar than he found there.

Overseas members

Someone who seemed part of Soho even when he was away from it was Stan Gebler Davies. In 1985 I ran into him at the *Spectator* when he was on a foray from Cork trying to sell some articles. He was renowned for not wanting to pay tax.

Stan could be very aggressive verbally. He was unusual in admitting that he was an alcoholic and continuing to drink doggedly. The doctor once said to him: 'What's the matter with you? You don't lie about how much you drink.' He was often pimply-faced and black about the eyes. His nose was bulbous and pitted. I saw him standing blinking in the morning sunshine in the garden of the *Spectator*, shaking and crapulous.

Another day he dropped in at 4 p.m. and joined the end of a *Spectator* lunch, being rude to another contributor and accusing him of blasphemy. That time he'd come to the *Spectator* to get some review books to sell at Gaston's bookshop off Chancery Lane, which offered half the cover price on new books, which it then sold on to libraries.

After he'd sold his books, we went to the King and Keys, the horrible *Daily Telegraph* pub in Fleet Street, then took a cab to the Coach. After that we went to the French, where I left him, unable to keep up.

Among the overseas members of Soho whom we were glad to see at least for the duration of their occasional visits was Robin Cook, who lived in France. Already in his mid-fifties, he had just published a crime novel, *He Died With His Eyes Open*, under the name Derek Raymond, by which he was to become famous as the author of repellently violent work.

In person he was reticent in manner, speaking with a slightly hoarse voice with almost a lisp. His face was thin, his teeth were bad and his straight grey hair escaped perpendicularly from a black beret that he generally wore in the Coach or French. His black leather jacket and black jeans did not distinguish him in Soho at the time, when, as I have said, all the young and some of the old wore black very day.

Robin was an Old Etonian, in attitude cynical and constantly amused by the seriousness with which France took his writing, inviting him on television chat shows with philosophers and historians. He drank pints of beer and seldom sprang to the chance of buying a round.

Robin Cook wasn't very nice, but niceness was no qualification for acceptance in Soho. He had doubtless, as he said, worked in porn shops and acted as a business frontman for the con man Charles da Silva (credited with selling a Grimsby fishing fleet sight unseen to a man he met in the first-class breakfast carriage of the train from Hull to King's Cross). But Robin didn't mind lying, so it was hard to know the true details of his life. He was on his fifth marriage.

18

Private Eye

Awkward people – Everything done in the pub – The first big libel –
The abandoned dining room – Quite drunk and very excited – 'Kiss
me, Chudleigh'

Awkward people

I don't know that Richard Ingrams much liked Soho, but he
made it the place where *Private Eye* took root and flourished.
When he was at Oxford in the late fifties, he had chosen for the
meeting place of his circle a greasy-spoon Cypriot café called
the Town and Gown, with neon lights and horrible food. They
had a table for lunch there every day.

When *Private Eye* set up shop in the sixties at 22 Greek Street,
'between a striptease and a betting-shop', in the words of Claud
Cockburn, Ingrams' journalist hero from the thirties, the offices
looked like somewhere 'into which some gangster had recently
thrown a more or less abortive bomb'.

It was no better when the magazine moved down the road
to 34 Greek Street in 1969. 'It was still another revolting office,
but this time it was above a Chinese,' Tessa Fantoni, the wife
of Barry Fantoni, told Ingrams' biographer, Harry Thompson.
'The street door was unlocked, so you'd go into the lavatory and
there'd be some junkie standing in the loo fixing themselves up.'

Ingrams was suspicious of swanky decor. When the *Spectator*
offices were redesigned in the eighties by Suki Marlowe, as she

was then (later Paravacini), he complained that they were now more like Harley Street than Grub Street. He always preferred down-at-heel places, just as he liked awkward people who would produce friction when they rubbed up against his colleagues. The Coach and Horses proved ideal.

Everything done in the pub

I didn't suspect it in the mid-eighties, any more than anyone else did, but after more than two decades in which the fortnightly satirical magazine had been identified with him, Ingrams was about to jump from the editorship, after installing his successor, Ian Hislop.

We hadn't seen much of Hislop in the Coach. Ingrams had met Hislop in 1980. He supplied jokes, notably a very funny parody of the regular *Sunday Times* feature, A Room of One's Own, with Bobby Sands as the subject. Bobby Sands, an IRA member imprisoned by the British, was at that time mounting a dirty protest and smearing his cell with excrement while wearing only a blanket. In his parody, Hislop wrote: 'He has chosen a simple pastel brown to decorate all four walls. "I think the effect is very soothing," he says, "and it sets off the subdued grey of my blanket. It cost me next to nothing".'

In 1984, when *Private Eye* had moved from Greek Street to Carlisle Street, on the other side of Soho Square, the staff continued to come to the Coach for lunch at the lavatory table, but not so dependably. Ingrams might come in with Christopher Silvester and Paul Halloran, but Hislop did not join them.

Christopher Silvester had found a job at *Private Eye* after working for Conservative Central Office before the 1983 election. Richard and Mary Ingrams even apparently thought he might be a suitor for their daughter Jubby. Silvester's nickname was the Spiv. He is the only person I can think of who carried an umbrella while wearing a leather jacket. His mousy hair curled over his collar and he took to wearing his keys or something on a chain in his trouser pocket.

Paul Halloran was described by Harry Thompson as 'burly, terse, unfriendly, suspicious, he rarely used a four-letter word when seven would do'. He was a stocky, red-faced Antipodean, often in a Hawaiian shirt, whose forthright remarks were as diplomatic as a broken bottle. I found him entertaining and frightening. According to Jane Ellison, a *Private Eye* journalist, Richard Ingrams enjoyed people's horror and outrage at Halloran. 'At the *Eye* lunches, Halloran used to get drunk and abusive, and Richard just sat there spectating.'

Occasionally, too, at the lunchtime table, that living shipwreck from the sixties satire boom, Peter Cook, would appear and launch into a stream-of-consciousness comedy fantasy as he consumed white wine from Norman's half-pint round-bowled glasses.

Each morning Norman would place a little 'Reserved' sign on the table while his mother sat there folding paper napkins and polishing forks. Sometimes only Tony Rushton, whom Ingrams called 'chief dogsbody and box-wallah', would come in for a sandwich.

'In the old *Eye*, everyone was much closer to each other,' William Rushton told Harry Thompson in the early nineties. 'Everyone went to the pub. All the decisions were taken there, at our regular table in the Coach. Now Tony goes and eats at that table alone.'

'Everybody used to go there at lunchtimes,' Ingrams recalled. 'Pretty well the whole staff of the *Eye* went to the Coach. We had our own table there, round the corner by the gents', which was very useful, because anyone who wanted us knew we would be there.' It was a subversive place to do important business, safely beyond the control of business managers.

When Tessa Fantoni, then still Tessa Reidy, came for an interview for a job as a secretary at *Private Eye*, she was sent over to the Coach and Horses, where she found Ingrams and others watching cricket on the television. At last Norman Balon took notice of her and asked: 'You here about the job?' Yes, she said. 'You'll do,' replied London's rudest landlord, and that was it.

The first big libel

Ingrams had, in 1971, forsworn strong drink. Norman Balon remembered him before then as 'an amazingly large drinker. He'd put it down by the ton.' But then Ingrams started to feel ill and was convinced that he was dying. 'The doctor said my liver was several sizes too big and I should give up drink,' Ingrams recalled. So he went to bed for the weekend and never drank again.

This went with one side of Ingrams' character. As his son Fred put it, he saw things in black and white, from a moral standpoint. Ingrams used to call the deep end of the Coach 'Winos' Corner'. To many who continued to enjoy a drink, it appeared that he was observing them from a distance and disapproving. That is how Jeffrey Bernard said he saw it. Certainly Ingrams, reasonably enough, regarded drunks as bores, the great public enemy. Even back in 1961, in the first issue of *Private Eye*, a front-page trailer had announced: 'Bore of the Week – back page'. And yet the whole social structure of the regulars in the Coach was itself designed to repel bores.

Private Eye had only found itself embedded in Soho in the first place because, in 1962, the prospering magazine had been sold for £1,500 to Peter Cook and Nicholas Luard, who ran the Establishment, 'London's First Satirical Night Club'. So Christopher Booker, William Rushton and Ingrams, together with Mary Morgan (later to be Mrs Ingrams) and Elisabeth Longmore (later to be Mrs Luard) moved from their offices in Covent Garden to the building where the Establishment Club was installed, at 18 Greek Street.

Private Eye's first big libel case, in 1963, was celebrated by the exhibition in the window of the new office at 22 Greek Street of a writ from Randolph Churchill, accompanied by a copy of the offending article and a cartoon of Randolph Churchill by Rushton entitled 'The Great Boar of Suffolk'. Some days later an injunction was obtained to compel the withdrawal of the little display. *Private Eye*'s own lawyers went into a panic upon seeing the Rushton cartoon. They sent a message: 'You did not tell us the pig was excreting.'

Ingrams' semi-detachment from Soho was reflected by his decision to buy a cottage with his wife Mary at Aldworth in deep Berkshire. He would shake off the dust of Soho from his heels at the end of the afternoon and head for Paddington. Mary Ingrams stopped working for the magazine in 1964 when her son Fred was born, and she rusticated in Berkshire alone.

The *Private Eye* people had already been familiar with the Coach and Horses when in 1969 the magazine moved in at 34 Greek Street, diagonally opposite. On the ground floor, downstairs from *Private Eye*, was Clementine's café and delicatessen. This had been opened the year before by the family proprietors of the old-fashioned French restaurant Le Petit Savoyard next door, which was still run by Isabella Martelli, who had opened it in 1907. It was quite a step from the satirical world of the swinging sixties back to the Edwardian days of the *entente cordiale*.

Norman Balon used to like to see how business was doing at Le Petit Savoyard by coming over from the Coach and Horses to borrow a lemon. Mrs Martelli died in 1970, and five years later Le Petit Savoyard became the Ming Chinese restaurant, where Jeffrey Bernard liked to lunch in the 1980s because the proprietor, Christine, was tolerant of him.

The abandoned dining room

For those who seldom visited Soho, the fortnightly Wednesday *Private Eye* lunches must have seemed even more peculiar. They were held in the dispiriting room on the first floor, 'designed by Stafford Cripps', as Jeffrey Bernard remarked of the austere decor. Perhaps because it had once been the Balons' dining room, it had an unconquerable air of desertion as though it was part of an abandoned house in a war zone.

For a long time it was hung with wallpaper of an outsize floral design, which was so bad that Richard Ingrams insisted it should never be changed. At last the room was redecorated in tasteful grey, but the chill atmosphere remained. Richard Ingrams had been presented for some achievement with a large framed cartoon by Scarfe, or possibly Steadman. He had never taken it home, and it remained propped up on the mantelpiece at one end, accentuating the bareness of the rest of the room.

Awkwardly, the room could only be reached by going round the end of the ground-floor bar counter, with permission, to reach the steep stairs up in the middle of the rear wall. The tiresome anti-monarchist MP William Hamilton once tried to ask Norman where he should go for the *Private Eye* lunch. 'Fuck off, I'm on the phone,' he replied. Hamilton did, and never returned.

For the *Private Eye* lunches, Norman supplied an unchanging menu, as agreed with Ingrams: melon, steak and chips then suet pudding with golden syrup. Ingrams cheerfully regarded it as 'disgusting', though it was surely no worse than the food provided later at the huge lunches held by the *Oldie* magazine at Simpson's in the Strand, over which Ingrams presided like a prep school headmaster.

'I always regarded it as a test of stamina for the guests,' he said of the *Private Eye* lunches. 'If they failed on the treacle stodge, which a lot of them did, it would always lower them in my opinion.' I must have passed the stodge test when I was first asked to a lunch in 1986, but I baulked at the custard. Perhaps that told against me. Ingrams was always friendly towards me, in those days calling me 'Hice' as a sort of nickname. But if I found him a little distant I was not the only one.

Quite drunk and very excited

One day in 1986 Dick West, a good friend and a veteran freelance journalist, turned up at the *Spectator* offices after lunch, quite drunk and very excited. It was an unusual combination with him. The excitement was provoked by the future of *Private Eye*, about which he cared very much. It was hard for a newcomer to Soho in the eighties to realize that it had only been a few years since he, like Jeffrey Bernard, had been a regular contributor, in the centre of the gang that produced it. Since then, Jeffrey had become hostile, while Ingrams chuckled at his drunkenness, and Dick had become distanced.

By 1986, Dick could look back with amusement on the years when *Private Eye* was one outlet where, as a freelance, he could place his stories. Standing at the bar of the Coach, he recalled one piece he'd written for *Private Eye*, over which there was eventually legal trouble. 'Richard Ingrams asked me if it was cast-iron.

'"Oh, yes," I said, "it has got a very good source."

'"Are you sure it's watertight?" he asked. "Is it really a good source? Where did you get it from?"

'"Yes, yes, very good. As a matter of fact I made it up myself."'

Dick was proud of never having had a staff job. He had reported from Vietnam during its war. One day he woke up in a field and didn't know where he was. He managed to get a taxi and told the driver to take him to town. As they set off he said: 'Oh, by the way, what's the name of the town?' 'Singapore,' came the reply.

By 1986 he looked a well-preserved 50, though he was already 55. His face was reddish, and his hair grey and well cut. He was about six foot, solid but not fat. Sometimes he would drink lime juice and soda or Perrier. Sometimes he drank pints of cider. Sometimes he drank a great deal of whisky. At Sunday lunchtime, perhaps after going to St Giles-in-the-Fields for a service according to the Book of Common Prayer, he'd drink Guinness. He preferred to drink standing. He sometimes had a hesitation in his speech.

Dick's views were unpredictable. 'What's spoiled Africa is socialism and democracy,' he said. He hated what had happened to the children in Biafra, which he blamed on England and the federal Nigerians. He blamed the Ethiopian famine of the 1980s entirely on its Marxist government. He was sympathetic to the

Vietnamese and the Thais. He found the roguery of Filipinos engaging, as he did that of the Trotskyist leader of the Militant Tendency in Liverpool, Derek Hatton. Dick was well liked, but *Private Eye* had stopped using his stories.

Ingrams had written a novel based on Dick, called *Harris in Wonderland*, which had come out in 1973. His co-author was Andrew Osmond, and the author named on the cover, 'Philip Reid', was a combination of their middle names. The novel was interesting to those who knew Dick West. An unlikely comic scene involved the accidental ingestion of LSD during a hippy happening at the Round House in Chalk Farm. Dick said that Ingrams had in mind a sequel in which the plot would culminate in Dick's imprisonment in a cage with one of John Aspinall's tigers.

'Kiss me, Chudleigh'

It was at the farewell lunch for Auberon Waugh in March 1986, a year of changes, that Ingrams had suddenly resigned as editor of *Private Eye*. Bron Waugh's plan on leaving *Private Eye* was to set up the *Literary Review*, a monthly that followed the simple plan of being filled with nothing but book reviews. I think his inspiration was *Books and Bookmen*, a periodical run on the same principle by Philip Dosse, who badgered people to write the reviews he wanted until they agreed. One was the Prince of Wales, who agreed to write about Queen Victoria. A reclusive man always short of money, Dosse had killed himself in 1980.

To found a magazine and club was a brave venture for Bron, then aged 46, who devoted every day to writing, in order to earn the money for the upkeep of Combe Florey, the house he had inherited from his father Evelyn, and to educate his children. He was able to buy a pied-à-terre in Hammersmith by selling for £240,435 a strange piece of furniture that had been given by John Betjeman to his father. This was the Narcissus washstand made by the Victorian architect William Burges. It features in

Evelyn Waugh's novel about an episode of madness, *The Ordeal of Gilbert Pinfold*, because, like Waugh, Pinfold was convinced that the removal men had lost an ornamental spout that went with the piece of furniture. Waugh, like Pinfold, was rattled to discover that the spout was a delusion.

Auberon Waugh was surprisingly full of energy, though he never seemed to do any exercise, and often had to spend a spell in hospital for treatment to his chest. This was the legacy of his days in national service in Cyprus, where, trying to unjam a machine gun, he set it off, shooting himself through the chest and shoulder, and losing a lung, his spleen, several ribs and a finger. It was on that occasion that, lying at death's door, he said in jest to his corporal of horse: 'Kiss me, Chudleigh.' Chudleigh, not recognising the Nelsonian reference, treated him ever after with suspicion.

The offices of the *Literary Review* were in Beak Street, in respectable west Soho, above the premises of the Academy Club that Bron also started, using his knowledge of wine. Bron wrote the monthly wine column for the *Spectator*, recommending disgusting white wine as 'ideal for weddings'. A measure of Bron's writing style is the scarcely credible simile he chose for one wine, which he likened to 'a bunch of dead chrysanthemums on the grave of a stillborn West Indian baby'.

Bron was as polite and reticent in person as he was outrageous in print. He hardly ever came to the drinking holes of Soho. Although he once wrote that he had never gone to bed sober for decades, he was too busy to spend time in pubs.

The Academy Club I found rather restrained and lacking in character when I went there. But it survived and improved in more agreeably unimproved premises from the early eighteenth century in Lexington Street, with Mandana Ruane, as she had become, installed as chatelaine for many years, and her dog Heathcliff ineffectually keeping guard of the door from the stairs up to the first floor.

After Bron left *Private Eye* and Richard had announced his resignation, Dick West had tried to stir up a move in favour of giving the editorship to Peter McKay (who'd returned from America the year before). Dick went for lunch with Peter Cook, Nigel Dempster, Patrick Marnham, McKay and others at the Gay Hussar at the top of Greek Street. Cook refused to be serious, but drank a great deal of wine.

It was from that lunch that Dick had come back to the *Spectator* in an elated mood, leaning on the doorpost of the little office at the back that looked out on the garden. He wrote a short leader on the subject while taking swigs from a quarter bottle of brandy. But in the meantime Cook had staggered over to the *Private Eye* offices in Carlisle Street and, spotting Hislop, shaken his hand, exclaiming: 'Welcome aboard.'

Hislop stayed.

19

The Enigma of Richard Ingrams

Live coals on the piano − Victorian digression − A kitchen in Chelsea −
It's a horrible life − Family territory − An eye for absurdity

Live coals on the piano

The most remarkable incident in the biography of Richard
Ingrams is surely the sudden appearance in the Ingrams household
in 1958, when he was 20, of an apparently deaf, deeply disturbed
Kikuyu boy of about 11 called Thieri.

Richard was at the time living at home between national
service and going up to Oxford. His brother 'PJ', 18 months
older than he, had simply brought the boy back from Kenya,
where he had been posted as a Guards officer. Their mother
Victoria had to look after him. It was an enlightening episode in
the life of the woman whose extraordinary qualities lie behind
the tenor of the Ingrams family story.

Looking after Thieri was a full-time task for her. He put live
coals on the piano. He often turned on all the taps in the house
and flooded it. He always put his pyjamas down the loo. He
did war dances in Cheyne Walk and tried to kill every passing
cat. Interviewed for a local deaf school, 'he climbed up the
headmistress, who was very tall and thin, as if she was a pole, and
damaged her back'.

Nagged by the authorities, Victoria Ingrams even told them
that Thieri was her son. Eventually, when no school could cope

with him, Thieri ended up at Lancaster Mental Hospital. But while he was still around, Richard, like the whole Ingrams family, had simply accepted him and shown him great devotion.

During her long life (1908–97) Victoria Ingrams exerted a remarkable influence, mostly from the kitchen of her house in Cheyne Row. It was over to this house that William Rushton, at school with Richard, would cycle during the holidays and automatically be fed in Victoria's kitchen. The death of Rushton's father brought him and the fatherless Richard even closer. It was to Cheyne Row that Mary Morgan came as a lodger before Richard did his national service. Only six years later did she become Richard's wife.

Victorian digression

Victoria Ingrams was named after Queen Victoria, whose doctor her father, Sir James Reid, had been. Nothing could rival his role in the death of the Queen-Empress (whom he called Bipps, to his family not to her face). As the Queen entered the last days of her life, unable to read because of cataracts and having lost half the weight that had made her look like a cottage loaf, Reid judged her state of mind as 'apathetic and childish'. It was apparently the first time he had seen her in bed, and he was 'struck by how small she appeared'.

Sir James found himself having to convince the Queen's children gathered at Osborne that she really was dying, despite her remark three days before the end: 'I should like to live a little longer, as I have still a few things to settle.' It was Reid who secretly telegraphed Victoria's grandson the Kaiser, informing him of the Queen's imminent death, which brought him hurrying to her bedside.

Hours before she died, Reid, as part of his scheme to let the Queen herself think she was not facing imminent death, got the Prince of Wales to silence the Bishop of Winchester's recitation of 'Lead, Kindly Light'. When she cried out to him, 'I'm very ill,' he replied, 'Your Majesty will soon be better.' He knew it was not true. When death came, it seems likely that the Queen's last words were not 'Bertie' but 'Sir James'. His final service to her was to ensure that the gold wedding ring from her Scottish servant John Brown, which she had worn ever since his death, was sealed with her body in the royal coffin.

Victoria Ingrams' mother had been a maid-of-honour to Queen Victoria. The Queen was quite put out by Sir James taking time away from her care in 1899 to marry her. Susan Baring had been 17 when her father lent £10 million to the Buenos Aires Water Supply and Drainage Company. It went bust, throwing the family bank on the mercy of a Bank of England bailout, bringing her mother to an early grave and her father to a disgraced retirement.

A kitchen in Chelsea

Victoria Reid found herself an even wider perspective than the Baring millions from which to view the world when she embraced Catholicism in 1932, partly influenced by the novelist Maurice Baring, her mother's brother. The brilliant prose stylist Ronnie Knox became her spiritual adviser, and for 35 years the parish priest of the church opposite the Ingramses' house was the well-connected Canon Alfonso de Zulueta, nicknamed Zulu.

To her, being a Catholic was of more than life and death importance. Under her maiden name Victoria Reid, she pops up in the life of the Catholic poet and artist David Jones. 'My mother had a most curious effect on her daughters-in-law,' Ingrams told the *Catholic Herald*. 'They all converted due entirely to her influence.'

Of her four sons, two, Peter John, PJ, the eldest, and Rupert, the third, were by agreement with her Protestant husband to be raised Catholics, with Richard and Leonard, the youngest, to be members of the Church of England. As soon as her husband died, she transferred Rupert to the Jesuit public school Stonyhurst, where she was to send Leonard, too.

By the eighties, Rupert had been killed in a motor accident and PJ in a climbing accident. When he was at Oxford, Richard had begun formal instruction in the Catholic faith with the university chaplain Fr Michael Hollings, but then let it drop. It was not until 2011 that he was to become a Catholic, too.

It's a horrible life

Although Richard Ingrams always seemed to view the world with an observer's amusement, he had spent much of his life in horrible circumstances. He hated prep school, where even his brother was against him. His father was distant, and died when he was a teenager. One day in the Coach, Gerry Lawless, a tiresome Irish socialist, accused Ingrams' father of having been a traitor. Ingrams shouted at him 'Get out! Get out!' Interestingly, it was to Norman Balon that he turned next, saying, 'Norman, this man is never to come into the pub again.' He was never more seen there from that day.

During national service Ingrams failed the board selecting officers and so spent his army career in the ranks. He served in Korea. The war had ended but it was an unpleasant place to be. In Malaya, to which he was transferred in 1957, Andrew Osmond, later a friend, remembered him as 'spotty and totally miserable'. It was more than ordinary acne, being a tropical skin complaint that left his face pitted, though his handsome looks and his demeanour still made him very attractive to women.

Ingrams' retreat to the country in 1964 with his wife Mary was seen by John Wells as the beginning of 'the great shut-off' for his friends in London. Then, just after Fred's birth that year, Ingrams' brother Rupert was killed in a car crash. A son, Arthur, never able to speak because of cerebral palsy, died, aged seven in 1977. Mary suffered from manic depression, which grew worse after Arthur's death, when she did not speak to her husband for eight months. John Wells remembered Ingrams saying that he treated Mary's rages like a kind of storm. He would sometimes stay with his old friend since Oxford days, Paul Foot, or with his mother.

Ingrams' elder brother PJ was killed on a mountain in Ecuador in 1979, while Richard was in the middle of the exhausting libel case brought by Sir James Goldsmith. In 1985 he had to give up work for three months after an operation on his back. The attractions of editing *Private Eye* were dwindling.

Eventually, as the eighties sped into the past, Mary left him. 'Mary wanted to get away and be on her own, where she could be free to drink,' Ingrams explained in an interview with Harry Mount. They were divorced in 1993 and she was to die in 2007.

Family territory

The Coach was a sort of family territory for Ingrams' children. Jubby, born in 1965, was in the mid-eighties beautiful, slim, lively and very welcome as a periodic visitor to the pub. She was given to sudden kindnesses, one day giving me her heavy black bicycle, which I happily pedalled home to Shepherd's Bush, where it was stolen after a while. But sometimes she looked tired and dark about the eyes.

Fred and Jubby, perhaps with an idea of being annoying, both agreed to appear in *Naked London*, a book of photographs published in 1987 by Naim Attallah, with whom Jubby had a job. Richard disapproved but did not take it out on Jubby, by her account. 'I realized there was no point in opposing it,' he explained later. 'If I had opposed it, they would have just gone on all the same.' But he was delighted when the book failed to sell.

In 1990 Jubby married David Ford, a businessman whose father was the remarkable Sir Edward Ford, ramrod-straight well into his nineties. He was the courtier who was to coin the term *annus horribilis* for the terrible year of 1992 in the Queen's reign.

His friend, the diarist of upper-crust life, Kenneth Rose, who never published his more exciting discoveries lest they alienate his sources, could not be dissuaded from suggesting repeatedly that the grammar of the phrase was defective, though it looked all right to me.

Jubby was to die in 2004, aged 39, of a heroin overdose.

Fred, a year older, seemed to possess an air of inextinguishable optimism and naive pleasure with the world. 'Look at this invitation that I've got to an arty party in New York on Monday,' he said one lunchtime in the Coach. 'I'm flying out on Sunday to make my fortune.' It didn't quite work out like that. He ended up as a painter. Francis Bacon bought a picture from one of his early exhibitions, and so did I. Now he paints mostly Norfolk landscapes.

Mary Ingrams had banned Fred and Jubby from seeing Richard's mother Victoria. But when Fred was at art school, his grandmother was shocked to find him living in a squalid flat with no sheets on the bed. She took him in and he spent two years living in her house.

It was Fred who surprisingly succeeded in introducing his father to the Groucho Club, which he found a welcome retreat from the noise of the Coach. In theory the Groucho was despised by habitués of the Coach because it stank of inauthentic advertising types. In practice Jeffrey Bernard enjoyed its tolerance of his drunkenness, and often staggered off there for lunch. He took me for lunch there once when I was homeless and hungry, and, since drink and amnesia went together, had to ask the waiter what he'd had for lunch the day before. (That was a socially easier incident than the day he kindly took me to a Greek restaurant and burned a hole in the tablecloth with his lighted cigarette by falling asleep before he'd even ordered.) Daniel Farson added the Groucho to his list of boltholes and once amused Ingrams no end by trying to introduce to him either Gilbert or George, being too drunk to remember which of the famous artistic pair it was.

In 1989, Fred's first child was born, a boy, whom he called Otis. He declared that he had named him after the lift, even though he could not have forgotten that Richard Ingrams had contributed to his school magazine the *Salopian* under the pen-name Otis. Richard had earlier used this as a nickname when writing home, in honour of Groucho Marx's Otis B. Driftwood. Mick Tobin took an avuncular joy in the new child, and from then on called Fred 'Father Fred'.

An eye for absurdity

Richard Ingrams relished absurdities. One day he was in the Coach with Christopher Silvester and chuckled over a fantasy being spread abroad by the black-clothed voice-over artist Bill Mitchell that Silvester was his son.

Many people have been unnerved by Richard Ingrams' silences. When others would laugh politely or throw a remark into conversation to keep it going, he often kept quiet. It made people doubt themselves. In the eyes of his old friend William Rushton, he was 'like a pipe-smoker who doesn't actually smoke a pipe – deliberate, reflective'. There is no doubt that Ingrams did not want to share his life's troubles with all the world. When he appeared on Anthony Clare's radio programme *In the Psychiatrist's Chair*, he seemed petrified of giving anything away.

At the same time, Paul Foot, his close friend as an undergraduate, remembered him as having 'this great internal resource, which flowed with his melancholy and with his religious commitment'. They used to go down to Cornwall and would sit on the cliffs or on Bodmin Moor. Foot would take a book, but Ingrams 'could just sit for hours without doing anything'.

When asked by a journalist what he'd like to have on his gravestone, Ingrams said: 'He made a nuisance of himself.'

20

The Lavatory Table

Space in the crush – Whizzing round Soho – A comet – Hot pavements

Space in the crush

'Ho! They won't drive me out!' exclaimed the caricature of a Cockney stick-in-the mud, all big nose, greased clothes and tufts of hair, in Colin MacInnes's *City of Spades* (1957). The Cockney character was a regular at the Moorhen (based on the Roebuck in Tottenham Court Road). 'They' were what he called 'darkies', devotees of the dancehall across the road, glad of the jukebox in the pub, a source of weed for passing trade and full of the energetic spirit in which MacInnes rejoiced.

The regulars in the Coach and Horses were not likely to be driven out by Africans and West Indians, who had long been present in small numbers in Soho. Nor was the Coach monopolized by the dominant minority in command of vice and crime – the Swiss, as it had been, then the Maltese, then the Italians.

But they were under pressure from young people.

These were not just students from St Martin's School of Art, but idiot youngsters from the suburbs coming for an evening of fun – drinking the fashionable lager of the moment from the bottle, and generally being annoyingly naive, brainless and prosperous. Most of all they lacked the death-or-glory commitment to a bohemian life without security.

The pressure was literal. The crowd was so thick that it was impossible to push through. The quickest way from the shallow end to the lavatory was out the door into Greek Street and in at the door in Romilly Street.

So the lavatory table which at lunchtime offered *Private Eye* the possibility of bread and brie became by night a rock and refuge. The regulars below middle age abandoned the tall stools at the bar and sat round the table: two on the settle, two opposite, a couple at either end. Tibbs the cartoonist, Jackie the barmaid on her break, Nick the cinema manager, Ann the barmaid, Ian the Hat, Fred before he became a father and domesticated, Glen the solicitor, Alan the stagehand, the Black Sheep (from whom I learned that having a bed at home was a waste of space), Pickles standing at the end of the bar, and a complicated shifting pattern of satellites. Mick Tobin liked sitting with younger people, and other older refugees at the lavatory table in the evening included Jeffrey Bernard and Graham Mason if still capable, Conan Nicholas, Diana Lambert and Michael Heath when he was around.

Whizzing round Soho

Diane Hills, the painter, counted as a regular, though her visits depended on her work and her moods, which were like sharp alpine peaks. I knew nothing of any past friendship between her and John Bratby. At this time she was constantly talking about her admiration for the painter Carel Weight. But Norman Balon had a fondness for her and she was always interesting if not always easy to understand. We generally saw her when she was towards the hypomanic, with continual jerky hand movements, and continuous disconnected speech.

One afternoon she came into the Coach after finishing a painting and said she'd have to drink to relax. She shook her head and looked up from beneath a dark-dyed fringe. She was wearing no make-up and the black bags under her eyes showed up. Sandy Fawkes said unkindly: 'She must have been punched in the nose.'

Maurice, who had already succeeded in relaxing, kept saying to Diane every few seconds: 'But how are you doing?'

I would have found it unbearably irritating, but Diane was in such a state of hilarity that she didn't get annoyed. Maurice and Sandy left. Diane went on. I told her I couldn't understand what she was talking about.

Alan Holmes, the stagehand, came in and had a pint. He did a couple of clues in the *Times* crossword. Meeting Diane's torrent of words he left, pleading work. A solid-looking CID man called Chris came in. He was not exactly unfriendly to Diane, other than by telling her not to speak to him. She took it all perfectly happily.

Another afternoon, I thought I'd had enough to drink and was on my way home when I was nearly run into as I crossed the road by Diane Hills in a Mini. I jumped in, and she careered round Soho a few times, looking for a place to park. I couldn't tell whether she was just elated or had had a bit to drink or something. Our voyage through Soho, accelerating, braking, careering round corners, backing and advancing in the face of traffic, was quite invigorating. I had a glass of wine with her in the French and made my escape.

A comet

The regulars round the lavatory table seemed like a solid core but new people appeared like comets for an unknown period, as though for our entertainment. Lord Patrick Conyngham made a mark when he wandered outside the Coach on a warm August night and, while he continued talking, leaned on a car. The alarm went off. Car alarms were a frequent nuisance in the eighties, easy to set off and hard to stop. Patrick repeated the performance carelessly once more. On the third occasion a policeman arrested him and took him to Vine Street station. He was charged with being drunk and disorderly. Andrew Tiffen bailed him out at three in the morning.

I didn't see him till later that day, dressed in a chalk-stripe suit that accentuated his tall and cadaverous appearance. He was talking to Jeffrey Bernard and the agreeable Stephenie Bergman, whose father had been Jack 'Kid' Berg, the boxer. Patrick had been found guilty by the magistrate and fined £40 with seven days to pay. This brought out the generosity of the regulars.

Jeffrey, who'd only recently been served with a bankruptcy order from the Inland Revenue for a debt of £598, had even more recently won £2,000 from Victor Chandler on a Yankee. He gave Patrick £100. Stephen Pickles gave him £40. Michael Heath gave him £20 or £30. So he was in credit.

Patrick was, in 1986, a poet. One lunchtime in the French pub he came over and took out some poems from a red enamel attaché case for me to give to P. J. Kavanagh, the poetry editor of the *Spectator*, for the favour of publication. They were pretty disjointed.

He once wrote a poem for me in the Coach called 'Banking on the Banks'. It was on the back of a bank statement, which recorded regular debits of £20 or £50 and a climbing overdraft for the month: £2,883.33, £3,154.58, £3,598.13. The poem, in ink, running where beer had wetted the page, began: 'The stain of time is not removed by any modern detergent.'

Patrick, then in his mid-twenties, was over six foot and bony. His eyes were sunken and tended to be surrounded by black. He was often in the French and Coach, and the Colony. He was open in conversation, sometimes loud in volume and would talk to anyone who was there. One week he was with a girl called Caroline who sold garden gnomes in Chelsea.

He was quite easy to distinguish from anyone else, and it wasn't apparent why he should wish to cement his identity, but one day he showed me his passport, which correctly recorded his first name as Frederick, and another day he gave me a black and white photograph of himself.

One Saturday morning he explained that he had been thrown out of the Colony on suspicion of drug-taking. He said that when he arrived on the pavement he was descended upon by policemen, just after he'd been handed a joint. He discarded the evidence but was taken to the station. On that occasion he gave his name and address and they let him go.

Conan Nicholas, that declared socialist, had told me that Patrick had been given free membership of the Groucho Club because of his title. But Conan also told me that, when Patrick resigned from the Groucho, after pissing out of a window, he'd asked for his subscription back. These two claims seemed irreconcilable. So when I next came across Patrick in the Coach one morning I asked him the truth of it. He confirmed he'd pissed out of the window and that he had been given his subscription back.

One of the barmaids, Deborah, talking with us when she was off duty, took against him, saying: 'Your trouble is you've never had to work for anything.'

It was certainly not easy for him to evade blame, being easily recognizable and resented for his aristocratic background. His most famous ancestor was Elizabeth, wife of the 1st Marquess Conyngham, the mistress of George IV and nicknamed the Vice Queen. Patrick's eldest brother, Henry, Lord Mountcharles, developed Slane Castle as a venue for rock concerts. His elder brother Lord Simon ran a wine bar in Edinburgh. Patrick stood to inherit no title and was looking for something to do.

He was certainly very pleased in 1986 when the musician Denny Laine said he'd got a deal to make a record using Patrick's lyrics. They were in the Coach one evening drinking Burton ale and planning to go off somewhere to celebrate. When I went out and came back an hour later, they were still there, drinking Burton ale. I don't know that anything came of the record plan.

Hot pavements

The summer of 1987 was crazy in Soho. After continuous rain and cold, the weather changed towards the end of June, so that it was over 80 degrees F by day, and still over 70 degrees in the small hours. People spilled out of the pubs and drank on the pavements: outside the Coach on the corner of Greek Street and Romilly Street; outside the decorative but tiny Dog and Duck on the corner of Frith Street and Bateman Street; outside the French in Dean Street and on the pavement on the far side of the road.

Diana Lambert's furniture lasted out the eighties as a source of drink money. She still cycled. Sometimes she looked after a dog, her mother's probably, and this got her into a mix-up. On the way home on a warm night she had settled down on the pavement for a minute to attend to the dog and sleep had overtaken her. That week, the *Observer* was running a feature on the scandal of London's homeless. Who should appear in a large, artily black and white photo poignantly illustrating their plight but Diana and her doggy companion?

By an irony, it was about this time that Diana tried to fix me up with somewhere to live when I was camping on Glen Reynolds' hearthrug with my possessions in two cardboard suitcases. She left a note for me saying that there might be a room at Dotty Phillips's. Dorothea Phillips had been Mrs Ogmore-Pritchard in the production of *Under Milk Wood* with Richard Burton in 1963 (and in the television version the next year). It was the nearest I got to Dylan Thomas, who died before I was born.

Dotty Phillips was always well turned out whenever she visited the Coach or the French, favouring scarves, beads and billowy blouses, I seem to remember. But she was 60 by then, and I wondered how she'd take to me as a lodger. Before I could go for an audition, a room turned up in Shepherd's Bush, and I took that opportunity to be saved from making my own appearance in the next *Observer* exposé on homelessness.

While her mother was dying, Diana managed to be barred from the Coach by Norman twice in a month. The first time it was for telling Norman to sack a barman. A few days later he did sack the barman, holding the door open like some Victorian paterfamilias for him to remove his few possessions. After Diana, who had acquired a plaster cast on her arm from a fall, was readmitted, her next offence was to say in a comically peremptory tone: 'Landlord, serve this customer.' Norman only served when he wanted, and she was barred again for a week or so.

The real problem came after her mother's death. Not only was Diana freed from the arduous journey by bicycle to north-west London, but she now had an inherited fund to buy whisky when she wanted some. She didn't eat any more than she had before but seemed more often to be tipsy in the morning. One day she was a strange colour. It wasn't just the dust from gardening. This was jaundice.

It turned out to be a sign of something serious. Liver, of course, but exactly what was not clear. 'I don't know, and I haven't asked,' she declared resolutely. Her decided attitude, if ostrich-like, was brave. God knows what she thought about when she was on her own. She went into hospital and did not come out. After so long struggling with poverty, she was killed by its relief.

21

Bruce

*At Jimmy the Greek's — 'Ruinously humane ideals' — A boozer —
Trouble with Jeffrey — Ice creams at Snow White — The big fall-out*

At Jimmy the Greek's

I hadn't had anything to eat all day when one August evening
I went down the steps into the cellar in Frith Street that housed
Jimmy's Greek restaurant. Bruce Bernard turned up. He hadn't
eaten all day either. At Jimmy's, with the kleftiko or kebab, they
would give you slabs of bread three inches thick and butter in
a little ceramic dish like an ink well. That and a Greek coffee
came to £3.85.

Bruce said: 'It's funny, I've been coming here for thirty years
and that waiter still doesn't like me.'

It was more common for people to like him without knowing
every detail of his daily life. He maintained long friendships
such as that with Lucian Freud partly because he didn't blab
confidences. Indeed, his long silences puzzled new acquaintances.
They often thought it was them.

In the mid-eighties, Bruce was in his late fifties, four years
older than his brother Jeffrey. He had never been as dazzlingly
handsome as Jeffrey, or his other brother Oliver, 27 months older
than he. In repose, his expression was hangdog, and his round
head gave him a Slavic look. He remembered that when he was
working on the building site opposite the French pub after the

war, passing women would call out: 'Hey, Poley, Poley, want a jig-a-jig?'

Like his brothers', his initials were reduplicative: B. B. Bernard. Very few knew during his lifetime what the middle B stood for. Marsh Dunbar knew but would not tell; even Jeffrey kept quiet about it. It turned out to be Bonus. I suspect his parents meant that he was a bonus to their son Oliver, but, as the Latin for 'good man', it seemed to me accurate.

He walked with what has been called a rolling gait. Most people didn't know that he suffered from sometimes agonizing gout, which was no joke. He had wanted to be a painter, but despite early sojourns in Paris and Cornwall after the war, he hardly let one canvas survive, certainly not be seen. He rented a stone barn for five shillings a week at Paul, near Mousehole, and picked potatoes to pay his rent. The studio where he worked and lived was up a ladder in the barn and through a trapdoor. Below it was a kitchen.

Decades later, Oliver reproduced a small image from 1950 on the cover of his collected poems, *Verse &c*, crediting it to 'Joe Hodges', a by-line that Bruce sometimes used, taken from his mother's maiden name. It shows something like a tree or cathedral stonework with cusped tracery. When asked in Paris what style of painting his was, Bruce had answered: '*Un peu abstrait.*'

That is how his manner sometimes seemed – *préoccupé*. A colleague from the *Independent* newspaper, the writer Kevin Jackson, said he spoke in a 'meandering, slightly plaintive manner'. It is true that he shared the Bernard downbeat enunciation, but, like his brothers, he relished a pointed formulation of words. In conversation in public, if he wanted to show friendliness he would give a soft punch to the upper arm.

Another judgement commonly held was that Bruce dressed as though he bought his clothes in charity shops. It is true that he often wore shapeless trousers and an old tweed jacket (over which he might put on a blouson-length leather jacket), but around the time of that meeting in Jimmy's he was regularly sitting over a period of months for Lucian Freud, so he had to wear the same clothes each time.

This was the standing portrait, with a shadow falling awkwardly across his head, later used as the poster for the Freud retrospective at the Whitechapel Gallery. It was to become the painting by a living artist that commanded the highest price at auction. About this painting, and another showing him seated, Bruce made the remark: 'It is indeed no ordeal at all to sit for Lucian, unless, like me, you do not like to sit or stand still for more than two minutes.'

'Ruinously humane ideals'

Bruce's chronic lack of money is often attributed to his integrity. He wouldn't do things commercially that he didn't believe in. Sometimes he seemed so serious that he was like a Wittgenstein who drank. When Ian Jack once made some remark to him about his 'career', he replied: 'That is one of the most horrible things I've ever heard. Disgusting! Awful!'

He liked to share presumptions with his friends about what was valuable in the world: of course Van Gogh was a superlative painter; of course Muhammad Ali was a noble man; of course Soho boozers weren't to be judged by their financial success. Jane Rankin-Reid, the art critic, called his set of attitudes 'ruinously humane ideals of artistic freedom'. Typically, Alexander Chancellor, his friend and admirer, gave this characteristic an edge: 'Integrity oozes from Bruce's every pore – which can be rather annoying.' There were other forces at work, too. One was his devotion to Soho. 'I've met all the people I've ever cared about in Soho,' he once remarked. 'I just hung about too long – a couple of decades too long.' In fact he never really left.

In a way, Bruce was a sort of gardener of Soho – he was more involved than a catalyst, as it were, which is unaffected by a chemical reaction. When, in 1962, Michael Andrews painted the Colony Room Club in action, crowded with only eight main figures, Bruce had been at the centre. As the writer on art Martin Gayford noted, Bruce remembered that Andrews 'at first shocked my humility by making me virtually the central figure, then shocked my vanity by bringing in Henrietta Moraes to obstruct the view'.

He was not entirely obstructed, for his face in profile emerges from behind her hair – or, rather, the hair of Virginia Law. It seems unlikely that Bruce got it wrong, but the figure in the foreground must be Henrietta's successor as the wife of Michael Law, Virginia Slater. She was convinced that it was so, she told me, and it is undeniable that the painting shows a fair-haired woman, when Henrietta was dark-haired.

In any case, Michael Andrews' intention was to give an impression of what the Colony Room was like. He had made pencil sketches of different people as studies for the oil painting, but the whole picture was not meant to be a series of portraits. Clearly enough, though, Bruce remains, in a triangle with Francis Bacon and Lucian Freud, at the heart of the dynamic.

It seemed quite normal that Bruce never owned a car. Many Soho hands didn't or couldn't. But the most demanding criterion for a thorough Soho bohemian was to have nowhere to live. Sometimes this was literally true of Bruce, as when he lodged in Rowton House, the vast dosshouse in Camden Town. But even when he was stably employed – as picture editor of the *Sunday Times Magazine* in its heyday, and later as visual arts editor of the *Independent Magazine* – he lived insecurely, in some interesting places.

One was in a lovely Georgian house next to the British Museum. But there he had no kitchen. Later he rented two floors of a house in Frederick Street, on the edge of Bloomsbury, in that knot of streets that Thomas Cubitt had built in the early nineteenth century as a sort of full-scale pattern book of his houses. It was sublet to him by a council tenant, which meant he could lose it at any time.

When visitors sat in his drawing room with its tall windows there, he would play, as loud as he wanted, which could be very loud, the 1958 semi-bootleg recording of the Maria Callas *La Traviata*. His love of opera had been consolidated by two years in the fifties as property master with the Sadler's Wells touring company. This particular recording is associated in my mind with French 75s, the cocktails made from gin, champagne and lemon juice, named after the 75mm piece of field artillery. They certainly had as devastating effect as the jokey name was intended to suggest.

A boozer

Bruce drank a lot, usually because he meant to. In later years, when I stopped drinking, he was practically the only person who disapproved of my decision. At the same time he did go to the trouble of arranging a tea party as a consolation. 'We could have coffee and chocolate eclairs, lemonade and Garibaldi biscuits,' he wrote on a postcard of a nude by Euan Uglow. 'The possibilities, if not quite endless, are dauntingly numerous, which just shows how sensible it is to stick to Scotch, beer and wine. Hope we meet soon, which is all the refreshment that I ask (apart from a small drink).'

Actually, he did knock off drinking altogether for a bit. I asked him what the result was – insomnia, or what? He replied: 'Oh, much worse.' But he categorized himself as a 'boozer', and he mixed with boozers. In pubs in the eighties he generally drank bottles of Löwenbräu blue-label strong lager. Unlike Jeffrey, who gravitated to vodka (except when eating) as the purest way to an alcohol hit, he remained discerning and would know the difference between Glenmorangie and Highland Park whiskies. Marsh Dunbar liked to joke that she couldn't forgive Bruce's assurance that after a while you stopped having hangovers; she had discovered this not to be true.

Sometimes drink accentuated Bruce's darker moods, but he was generally quizzically funny when having a drink. Like his brothers, he enjoyed finding humour in a choice of words. One morning, in the *Spectator* pub in Doughty Street we were having a drink and he was looking at the new issue. He came across a cartoon by Ray Lowry, who drew with a very individualistic style, of two stormtroopers, one of them saying: 'You know what I miss? Jewish jokes.' Bruce's lugubrious features became animated and he let out a laugh like a shout, holding the magazine in one hand and thumping the bar with a fist.

That was only a few years after I first saw him, when I had slowly twigged that this was Jeffrey's brother. There had seemed to be no connection between them. Jeffrey was talking with some regulars in the Coach, at the bar, sitting on the tall stools. Bruce was standing behind them at a distance, with a bottle of blue-label beer on a table and a round glass in his hand, not speaking. Jeffrey often proved a cause for anger.

Trouble with Jeffrey

In 1986, a collection of Jeffrey's columns came out in a book with the simple title *Low Life*. I was in the Coach, as was my habit, to deliver the week's new edition of the *Spectator* to him before it was in the shops. First Bruce came in. I showed him the review in the books pages, at that time and for long after brilliantly edited by Mark Amory. The review was by Sally Vincent. He read it very slowly. I bought him a bottle of Löwenbräu blue label (£1.08). He later reciprocated with a pint of Burton for me (same price).

Bruce said: 'Don't show that to Jeffrey. He'd only half like it. Between you and me, I'd recommended Sally to Mark as a reviewer.'

I wondered which half he wouldn't like. Would it be the bits about his false stories about her? 'I never did fling open a window and hurl sleeping tablets at his lovesick head while bawling that he should do his appalling self in. But I've always found it almost as plausible a tale as every one he's told. I didn't black his eye in a lover's tiff, either.' Or would it be the bits about his single-minded, 'fascist' pursuit of his discovery that 'the way to prolong your life, or at least make it seem to last for ever, is to piss it up the wall'.

That was why, she said, he was, in his way, 'as beguiling as a Nuremberg Rally. He's not remotely sentimental himself, he merely arouses the sentimentality in others by being so very dramatically more-suffering-than-thou. Plus he knows what he likes. I mean, he really knows what he likes.'

Jeffrey came in, and I gave him the copy of the *Spectator*. He read the review and said (*said*) he was delighted.

Ian Jack once asked Bruce whether he had resented Jeffrey's celebrity. 'No, I was rather proud of him,' he replied, 'but I think Jeff wanted me to resent him, and I resented his wanting my resentment.' Periodically Bruce resented Norman Balon's proprietorial attitude to Jeffrey, too, as did Oliver Bernard. None of the brothers were to be taken as copies of each other. Each had been to a different school: Jeffrey to Pangbourne naval college; Bruce to the liberal Bedales; Oliver to Westminster before he decided to leave, or had to. Perhaps, by way of education and provoking a reaction, the schools had left their mark, but it was hard to think it was the schools that had made the brothers so different.

The year after *Low Life* came out, Bruce had a party at Kettner's for his own book, one of a series on paintings. This was about images of the Virgin Mary and was called *Queen of Heaven*. Bruce didn't make much money from his books until much later, in fact not until the eve of his death, with *Century*. Even then, he remarked before it was completed: 'I've never been on such a tightrope, financially.'

In the Coach and Horses before the Kettner's party, Jeffrey was talking to Graham Mason and me. 'I've been evicted from the Chelsea Arts Club and I've got nowhere to go.' He didn't mention that Allan Hall had let him use his flat at Marble Arch. 'I don't really want to go to Bruce's party,' he said. 'I need something to eat.' He had to get his insulin balance right.

Bruce came into the pub and said nothing. After a while he shouted at Graham: 'So *you* won't speak to me now!' Graham immediately made an effort to be nice to him. But Bruce kept clutching his bottle of blue-label beer in a rage and muttering 'You bastard!' at Jeffrey.

Oliver Bernard arrived, and things calmed down. Jeffrey left to get something to eat. At the party upstairs in Kettner's, I feared he wouldn't turn up. By that stage in his life, he, like Graham Mason, found it difficult to last into the evening without getting incapably drunk, even if he wanted to.

But after a while I saw him trying to get up the stairs to the second floor. He stumbled and slipped a couple of steps. He tottered into the crowded room where the publisher was making a speech, and spent the rest of the evening on a chair next to the bar looking washed out: head down, hair falling over his face, holding on. It was the familiar condition of many regulars that we casually called 'pissed'.

The party was a mixture of publishing and arty people, and old Soho hands. It was a good example of Soho democracy: the rich and famous Lucian Freud was there and so were the penniless Canadian Jo and Brendan, whom I'd known earlier as friends of John Heath-Stubbs. Daniel Farson was talking a lot and drinking a lot. Graham Mason met a large number of people whose identity he could not remember. Marsh Dunbar, with her dried-up face, was dressed smartly.

When I thought it time to leave, I said to Bruce: 'Thank you, I enjoyed the party.'

'Oh, did you,' he replied. 'I didn't like it very much.'

Ice creams at Snow White

Bruce hatched a plan to go and see the film *Snow White* at the Odeon, Leicester Square. He had a trick of breaking out of Soho. He'd planned other outings – one to see Ken Dodd at Skegness, another, arranged decades in advance, to see the millennium fireworks on the Thames, for which he'd booked a room with a balcony at the Howard Hotel. He just managed to live long enough; the hotel has since been demolished.

For *Snow White* he took a woman friend and her two children, Stephen Pickles, Marsh Dunbar and me. Jeffrey had refused to come. Graham Mason had become angry at the very suggestion

We had seats in the circle, thanks to Nick Robson, the regular at the Coach who managed an Odeon cinema, and had therefore been nicknamed by Graham 'Nickelodeon'. (The old song went: 'Put another nickel in / In the Nickelodeon / All I want is loving you / And music, music, music.') At the screening of *Snow White*, Bruce bought us ice-cream tubs with little wooden spoons. He had seen the film when he was eight, Marsh when she was six. She laughed at the Prince. Pickles shed a tear at the resurrection scene. Bruce's stone face was unreadable.

I shared a birthday with Bruce's mother. I don't think I appreciated enough at the time some of the presents he gave me, not only copies of his books, such as *Vincent by Himself*, a happy marriage of Van Gogh's pictures and letters, but also photographs he had taken. One of them is well known: the still life of two prints of photographs of Michael Andrews taken by John Deakin and curled back as they stand on the mantelpiece.

Another is not at all well known: a scene at the Derby funfair, with Ann Robson sitting happily in the car of a big wheel with me next to her gripping the rail, out of a fear of heights, while the fairground hand leans casually on a guy rope. A line of light bulbs makes a kind of valance at the top of the picture. If it had not come out so well, Bruce would not have given it to me, but destroyed it.

The big fall-out

It was not easy to give Bruce a label. He angrily denied being an art historian, though he was. He worked as a picture editor and it was by his eye for remarkable photographs that he made a living, notably with the *Sunday Times Magazine* when it was renowned for its use of pictures. The fruit of his talent – the apples of his eye – were memorable books of photographs: *Photodiscovery* on the century 1840–1940, and later *Century*, the historic portrait in 1,000 photographs of the twentieth century, weighing 13lb and coming with a carrying handle. A selection from the vast Hulton Deutsch Picture Library, *All Human Life*, went with a show at the Barbican, and *100 Photographs* was a posthumous selection from the collection he put together for James Moores.

Kate Bernard, Bruce's niece, remembered her father saying of Bruce: 'He was so good at looking at paintings and photographs, it's not surprising he was extremely good at looking at people.' That was one reason that painters like Bacon, Freud, Frank Auerbach and Michael Andrews allowed him to photograph them at work, which most painters enjoy no more than Bruce did when he was painting his own unseen canvasses. He wouldn't even allow anyone in the kitchen when he was cooking, which he did very well.

I don't think his secretiveness was due to shyness or an unassuming nature. It was policy. If he mentioned enjoying partridge for breakfast with Lucian Freud, it was not the sort of thing he announced to the world, as Jeffrey would announce the meanest characteristics of his friends. Bruce's love life was peculiarly discreet. He admired the beauty of a young woman from the Basque Country, Anabel Arregui, and her intellect, temperament and devotion to the violin. She worked as a barmaid in the Coach and Horses, but they had little social contact there. He formed a lasting friendship with the painter and lecturer in art Virginia Verran, too, who possesses a remarkably original freshness of outlook and a different kind of beauty.

Before Bacon died in 1992, Bruce fell out with him in a big way. From 1987 he had worked on a book on the painter, to be called *About Francis Bacon*, with reproductions of his pictures, press notices from 1931 onwards and a biographical narrative supported by photographs of him and his friends. He got the brilliant Derek Birdsall to design it, and Bacon thought the dummy he produced 'marvellous'. Bacon's agents, Marlborough Fine Art, gave full cooperation.

Bacon took home a copy of Bruce's biographical narrative and rang him early next morning to say that owing to insomnia he had read it during the night and 'rather liked it'. Bruce agreed to remove an anecdote that would cause someone embarrassment.

Bacon took Bruce, Birdsall and some of his family out to lunch, during which he charmed them 'with his generosity and customary enjoyment of such occasions', as Bruce put it. After seeing some colour proofs which were not yet adjusted, Bruce felt 'other unspoken doubts' had been triggered.

With less than a fortnight to go before the book was due at the printers, Bruce got a phone call from Bacon saying he wanted to see him urgently. Next morning, Bruce went to see him and, after an offer of tea, was told that Bacon insisted that all the photographs, the biographical narrative and any reproductions of works before 1944 should be removed. This would destroy the whole concept of the book. Neither Bruce nor his publishers could accept it.

'Friendly agreements,' Bruce later reflected ruefully, 'are, by their nature, vulnerable.' The book, Bruce firmly believed, had been 'an interesting tribute to him and his work', blocked by 'unquestionably bad faith of his part'. It was a hard blow for Bruce: the end of a friendship of 40 years and the destruction of a piece of work that he was uniquely qualified to produce.

22

The Red Baron

Dead drunk − The Derby coach − The big wheel − Casualties

Dead drunk

The most vivid visual memory of the trip to the Derby on 1 June 1988 was of the Red Baron lying on the grass stiff and unmoving on his back in the sunshine, his bow tie a little crooked, exposing the stud of his stiff collar, but his monocle still wedged in its place. Someone had put a posy of flowers in his hands clasped at his breast. An empty bottle of champagne lay by his side.

It had been an early start that day, but this was a man accustomed to applying himself to drink. One Saturday morning when he came into the Coach and was asked what he'd been doing, he said: 'I haf been sitting in the bath drinking cider.'

His name was Christoph Schliack, and he was addressed by regulars as Christoph, though his nicknames included the Red Baron, for he presented himself as a stage German. He was about 5ft 4in tall and he often spoke in a sort of ululating moan. 'Lunch! Tsis is lunch in a bottle!' the writer Michael Bywater remembers him exclaiming after a gulp of Guinness. 'I vill hev no other lunch from now!'

A few months before the Derby he had come into the Coach early one evening, his roly-poly frame clothed in a waistcoat, denim jacket, trousers and black shoes, with a tweed cap on his head and a monocle in his eye. He said to Jeffrey Bernard: 'Do you know what Randolph Churchill said when he first read the Bible?'

'No,' Jeffrey replied, 'and I don't want to know. Why do you treat me like I don't know anything or anybody?' Raising his voice to a shout he continued: 'I knew Dylan Thomas, I knew Ian Fleming. I knew Ann Fleming ... I even know Christopher Howse,' he ended with a smile. Christoph didn't spot the joke and kept repeating: 'I apologize. I apologize.'

The Derby coach

Christoph Schliack had followed an unusual career, coming from Hanover 20 years before to read Chinese at Leeds University. 'He habitually wore an academic gown, a formal dark suit, a stiff wing collar and a monocle', a contemporary remembered. He qualified as a barrister but never practised, making a living by editing legal journals.

He had joined a pretty mixed bunch of Jeffrey Bernard's friends that Wednesday to go down to Epsom by coach. Nominally the outing was under the auspices of the Groucho Club but Jeffrey had recruited the 40 participants mainly from the Coach. There were a couple of barmaids, a stage-door keeper, a VAT man, a plainclothes policeman, two pornographers, half a dozen journalists, a jobbing builder, quite a few layabouts and some women who came into the category of 'wives'.

Jeffrey had been up since four, writing his column for the *Spectator*, as Wednesday was its press day. Some of the party had started drinking before breakfast of kedgeree at the Groucho at 8 a.m. There was champagne available on the coach, but Graham Mason, who disliked champagne, had brought his own bottle of vodka. By the time we approached Epsom Downs at 10 a.m. it was getting dangerously low. 'Oh, what am I going to do this afternoon?' he wailed.

One of the Derby-goers must have had a puzzling time, as I found out a couple of weeks later. Jeffrey was trying to fix up a free flight to Thailand, where he'd been offered a free week in the Oriental Hotel, Bangkok. So he detailed me to find out the name of a man from British Airways who'd been at a *Spectator* lunch with us both. I checked and told Jeffrey that he had been on the bus to the Derby at Jeffrey's invitation. Jeffrey had forgotten he'd asked him, didn't recognize him on the bus and spoke not a word to him all day.

As the coach crawled through the suburban traffic, Norman Balon strode up the aisle and picked up the microphone next to the driver's seat. 'During the delay, Irma Kurtz will give private consultations on your emotional and sexual problems.' Looking up and down the coach, it would have taken the agony aunt of *Cosmopolitan* all day to make much headway with the problems on offer.

In any case, the emptyings of a pub are not easy to accommodate two by two on a coach. Granny Smith, the stage-doorman, sat happily enough next to Nissa, the Maltese builder. The theatre carpenter Mick Tobin, in his flat cap, sat next to the long-haired publisher Stephen Pickles.

All three of the Bernard brothers were, for a wonder, on the coach. Bruce sat next to the beautiful Spanish violin-playing barmaid Anabel. Both of Oliver's daughters had come along. Finola Morgan from Islington had accepted Jeffrey's invitation to be there. Graham Mason was sitting next to the CID man whom he mockingly referred to as 'Jeffrey's Policeman'. I was sitting next to a pleasant unmarried woman called Jinty, which provoked Norman to make lewd and unkind remarks.

But the one person whose approach caused an awkward shuffling was the Red Baron. No one wanted to be landed with him for a couple of hours. From the security of my seat I could hear snatches of his conversation or monologue drifting down the coach. 'He voz a very good Gaelic scholar ... that voz before the Battle of Blenheim ... No, you are quite mistaken there.'

The big wheel

Pub regulars look strange by outdoor daylight, their clothes shabbier, their faces paler and less defined. A trip to the Derby was theoretically a treat. In practice, there were difficulties. Getting drunk was an obvious hazard, and wanting to go to the lavatory another. There were longueurs, since the horses didn't run all the time. Jeffrey had named a dead cert a couple of months earlier and I smugly backed it for the big race while the odds were still long. They shortened when it won a couple of other races with ease. Then, a fortnight before the Derby it was withdrawn, so I lost my stake.

I was with all the other amateur gamblers scanning the form in the paper and taking a fancy to a horse's name. In his Low Life column Jeffrey recorded that I'd chosen some shrewd winners. I don't remember. Did I back some winners or was that just a line Jeffrey put in to highlight the improbable?

There was time to visit the funfair before the first of the six races at 2.15. Ann, the Scottish barmaid, wanted to go on the big wheel. I did not want to go on the big wheel, because I fear heights, but I did want to go with her on the twin-seat bucket with its snap-to bar across, which I grasped with unnecessary force. It was extraordinary to be up in the breeze of the sunny Downs, with the smell of petrol fumes, burgers and mud from below, looking over the rolling course and the rows of coaches and lunch tents, and to hear Ann's cheerful mockery of my terror. As the car came down at the end, and the swarthy fairground man leaned towards the bar to release it, Bruce Bernard clicked the button of his camera.

After lunch, Jeffrey took a nap on a groundsheet in the sunshine. Finola sat by him. Bruce won a couple of hundred on one race, then lost £50. For the Derby, Jeffrey put £100 on Al Mufti, 'a quality horse with impressive hind quarters' as he was described in some form book. He came tenth.

Casualties

There were some casualties by the ends of the day. Stan Gebler Davies was lost and the coach left without him. Graham Mason was so drunk that when he reboarded the coach parked on the grass he negotiated the sloping floor as though it was a notorious rock face.

On the bus back from the Derby, Bill Mitchell was astonished by the behaviour of the Red Baron. 'Hey, we just do this as a jest,' he said, 'but this man *means* it.'

The next year, Christoph Schliack was found murdered in his small flat in Shepherd's Bush, aged 40. 'He was stabbed repeatedly,' wrote Giles Tremlett, now a distinguished foreign correspondent, on the front of the local paper. 'Upstairs nobody heard a word.'

'With his monocle, Bavarian style trilby hat and fine country-gent clothing, he was a caricature of the German aristocrat. On the Uxbridge Road he was known as the Prince or the Kaiser – depending on which pub he was in.' Or, in the Coach and Horses, the Red Baron.

23

Oliver

Three smells – 'Your bloody family' – The meaning of Walberswick –
Two clean panes – 'Comparatively desert air' – She picked up a knife

Three smells

Three smells remind me of Oliver Bernard: the strong tobacco
he would tamp into his curved-stem pipe; the aniseed of Ricard,
his preferred drink; the woodsmoke from the fire at his one-
room cottage in Norfolk.

The eldest of the Bernard brothers, who outlived the others,
he was 60 in the mid-eighties. He had just spent some weeks in
Norwich jail (where the other, much younger, prisoners called
him 'Pop', and he yearned for silence from Radio 2). It was for
cutting the wire at a nuclear weapons base. He had recently
become a Catholic. He wore sandals (without socks).

Like his brothers he enjoyed playing with words, which was
just as well since he was a poet by vocation. 'I quite missed you
the day you left,' wrote his brother Bruce to him in 1949 from
the village of Paul in Cornwall, where he had gone to try to
paint. 'I had no one to make puns to and had to make them to
myself, a crafty tear now and again trickling down my wrinkled
old cheek.'

After the war Oliver had lived in Paris for a bit and had been
amused by the stamps that entitled card-holders to a daily ration
of bread. Each one bore the French word *pain*. The whole sheet

told a hard tale of the quotidian human condition: '*Pain. Pain. Pain. Pain.*'

He was still only 14 when he discovered Soho, which came to mean home to him, 'a village where I was known'. At first he visited the place to fetch supplies for his mother from the Continental grocers to take back to Holland Park. 'I must have looked about me,' he was to write in his memoirs, *Getting Over It*. 'People stood on the pavement and talked outside the Bar Italia and outside Parmigiana's on the corner of Frith Street and Old Compton Street. There were still yellow horse-drawn Carlo and Gatti ice-carts, traces of straw, nosebags and horse-dung.' In 1942, aged 16, Oliver ran away from home.

He gravitated to Soho. It had the attractions of drink, women and talk that wasn't at all small talk. There he embraced a culture in which 'it was all right to be very poor, and people borrowed shillings off one another'. Best of all 'you could sit and talk for hours without needing to justify your existence'.

If Soho exerted a pull, his family gave him a push. On the dust jacket of *Getting Over It* he put a photograph of his mother with the three boys in 1939, after the death of their father, in summery attire in the garden of a villa between Monaco and Menton. His mother is looking at Bruce, who stands with his hands on his hips. Jeffrey is crouched leaning towards her on a balustrade. Oliver is looking away into the distance, towards the sea.

He was the handsomest of the boys. John Deakin caught him in a photograph aged 26 looking extraordinarily like Rimbaud, whose poetry he later translated and performed in mesmerizing monologues. A less fierce photographic portrait by Deakin took up the whole of the dust jacket, back and front, of Oliver's volume of poetry *Country Matters*, published in 1961. As time passed, an abrasion tended to form down the nose where it straddled the book's spine. George Barker had upbraided him with vanity for the design. George Barker was someone whom Oliver said he had hated quite a bit at first, when he met him in the late forties, but had then grown to love for the next 42 years till George died, aged 78, in 1991. Barker said what he honestly thought about younger people's poetry, including Oliver's. Of his *Moons and Tides, Walberswick,* Barker said: 'The only imagist poem' – an opaque remark.

If Jeffrey said he was embarrassed by having 'fancied' his mother, Oliver was deeply wounded by her behaviour. He hated her unkindness to their sister Sally and the way she would ask him 'in a theatrical way, so that I knew she wasn't being herself, "Do you love me, darling?" (Do you LOHVE meh?)'.

A poem in *Country Matters* declares: 'My mother died appallingly … of cancer and the old complaint / do you love me darling no / but I never answered till she lay dying … and what I said / was oh mother you know I do / I do she died is this a pattern?'

'Your bloody family'

There had been an interlude of benign development when Oliver was nine. He was sent with Sally and Bruce to Bunce Court school, made up of seven or eight British children and 120 German Jewish children who had arrived en bloc from somewhere near Mannheim at the beginning of the Hitler period. 'The wonderful thing about it was the way it allowed things to happen,' Oliver recalled. 'Not only was no one ever physically assaulted there by a member of staff in the name of discipline, but no one was afraid of anyone. It was a community. We dug our own swimming-pool; we went on a huge bike ride and camped somewhere near Rye …'

When I once sent him a postcard of a seventeenth-century family he begged me not to send him any such picture again. 'I used to wish that I was an orphan and that everybody would die,' he recalled. His parents' marriage seemed a rerun of the violent instability that his own father recounted in his memoirs *Cock Sparrow,* published in 1936, shortly before he died. To Oliver's father, Oliver P. Bernard, the smell of Pears' soap reminded him of 'brutal thrashings for misunderstood reasons, by a father who thought sons could and should be moulded by force to another's will'.

In the late thirties, at the last home they had in the country, at Oxshott, Surrey, the young Oliver saw his father Oliver in the kitchen 'transformed with anger', almost throttling his mother one evening. In the garden there, he first 'put into words the thought that it would be better if both my parents were dead'. It was a variation on the childhood experience of his father who, resenting his own parents' early death when he was 13, leaving him hungry and lonely, ran away to sea, serving in a tall ship on the timber route from the Baltic, and happy enough on his return to find the shelter of a cubicle at the Rowton House at Newington.

His son Oliver, on the first day that he had run away from home, found a job and lodgings. At that time, too, he became a member of the Communist Party, which lost its sway over him by the end of the war. He was in the years to come to find work as a kitchen porter, builder's labourer, coal-heaver, tramway repairer, farm labourer and furnaceman at a gasworks.

He particularly relished his dangerous work in the No. 4 Retort House at the East Greenwich gasworks, on the site of which the Millennium Dome and then the O2 Arena were later built. The scale was gargantuan, satanic. The retorts in which gas was removed from the coal were long elliptical tubes lined with fire bricks, in great blocks 20ft high and 20yd long. Five blocks went the length of the house, five rows of these blocks took up its width. Railway lines to deliver coal entered the house halfway up, level with the banks of retorts.

After a few hours' cooking, the coal would have given off its gas, tar and ammonia, and been converted into bright red-hot coke, actually burning as a ram pushed it into vast chutes with barred grilles at the bottom, which could not be released onto conveyor belts until the coke had been 'watered down' to extinguish its fire.

Watering down was one of Oliver's jobs during the winter of 1952–3. He would hold a high-pressure hose with a curved and rigid nozzle and approach the mouth of the chute crouching, shielding his face from the blistering radiation of heat from the burning coke. He could not open the valve until the nozzle was over the edge of the chute, and then he must be absolutely sure not to come into contact with the explosion of superheated steam that occurred as soon as the water hit the coke.

Just as dangerous was the job of charging retorts with new coal. Soon an 8ft plume of flame was roaring out of the filled retort. A man with a steel bar would catch the cast-iron door of the retort and slam it shut, transforming the plume of flame into an oval sunflower with the door as its centre. Then the man would reach forward and turn a handle with a gauntleted hand to tighten it and seal the fire inside.

Oliver liked and respected many of the men he worked with, but none were so clean-spoken and solicitous as those he worked with at the gasworks. 'Don't get your nose over the hot coke when you turn the water on', he would be advised. 'Watch how you tread here, it's a bit greasy.'

It was certainly more satisfying than the five or six weeks he tried as a rent boy at the age of 15, for which he had neither the aptitude nor the callousness required. He was to look back on his years as a young man as 'a more or less uninterrupted series of sexual and emotional adventures with women, including adultery, fornication, unsuccessful love affairs, betrayals of friends and multiple infidelities'.

After running away from home, Oliver had soon joined the RAF and was sent for pilot training in Canada. He did not see his mother for three and a half years, or even write. On his return to England he made a kind of peace with her and found himself on terms of friendship with Bruce. They took two girls to see the Picasso and Matisse exhibition at the Victoria and Albert Museum in January 1946. On leave in London that year he went five times to see Marcel Carné's *Le jour se lève*, with Jean Gabin giving his tobacco-smoke-filled, suicidal, nocturnal reminiscences. Instead of saying, 'Let's go to a film', he and Bruce would say, 'Let's go and see *Le jour se lève*'.

Decades later he was to remember an incident at the Caves de France in Dean Street one afternoon. He walked in out of the sunshine, and Nina Hamnett was sitting at the far end of the dimly lit bar with her money in a tobacco tin in front of her.

'Hello, Oliver! How are you?'

'I'm very well, thank you, Nina. How are you?'

'Oh, all right. How's your bloody family?'

'That is a very understanding remark. Have a drink, Nina.'

'No, I'm going to buy *you* a drink. What are you having?'

I didn't know all this in the mid-eighties when Oliver visited London. It was always a sort of treat for me. There were puzzling things about him. He was the only person I knew who had fallen out with Marsh Dunbar, whose lover he had been for a time, as he had been in Paris in 1947 of Jeffrey's first wife, before their marriage.

What I did see was the same sort of moral courage that Bruce often displayed. Oliver visited their sister Sally, the eldest child of the family. He blamed his mother for hating her and implicitly for the mental breakdown she suffered as a young woman. 'It was my mother's fault that my sister went mad,' Jeffrey once said over lunch. 'She didn't like the competition and was awful to Sally. She was mad from the age of twenty-five. She used to sit in the French. Gaston would give her money. One day an American came in, and, the way Americans do, started to talk to her. She just hit him a tremendous whack across the head which sent him flying and said: "Hello".'

It wasn't funny about Sally. Jeffrey could not bring himself to go and see her in her sheltered housing. Sally outlived Jeffrey and Bruce, and Oliver sent me a photograph of her in her beauty when at last he attended her 'very pared-down' cremation.

He included in his last volume of verse an affectionate poem for her which incidentally contained a few lines that exactly reflect the way that he would sometimes talk:

A friend I used to what is called create
What are called brochures with and trade and technical

Advertisements for engineering firms
Says that there is a Transylvanian
Victoria and Albert sort of posh
Hotel at the end of the dam with fishing
Rights and a panelled library and solid
Sun never sets type comfort.

The meaning of Walberswick

If anyone had asked me what Oliver was, I'd have answered: 'A poet.' It was because he was a poet that he translated poetry so well. Since he was translating from French, it was as well that he had come to know the language thoroughly, living in Paris and teaching in Corsica, where he set himself to learn to write. There was an element of self-discipline, too, in his deciding to take a degree in teaching, which he did at Goldsmith's College from 1950 to 1952 while busy with much else – drinking, writing, singing late at night in Soho doorways while it rained, 'having what's called a good time' in his own words, and splitting up with his first wife.

His translations of Rimbaud's *Collected Poems* for Penguin came out in 1962, and in 1965 Penguin published his *Apollinaire*. Revisions of the Rimbaud went towards a bilingual edition that he achieved before his death. Performing Rimbaud's *Une saison en enfer* in his own translation, Oliver made use of a table, a chair and a pipe, lit as punctuation. He had the plangent Bernard voice, which he used to good effect. There are some commercial recordings of his readings. He had won the Poetry Society's Gold Medal for verse speaking in 1982.

When working as an extra electrician at the Fortune Theatre in 1954 he had met Joyce Grenfell and they became friends. 'She liked blue and white crockery and a good cup of tea,' he remembered. He lent her some poems which she took to Walter de la Mare, who said they were 'real poems' and asked them to tea. The writer was in his eighties and lived in a flat in an early

Georgian house in Twickenham where Tennyson had once lived. He appeared 'in a dressing-gown, neckerchief, shirt and slippers all of different shades of blue,' Oliver recalled. 'He seemed to me in fear of death.' But he sang old music-hall songs, alternating with Joyce Grenfell. He did die less than two years later.

One summer in the eighties Oliver gave an unbirthday party, not at his house in Kenninghall, but at a place that had played a crucial part in his career as a poet 30 years earlier: Walberswick, the less well-heeled twin of Southwold on the other side of the River Blyth by the sea, but separated from it by the smaller River Dunwich, which runs a strange course parallel with the shore. There was plenty to drink and many unusual people.

Oliver had been lent a cottage in Suffolk in the early fifties by the poet Philip O'Connor, who also lent him a bicycle to reach it, all the way from Charlotte Street. In Suffolk Oliver worked as a farm labourer, using horses, not tractors. By a farming couple he met then, he was lent a big house by the water in Walberswick from the autumn of 1957 till the end of spring in 1958. There he had the best few months of his life, from the point of view of writing.

He dedicated his verse sequence *Moons and Tides, Walberswick* to his benefactors there, and he thought the sequence worth reprinting in *Verse &c.* This, his last volume, omitted most of his early verse, but did collect up between covers selections from *The Finger Points at the Moon*, a collection of inscriptions from the walls of Paris from May 1968, previously published in 1989 as stapled A4 sheets to mark the retirement from the French pub of Gaston Berlemont.

Two clean panes

Since I saw them so often, Jeffrey and Bruce hardly ever wrote to me: invitations, mostly. Oliver, living in Norfolk, wrote often and well, either in his italic black script or typewritten (and, like Jeffrey's Low Life copy, seldom mistyped or corrected). Francis

Bacon in his droll way had once commented on Oliver's life as a country mouse: 'I wouldn't like living in the country, because of all the *horrible little apple trees* there.'

Oliver's letters were about books and people, weather and things around him, plans and, as the years went by, deaths. He used scrap paper when possible (such as the back of a Norfolk Festival of the Spoken Arts certificate, 1981), until he won some prize of a supply of A4 paper with a small colour picture of his house in the village of Kenninghall at the top left. It was a remarkable house in a way, at the end of a row, timber-framed with thin wattle-and-daub walls, whitewashed.

Mallows bloomed in the garden next door and sunflowers in his. Inside, the one room on the ground floor had a window onto the street and, at the side, facing westward, two casements side by side, of eight lights each. The glass in the right-hand casement was dirty and brown; that in the left had two panes clean and transparent, at the eye level of someone sitting down. These were in front of Oliver's desk.

At the desk, with its manual typewriter, stood an office chair, the kind with roller-casters radiating from a central column supporting the seat. Cobwebs hung at the windows and from the ceiling. A wood-burning stove sat in the chimney space, each side of which was a steel-framed chair. Round logs were stacked by the stove, and across the chimney-hearth strings were stretched from which a shirt hung drying. A beam ran across the yellowing white-painted ceiling.

All the room was a jumble of oddments. A clock with a china face bore the CND device in black. A small Japanese-figured paper lampshade lay on the windowsill. Shelves of books filled the wall between the front door and the desk, and the back wall, too, and more books and papers were piled on the table and the floor.

Between the desk and the back wall hung photographs, black and white ones in frames and newer colour photographs unframed. There was a framed photograph of the painters usually known as the two Roberts, Colquhoun and MacBryde, on the chimney breast, the one taken in 1949 by Felix H. Man, I think it was.

Out of the back wall a door opened into the lean-to lavatory, with its pedestal raised up a little, fixed on a piece of split, unpainted wood. Next to the lavatory was a tiny kitchen with a small window above the sink looking onto a small garden, mostly above a septic tank.

The coming of mains sewerage formed the subject of one letter, full of optimism. 'The new first-time Kenninghall sewers are being laid, apparently most efficiently and speedily, by some amazingly polite and pleasant workmen and their ferociously modern equipment, which includes heavily vibrating rollers for finishing off filled-in trenches about three and a half feet wide and seven feet deep. They've just got past my front door, but I'm off to London tomorrow to sit (again) for my painter friend to whom I read novels and biographies, and who cooks nice little lunches, as nice as they are little. I hate having too much to eat.'

When Oliver made tea in the kitchen, with water from a filter jug in an electric kettle, he poured the boiling water over leaves in a tea strainer held over a mug. This was a method he had adopted from Jeffrey. Bruce's variant was to put lots of tea in a warmed pot, add the boiling water and then to pour out the cups very soon, catching some essential solubles but not the tannic remainder.

It tended to be chilly in the house even in summer. Beside the chimney a door opened onto a very steep stairway, up to his bedroom. He had an electric blanket, but he did not get double glazing to reduce the winter freeze until his last winter.

'Comparatively desert air'

A page of one letter was full of etymology about goads, gadflies and gadding, taken from H. C. Wyld's *Dictionary*, a copy of which he'd just bought for 50p at a garden party raising funds to repair a Norfolk church. 'John Heath-Stubbs told me about

Wyld's dictionary a long time ago,' he explained, 'saying that it was better, etymologically, than the Oxford dictionaries. I think it may be that Prof. Wyld taught Heath-Stubbs.'

'I'm struggling to translate Aragon: *Le Crève-coeur* (Almost impossible.)' he wrote another day. 'I had cold pheasant on hot toast for tea just now, which is a discovery of mine, I like to imagine, and very good.'

'There is in a Wm Morris prose romance called *The Water of the Wondrous Isles* a rather gloomy place called the Black Valley of the Greywethers. I think it is the best of those books. It has a heroine rather than a hero. Some, indeed most, critics are a bit impatient about these Morris books with their artificial language (somewhat like Malory) but I've enjoyed them all.'

'Who was Monna Vanna?' he asked in another. 'I know that Mopsa is a silly peasant girl character in Sidney's *Arcadia*. I have to read a Heath-Stubbs poem mentioning both.'

'I'm sending Lewis Wolpert one of the copies of my last collection which I failed to flog at Torriano Meeting House on Sunday. It was so packed (to hear John Hegley rather than me) that people were sitting on the table where the books were displayed and none got sold.'

Oliver had driven me one day over to Thornham Parva, where I wanted to see the altarpiece, an astonishing fourteenth-century painting, made locally and surviving by a miracle. The predella that once went with it is in the Musée de Cluny in Paris. While I looked at the altarpiece, Oliver stayed quietly in the church, reading the visitors' book. He found one entry that said the church was 'almost too beautiful', but it then went on to complain about a bush in the churchyard. He sent me a good colour reproduction of the altarpiece, which hangs framed on my wall.

A poem of his, long enough to be published as a pamphlet, was *Quia Amore Langueo*, a version in modern English of a medieval poem about the Virgin Mary. An edition of the poem had been published in 1937 with wood engravings by Eric Gill, but Oliver's was the first translation of the full poem. He republished it in *Verse &c.* It was dedicated to the Carmelite nuns at Quidenham in Norfolk, over to whose monastery he would walk from his house in Kenninghall for Mass day by day.

'Between Kenninghall and East Harling,' he wrote one spring, 'the roadside verge on the south-facing side has two 25-yard-long patches of violets, one mixed violet and white, the other entirely white. It is not a stretch of road to walk on (narrow, with fast traffic), so there they flourish in the comparatively desert air.' When he died he left me the Gill-illustrated *Quia Amore Langueo* together with his own version, in a little box labelled in his italic hand.

She picked up a knife

In reply to a remark I made about about Savonarola, he wrote: 'Bruce once wrote in a letter from Cornwall: "Guess who knocked on my door the other day. Savonarola? No: Harry Barnes." Barnes was a tough guy in Soho, and a faker of paintings, not a very nice person. But Bruce was as isolated in Cornwall as you could well be. And Harry might have had a bit of tobacco on him. But neither of us was very fond of Harry. I see now that Bruce was painting at the time, and Harry's knock may have had rather a threatening sound. But I should like to exchange my prejudices about Savonarola ("iconoclast") for some real information.'

That letter from Bruce must have been written a couple of years after Oliver made an entry in a diary of a leave from the RAF to London in 1946. 'Arrived at Piccadilly Circus, quarter to seven and went to Bianchi's for spaghetti. Met Harry Diamond on the way to the Duke [of York, Rathbone Place]. Bruce was there, so were the Schnorrer and the Fine Doll. I roasted chestnuts and bought people drinks.

'Robert MacBryde and Nelson [Pollard] and I went to Tony's [café] and waited and waited. A brawl started over Dinora [Mendelson]'s alleged insulting some awful tart (who had got three years for slashing someone and who screamed filth, undressed, tore down the lapels of Bruce's overcoat, pulled my hair, and tried to get at Dinora again. Her girlfriend picked up a knife which Bruce tore away from her. She shouted at Harry Barnes, who hit her, saying "You'll get no porter out of me.'"

Oliver, Bruce and Robert MacBryde then dossed down at Nelson Pollard's and had breakfast next day at Tony's in Charlotte Street again. It doesn't sound very pleasant, but it does sound exactly the way Soho enveloped young people in the forties – or the eighties.

24

A Painter Upstairs

Art in the attic − Beheading the Queen − Crushed images − A chair portrayed too − Ludomania − Steadily burning

Art in the attic

One of the first full-length, life-sized portraits produced by Rupert Shrive in his studio on the top floor of the Coach and Horses was of − a mouse. Name unknown, it had perished, perhaps of starvation, in that lofty, unpeopled space visited only by the occasional pigeon that had found its way through a hole in the roof.

Norman wasn't very pleased when he saw the portrait of the mouse. Indeed, he wasn't pleased about most aspects of allowing a painter to set up a studio in his childhood home, where his bedroom had been. Despite that, Rupert managed to stay for five years punctuated by regular rows. Norman didn't like people tramping upstairs via the business side of the bar, the only means of entry, and he didn't like people beyond his control getting up to heaven knew what. It was bitterly cold in the studio in winter and Norman feared that a heater would set the house on fire. There were other unexpressed feelings of insecurity in ceding sovereignty over his demesne. Yet this little bit of territorial patronage was surely Norman's greatest service to art, beyond getting generations of painters legless.

Rupert had been working in Bobby Hunt's picture library, managed by Graham Mason. He was ten years younger than I was, tall and dark-haired with a long face a bit like a horse's or sometimes like that of one of the Toledan gentlemen painted by El Greco. I knew he'd been to Norwich School of Art and then to St Martin's, but so had a lot of people. I hadn't imagined that he was a real painter, just part of the confused pinball trajectories of drinkers between the Coach, the French and the Colony.

Graham Mason, sitting at the bar of the Coach and Horses at lunchtime, would shake his head sadly, take in a good lungful of smoke and say: 'He isn't very bright, you know.' It wasn't true and he didn't believe it, but it was a formalized way of saying something peculiarly annoying, just as he would say of me: 'Don't mind him. You see, *he lives with his mother.*' I didn't, but I didn't react in rage either, so he stopped saying it. Rupert just laughed at the jibe, too. He clearly had a gift for making friends in a number of languages, which was no sign of dimness, but I was nowhere nearer suspecting he could paint. Then I saw a picture he had painted.

It was in the unpromising gloom of the lobby of a little house near Valencia where he was living for a bit. As usual he had girlfriend trouble. In fact the trouble was so bad that I think I shouldn't write about it here. She died after an illness, but he is still alive, and it wasn't in Soho, so it's not necessarily our business. But that painting convinced me he could paint.

It was a landscape, with trees, and Rupert is a portraitist, I hope. Actually, Raffaella Barker, the novelist, one of George Barker's daughters, says her favourite painting is a picture by Rupert of Weybourne in Norfolk, with a black dog on a clifftop. To her it represents the Norfolk legend of Black Shuck. 'If you're walking along the beach and you hear Black Shuck's breath behind you, you must not turn around or you'll see his red eyes and you'll be dead in twelve months.' Rupert has gone through alarming patches of abstraction, but my spirits rise whenever he returns to portraits.

Beheading the Queen

There were other promising young painters in Soho at the end of the eighties. Justin Mortimer, who was studying at the Slade, was seen in the French and in the Colony, often in company with the artist and designer Kathy Dalwood. She was one of the women there at the time with the most interesting things to say. Her father was Hubert Dalwood, the sculptor, who had died in 1976 aged only 52. The most popular artefact she made connected with the Colony was an aluminium ashtray with hemispherical holes in it like cheese.

Justin was to win the National Portrait Gallery's BP Portrait Award and count the Queen among his sitters. In his portrait of the Queen, commissioned by the Royal Society of Arts, he placed her head a small distance above her body, on a custard-yellow ground. The *Daily Mail* ran the headline: '"Silly" artist cuts off the Queen's head.' It quoted Brian Sewell, the punchy critic with a mannered voice. 'I actually think Justin is a very promising artist,' he said, 'and I have bought one of his works myself in the past, but this is just ridiculous.'

Justin valued figurative art and asked why it couldn't be about modern life, as conceptual art claimed to be. Later, his paintings reflected some of the miseries of the modern world, disturbing but still well made.

Crushed images

Michael Peppiatt included Rupert under the heading 'School of London artists', along with Bacon, Auerbach and Paul Simonon (also known as the bassist in The Clash), in his collection *Interviews with Artists 1966–2012*. The interview was in Paris after Rupert had left Soho to live and paint there.

In it he tried to explain why he had taken to crushing up portraits to capture 'fleeting presence, like the faces you see flickering up in a fire'. This technique developed from something he discovered when he was working in his studio in the Coach. 'I ripped up some drawings in a rage, and when they were on the floor I realized that if you shuffled five or six pieces around you could turn them into what I then termed "visual anagrams".'

Having painted half a dozen flat paintings as well as he possibly could, he did not find the process of screwing them up and crushing them pleasurable. 'I always try to preserve the features,' he said, 'I want to be able to see the eyes.'

It was partly that he wanted to make an image that the spectator has to walk round. With a picture like Piero della Francesca's *Baptism* in the National Gallery, he explained, there is 'a particular point where you have to stand and then this glorious geometric harmony falls into place'. But with El Greco, a painter he much admires, 'his compositions catch your eye as you walk past. They're flickering flames of composition that take your eye up, largely heavenward, and I like that very much, and it's something I want to explore.'

In part, too, it was a way of taking advantage of accidents. 'I discover something in the studio, some way of working, some shape, some combination of something, and within half an hour of leaving the studio I see the same thing there on the street that I'd never noticed before.'

A chair portrayed too

It had been Fred Ingrams who first did some painting upstairs in the Coach, and, after Fred had fallen into gainful employment for a spell, Rupert persuaded Norman to let him do the same. The first three storeys of the building have high ceilings, so the stairs zigzagging up to the third floor are steep.

The studio was bare and light, with a window looking south onto the blank brick side wall of the Palace Theatre in Romilly Street and another facing west over the side of Kettner's in Greek Street. The corner between the windows was rounded, as can be seen on the outside, above the red and gold wall sign that proclaimed the pub to be 'Norman's'.

The bare floorboards were attractive in their way. There was a gap where a board had been broken somehow, and a square-headed nail remained there, fixed in the joist and bent a little to one side. The only piece of furniture was a large armchair, the green upholstery on the arms of which resembled an irregular mossy bank in a Devon lane. Both the nail and the armchair figure to their advantage in a large canvas Rupert painted of me when the eighties were over.

Being painted is not an ego trip if the painter is any good. It is alarming to see yourself as another sees you, though it is a fortunate opportunity. Sitting in an armchair with my left leg crossed over my right for regular sessions was a comfortable enough occupation, even though I had initially put my foot on the floor in a position slightly out of true, by which I had to abide as the weeks went by.

The canvas was 6ft by 4ft, and there was room for an appreciative treatment of the floorboards as well as the variegations of the worn and battered armchair. It was not that the portrait of the armchair flattered it, but that a careful rendition respected its individuality.

The smooth curve of the plastered wall behind the armchair made for an interestingly shaded background. It was punctuated by a postcard pinned to the wall of Zurbarán's *Agnus Dei*, a lamb lying with its feet bound, which is in the Prado. In an earlier draft, the postcard had been of Géricault's *A Horse Frightened by Lightning*, but the lamb for sacrifice was reckoned to be a better emblem for my new job as an obituaries editor.

Ludomania

There was a homeless woman, Pam Jennings, whom I'd seen around Pimlico, where she slept in a hostel. She spent much of her time asking for money in Soho, going into pubs including the Coach, from which Norman chased her if he caught sight of her. She was short and round-headed, with close-cropped hair and a cheerful, fairly innocent, if troubled disposition. She would hug someone who gave her a pound.

She smoked, but did not drink. Her hostel cost £7 a night, but she spent so long collecting money because she was addicted to one-armed bandits. While she played she would rub together two pound coins between her left thumb and finger and two between her right. No doubt she craved the experience of playing the fruit machines. It was not a pleasure in itself, but a relief from the anxieties of life outside the habit. Hers was a mirror of the dependencies of the daily drinkers around her.

Rupert had a brilliant idea and painted a simple watercolour of her, which was turned into postcards that she could sell for £1 each, a step up from basic begging. She enjoyed the distinction that the arrangement brought.

Steadily burning

One artist who couldn't be taken for anyone else was a Soho fixture at the time, Christopher Battye. He had a wonderful face dominated by a big squashed nose the shape of a stingray. Yet he fell in with an unnecessary plan to distinguish himself from the rest of the world of Soho by dressing as a fifties Teddy Boy, with long-jacketed bright blue suits and bootlace ties.

He was in his forties and spoke with a Liverpool accent (though he was born in Lancaster), in a resigned manner that went with his hangdog putty features. A black and white photograph in the National Portrait Gallery by Michael Woods shows what he looked like in the eighties. His unmistakable paintings and prints (in vivid colours with scintillating outlines) celebrated drink sexual attraction and violence, each item sometimes standing metaphorically for another. His *Friday Night in the French*, for example, showed men and bare-breasted women pouring drink into their upturned mouths, like monstrous fledglings crowded into a smoke-filled nest.

In the next decade, Young British Artists, as their species was known, were to colonize the Colony, the foremost being Damien Hirst. He was perfectly agreeable if often wildly and incoherently drunk, which he isn't now. But his art was not painting, and nor was that of Sebastian Horsley, who was actually older than Hirst but arrived late in Soho to show himself off and then finish himself off with drugs.

Between the rising stars and the burning sun of a Freud or Bacon, Christopher Battye was representative of a more constant constellation of painters that burned steadily in the eighties, sometimes consuming themselves as their flame flickered.

25

The Last Lamplighter

Cadging, stealing, verbal attack – The end of Paul Potts – This is worse – Last laughs – Leaving the taps on – Death of the eighties – A leg in the bath

Cadging, stealing, verbal attack

It was greatly to the credit of one of the French pub's oldest customers, Stephen Fothergill, that he remained on friendly terms with the poet Paul Potts until the latter's death in 1990, by which time most of his associates had long abandoned him. It is true that the writer Craig Brown, a man remarkably open to humanity, enjoyed conversations with Paul Potts in the Colony Room Club in the seventies, but Stephen even went to visit him when he was bedridden.

The principal enemies of Potts's popularity were his constant cadging of drinks and money, his theft of friends' books and shirts, his wounding outbursts of verbal abuse and, later, his strong and offensive smell.

Stephen Fothergill was to me a familiar and welcome sight in the eighties in the French pub, late in the evening. Tall, with a sharp nose that often seemed nipped with cold, grey-haired and dressed in a long, drab raincoat, he spoke quietly and occasionally laughed lightly with a noise a little less than a snort.

'If I ever need to remind myself of the virtues of constancy and good manners, or of the fact that people can hold very different views from my own without its actually mattering,' wrote Oliver Bernard, who had known him since the forties, 'I'm always glad to see Stephen, because he reminds me of them.'

Despite Stephen's diffident air, he had been involved in some hair-raising incidents. He had been in Soho before almost anyone then alive, it seemed: since before the war. He had first met Paul Potts in 1939, trying to borrow money in the Wheatsheaf pub in Rathbone Place.

After being honourably discharged from the army, which even in wartime found him more trouble than he was worth, Potts ran into Stephen one day in the Swiss pub in Old Compton Street. Stephen was impressed by his manner of drinking, which was to swallow in seconds any pint of Guinness bought for him. After a few pints he proposed buying Stephen lunch at an Italian restaurant. Much of Potts's spaghetti ended up on the cloth. At the end of the meal, he announced without embarrassment that he was broke. Stephen paid the bill. As they parted at the door, Potts said: 'Can you lend me half a crown, old boy? Bus fares, you know, and my entrance fee to the French tomorrow morning.'

With his entrance fee to buy a first drink for himself, he hoped that someone else would pay for subsequent drinks. Paul Potts existed mostly by this exhausting method of getting drinks and asking for small loans – 'marathon tapping stints' as Stephen neatly phrased it. He was left with little time for productive writing, but his most notable book was *Dante Called You Beatrice*, published in 1960. John Heath-Stubbs and David Wright had included one of his poems in *The Faber Book of Twentieth-Century Verse*.

Oliver Bernard was one man who found Paul Potts's cruel tongue impossible to endure in the late fifties. Oliver had been delighted that some 300 lines of Apollinaire in his own translation had appeared in *Encounter*, thanks to the support of Stephen Spender. One day, in the Caves de France, which people used as an afternoon drinking club, Paul Potts shouted out: 'Here's Stephen Spender's little sexy boy!'

Oliver found that others suffered worse. John Stephens, an actor and poet 'who worried about his dark good looks', put up

Paul Potts for a few days and, as was often the case, suffered theft of his shirts and books. Reproached, Potts shouted at him in the street, calling him a 'damned half-caste'. As Oliver put it, 'For me Paul Potts's mind is a mystery I am in no great hurry to solve.' He avoided him for the rest of Potts's life.

On one occasion the tables were turned. Jeffrey Bernard, on the run from the army in the early fifties, counted among the clothes that he carried in a holdall a white shirt with the name on the neck band: PAUL POTTS.

The end of Paul Potts

Stephen bore witness to Paul Potts's physical courage and his quality of being 'incapable of penning a single sentence that did not come from the heart'. But he couldn't deny that by the eighties his refusal to wash and his double incontinence meant that 'as he entered a pub a terrible odour rapidly filled the whole room'. Even the tolerant Gaston Berlemont felt bound to have a word with him. 'It really is too bad, sir,' he said. 'As soon as you come into the pub my customers leave in droves. You really must do something about this awful smell, otherwise … well, it's quite impossible.'

Potts took to his room in Highbury, and only dark rumours of the squalor he enjoyed, in which excrement figured prominently, filtered back to Soho. It was not until he heard that Potts now had a home help from the council that Stephen plucked up the courage to visit him.

After being thrown a pair of dirt-encrusted keys from an upper window, Stephen found Potts lying on top of his bed in an overheated room that, thanks to the daily helper, smelled of nothing worse than ammonia. After Stephen had fetched supplies, Potts hungrily consumed a bag of peanuts, some bananas, a slab of nut chocolate and a vanilla ice cream, at the same time taking gulps from a mug of lager laced with whisky. He made no attempt to wipe ice cream from the beard he now wore.

They were interrupted by the home help, who chided him with: 'Paul! You know you mustn't eat lying on your back.' A pocket in his oesophagus had recently landed him in hospital, for the removal of accumulated food that had lodged there. But only after a tirade of four-lettered abuse would he now heed his good-natured helper's admonitions.

By Stephen's account, Potts's death after he had set his bed on fire with his pipe was accompanied by no pain. Somehow his nerves had been deadened and, despite his burns, he met the firemen, alerted by the smoke from his room, with indignant orders to fuck off and leave him in peace. He died shortly after being taken to hospital on 26 August 1990, aged 79.

This is worse

Stephen had experienced worse, nearer home, as he told me quietly in the French one evening and later wrote about in his short, spare memoir. 'In those days I was working as a lamplighter and learning to play the trumpet,' he explained. That was in the fifties, when he lived in an unfurnished room in Delamere Road, near the house shown in Freud's *Interior at Paddington*. But Stephen's room faced the wrong way for a view towards the Grand Union Canal.

A week after they first met, Jackie moved in with him. It was a brave move. There was no bathroom. A Primus stood on the carpetless floor where old newspapers and magazines lay. Quart beer bottles stood about, awaiting return for the twopence deposit reclaimable on each. An orange box sheltered some books, a couple of enamel mugs and a packet of biscuits. On a refectory table were the instruments of Stephen's vocation: a trumpet and a pair of bicycle clips for him to cycle off with his extendable ladder to tend the gas lamps of the locality.

He remembered Jackie as warm-hearted, fun-loving, quarrelsome, pig-headed and violent, smashing a milk bottle on his head when she suspected him jealously of flirting with a middle-aged woman who lived upstairs. Despite a private school education, she exhibited surprising ignorance, thinking Ireland still to be part of the United Kingdom, for example. They married, despite his opposition to the institution, to get a tax rebate. The pawnbroker was a regular destination.

When a hypodermic fell out of her handbag and Stephen realized she was injecting heroin, he hit her, 'an action for which I have always felt ashamed'. She went to the Maudsley Hospital for a 'cure'. She relapsed and took another cure. Then another. Prescribed a regular dose of heroin by a GP, as could then be done, she resorted to dealers to top it up.

At another flat with more room, they began to live separate lives. She became a semi-invalid after a stroke and suffered from emphysema caused by smoking too many small cigars. She had a fall and broke a hip. An operation was successful, but she developed pneumonia and died, aged 58.

Jackie's story formed a chapter in *The Last Lamplighter*, published by the editor of the *London Magazine* for 40 years, Alan Ross, as one of his last projects before he died.

Last laughs

If there was a slightly icy air about some of Stephen's conversation, because he did not express overt emotion, he was aware of the comic accompaniments to the inevitable tragedy of Soho lives. At the Coffee an', a bohemian joint in St Giles's Passage, Stephen witnessed the owner, Boris Watson, of Bulgarian descent, kill a man. In an argument he hit him on the head with a steel used for sharpening knives, and he reeled from the café bleeding heavily. Watson was acquitted of manslaughter and went on to start the Mandrake Club, underground in Meard Street.

Stephen had for decades been a friend of the often absurd poetry publisher Tambimuttu, one of whose characteristics was extreme tactlessness. 'Why are you always so red?' he asked a young man in the French who tended to blush. 'Is it a disease or something?'

Tambimuttu returned to England after 20 years away. In the early eighties he was living in a flat above the October Gallery in Old Gloucester Street, that strange mix of early Georgian houses and hotel service entrances on the edge of Bloomsbury. Tambi, as Stephen knew him, had to climb an iron staircase to reach his door, and one evening slipped and fell. He had only days to live.

The wake was held at the October Gallery, where Eddie Linden, the editor of the poetry magazine *Aquarius*, got very drunk and declaimed poems to the captive audience. Their ordeal was ended only when the gallery owners announced that they must vacate the room because it had been booked for a belly-dancing class.

Leaving the taps on

By the end of the eighties, when Lucian Freud had painted him wearing his characteristic checked cap, which he generally kept on while sitting in the Coach and Horses, Mick Tobin sometimes found life got him down. At his newspaper pitch in Charing Cross Road he would often be asked brusquely by tourists for directions to various theatres.

'It's by the school,' he would say.

'What school?'

'The school where they teach you to say please and thank you.'

He found it harder to get odd jobs, though a snowy week spent selling newspapers at a pitch outside the American embassy in Grosvenor Square was turned into a lark by his borrowing a fur hat and fixing a Russian badge to it. His carpentering was not always reliable by now, and he needed the advance of some 'moving-about money' before he could get stuck into a job. Once he spent the £30 moving-about money that Sandy

Fawkes had given him to put up some shelves. Pickles paid her the money from his own pocket, with the cover story that Mick was not well and had entrusted the funds to him to give back.

Often skint by Saturday, unless a fortunate horse supplemented his income and pension, he took to spending most of Sundays in bed. But he found that his rest was disturbed by a deep-bass rhythm from a clothes shop beneath his flat in Covent Garden. Remonstration had no effect, and one day he put the plug in the bath, turned on the taps and went out. He admitted the crime to the police and received a suspended sentence.

In his last years Mick took to sleeping in a chair to ease his breathing. He was eventually admitted to the Middlesex Hospital with cancer of the throat. Friends took him cans of Guinness, which soon no longer fitted into his bedside locker. He resented being told that he should not drink in the hospital because some of the patients were alcoholic.

He reacted with horror when I gave him as a present a betting slip for a wager I'd put on a horse in an approaching race, fearing a win would bring death with it. He was petrified by the suggestion that he should go to a hospice staffed by nuns; nuns had been his nemesis when he had been a naughty young boy.

As the disease grew, the nights were the worst, when he sat in a darkened room, alone with his fears and a feeling of choking, and his throat burning with radiation treatment. As a seasoned boxer he asked indignantly: 'They talk about fighting cancer. What am I supposed to do, go the distance with it like Randolph Turpin?'

He was pleased when friends came to see him, including Jennifer Paterson and Lisa Stansfield, who had often enjoyed a drink or two with him at the Coach and the Colony.

Mick's funeral was at St Patrick's, Soho Square, and Jeffrey Bernard had agreed to say a few words. 'I still can't think of what to say about old Mick', he complained in the *Spectator* as the time grew nearer. 'I shall probably make the relations angry by not being too serious, but then there are so many things about death that are not too serious unless you count your own and even that will make the wintry, thin lips of friends and acquaintances distort into a smile.' In the event he recalled the occasion that Mick and he had the job of sticking the little stars on the nipples of some exotic dancers.

Death of the eighties

The death that sealed the death of eighties Soho did not come till 1992. On 28 April Francis Bacon died. The reaction in the Colony Room Club was beautifully caught by the photographer Craig Easton, for the *Independent*. He found only Ian Board, Michael Wojas and Graham Mason in the club, where the afternoon spring sunshine had turned the window to Dean Street into its habitual portal of glory.

Nothing is being said. Each of the figures is smoking a cigarette: Ian on the perch, smoking his menthol brand, with a woollen scarf round his neck, has his feet, encased in horrible green shoes, up on the neighbouring stool; Michael, below a print of Bill Brandt's stark portrait of Bacon on Primrose Hill, has his arms hugging his body, a normal pose; Graham with his legs twisted round a stool, about to exhale, has his soggy face turned to the ceiling.

Certainly Ian Board had no high ideas about death. 'Chuck me in a bin bag,' was his attitude to his own passing. When I visited him in hospital during his mortal illness two years later, he had plenty of vodka to offer me, which I drank, as though in some primitive ceremony, from a disgustingly beslobbered toothmug. Michael had his own fears to which I was not party. I knew that he could only sleep by rocking to the sound of the radio left on. Graham expected to die before Marsh Dunbar, but he was wrong, and was left alone for a year, with almost all his friends dead, imprisoned by emphysema in his flat, with a cylinder of oxygen by his armchair and bottles of white wine, regarded as a benign alternative to vodka, within reach, while he looked from the window over the view of the Thames, still very angry.

A leg in the bath

Jeffrey Bernard was in a wheelchair, which can at least be a platform from which to avoid overt criticism of one's efforts. He would emphasize a point in conversation by waving his stump.

Sometimes I would wheel him home from the Coach to his warm, characterless flat high up in Kemp House, a modern council block behind the King of Corsica in Berwick Market. He had an artificial leg, which he had neither the strength nor inclination to learn to use. It stood reproachfully in the bath next to a bucket with some underclothes soaking in a solution of Jeyes Fluid.

It had been quite an achievement to survive, first, the removal of the orange-sized sebaceous cysts on each side of the nape of his neck, then the amputation of his leg below the knee, as a result of gangrene setting in as a complication of diabetes. Visiting him after the cysts were cut out I met the surgeon in the lift, who praised Jeffrey's game courage. In the ward, Jeffrey was full of a report he had read in the paper of a man whose child had been caught by the blades of a helicopter. 'They could hear the screams over the rotors,' he said.

Some time after the week that a line appeared in the *Spectator*, in place of his column, 'Jeffrey Bernard has had a leg off', he tried to push me away. I didn't understand why at first. He had gone on a foreign freebie paid for by a magazine, assuring them he had travel insurance. He was taken ill abroad, and it soon became clear that he had no insurance. A friend of mine at the *Daily Telegraph*, of more robust confidence than I possessed, spent some time on the telephone convincing the magazine that it was nevertheless its duty to bring Jeffrey safely home. This it did.

When he wrote about it in the *Spectator*, he remembered 'hours and hours in one of the world's poshest hotels, La Mamounia, where I lay writhing in my own vomit and excrement waiting to get out of the country'. I visited him recovering in the Middlesex Hospital, where he was sitting enjoying a smoke on the landing, where it was still allowed in those days. He was in

St Paul's ward, and he incorporated in his next column a fact I'd mentioned in conversation, that St Paul had been a tentmaker. Many of his conversations, when he could remember them, were rehearsals for his column. After a while I said I'd better be going. 'Just go then,' he said. 'All you did was keep looking at your watch anyway.'

It might not sound deadly by the standards of Soho vituperation, but it was intended as a rebuff. Slowly I realized that he resented my interference in helping to bring him back, when he had preferred to die abroad. I didn't stop spending time in his company, but a chill had been introduced.

Jeffrey's kidneys failed, and he had to be given regular dialysis, which he found boring and irksome at best. He decided to decline further sessions and invited family and friends to his flat to mark the decision with a drink. I didn't go.

Envoi

A book that the actress Diana Lambert gave me one day in the Coach and Horses was *Trilby* by George Du Maurier, published by Osgood, McIlvaine & Co., in blue cloth with the heroine in gold blocking on the front cover. The melodramatic plot, of Trilby the artist's model hypnotized into stardom as a singer, may be funny when it doesn't mean to be, but the incidental evocation of bohemian life in the Paris of the 1850s provided an intriguing commentary on life in the Soho of the 1980s.

In 1856 Du Maurier was seeing if he could be a good painter, and he mixed with painters, one of them being the American James McNeill Whistler. But there was something unreal about Du Maurier's bohemianism, as there was about his own self-image. He thought he was descended on one side from George III and on the other from a French aristocrat; only research by his grand-daughter Daphne Du Maurier revealed that neither ancestry was true. Du Maurier gave up trying to be a painter when he lost the sight in one eye, and he had to settle for being an extremely successful novelist and a cartoonist for *Punch*. (His most celebrated gag was The Curate's Egg.)

If bohemianism meant, as in the 1860s it was said to mean, the artistic way of life of someone who 'secedes from conventionality', then Soho in the eighties was bohemian. The term had always possessed a different flavour according to the direction from which the bohemian came to it. To the 6th Duke of Sutherland a visit to the Colony Room Club had a grubby frisson absent from the impression it made on the skint retired stage carpenter Mick Tobin, even if Mick did familiarly address Maria Callas as 'Cally' and Lucian Freud as 'Lu'.

I don't know that sex defined the unconventionality of Soho in the eighties. Clearly there was far less disapproval of unmarried liaisons and homosexuality than still held sway elsewhere at the time. But it seemed to me that a disregard for money and conventional success proved a more challenging school of virtue there. All the same, it was less like a monastery than it was like a lifeboat.

Otherwise, what did it all add up to, Soho in the eighties? Will its traces be obvious in the art and literature still enjoyed in a hundred years' time? Obviously a painter like Francis Bacon would not have painted as he did if he had not fallen into Soho. It was a part of his rhythm of life, and the same could be said of other painters of the so-called School of London: Lucian Freud, Michael Auerbach, Michael Andrews, even if Soho had first scoured their experience in earlier decades.

There's no great Soho novel of the eighties, but plenty of people active in the arts as publishers, actors and journalists saw their work moulded by their time there. Some it destroyed. Already, to read Jeffrey Bernard's columns from the *Spectator* in that decade is quite shocking. The attitude to women is sometimes painful, if sometimes only intended as another blow in the battle of the sexes.

For me, Soho in the eighties was a love affair, if a dangerous liaison. It was no great achievement to survive it, for it was Soho that fell away from me and disintegrated. If only, one is tempted to think, some narrow academics and dull management types today could be transported back 30 years and thrown in at the smoky deep end with those monsters who felt at home there, then they'd wake up. But would they?

Even now, a lot of commentary on Soho in the eighties reads anachronistically, falsifying the emphasis, dynamic and whole flavour. Of course I put a foot wrong many a time in that decade; I have not been trying to defend my record. But I'm glad I was there.

Acknowledgements

Robin Baird-Smith of Bloomsbury Continuum is warmly thanked for his encouragement, patience and understanding. Jamie Birkett of Bloomsbury Continuum was unfailingly helpful. I thank my old friend Rupert Shrive for his memories and for kindly letting me use the image for the dustjacket and his head and shoulders of Graham Mason as one of the plates. My even older friend Michael Heath still surprised me with fresh observations and kindly let me reproduce one of his strips from The Regulars. Maurice Lipsedge ran his sharp eye over the typescript with good effect. Lucy Davies was helpful in sharing her knowledge of photographs. I owe thanks to Emily Faccini for her care over the map and to Richard Burgess for his skill in drawing the plans. To all those at whom I shouted in the eighties, or who shouted at me, I owe the greatest thanks, especially to the dead.

Bibliography

Abrams, Robert C. (2015). 'Sir James Reid and the Death of Queen Victoria', *The Gerontologist*, vol. 55, issue 6.

Balon, Norman (1991), *You're Barred, You Bastards! The Memoirs of a Soho Publican*. London: Sidgwick & Jackson.

Barker, Sebastian (1979), *Who is Eddie Linden?*. London: Jay Landesman.

Barrow, Andrew (2002), *Quentin & Philip: A Double Portrait*. London: Macmillan.

Bernard, Bruce (1980), *Photodiscovery*. London: Thames & Hudson.

— (ed.) (1984), *John Deakin: The Salvage of a Photographer*. London: Victoria and Albert Museum.

— (1985), *Vincent by Himself*. London: Orbis.

— (1994), *All Human Life*. London: Barbican Art Gallery.

— (1999), *Twelve Photographs of Francis Bacon*. London: The British Council.

— (1999), *Century*. London: Phaidon.

Bernard, Jeffrey and Taki (1981), *High Life, Low Life*. London: Jay Landesman.

Bernard, Jeffrey (1986), *Low Life*. London: Gerald Duckworth.

— (1987), *Talking Horses*. London: Fourth Estate.

— (1989), *More Low Life*. London: Pan Books.

— (1996), *Reach for the Ground*. London: Duckworth.

Bernard, Oliver (1961), *Country Matters*. London: Putnam.

— (trans.) (1962), *Rimbaud: Selected Verse*. Harmondsworth: Penguin Books.

— (trans.) (1965), *Apollinaire, Selected Poems*. Harmondsworth: Penguin Books.

— (1983), *Poems*. Kenninghall: Samizdat.

— (1989), *Moons and Tides, Walberswick*. Southwold: Southwold Press.

— (1990), *Getting Over It*. London: Peter Owen.

— (2001), *Verse &c.* London: Anvil Press Poetry.

— (trans.) (2012), *Rimbaud: The Poems*. Manchester: Carcanet Press.

Bernard, Oliver P. (1936), *Cock Sparrow*. London: Jonathan Cape.

Calvocoressi, Richard (2017), *Michael Andrews: Earth Air Water*. London: Gagosian Gallery.

Corrigan, Felicitas (1970), *George Thomas of Soho*. London: Secker & Warburg.

Dark, Sidney and Rowland Grey (1923), *W. S. Gilbert: His Life and Letters*. London: Methuen.

Farson, Daniel (1987), *Soho in the Fifties*. London: Michael Joseph.

— (1988), *Sacred Monsters*. London: Bloomsbury.

— (1998), *Never a Normal Man: An Autobiography*. London: HarperCollins.

Fawkes, Sandy (1993), *The French: A Personal History*. London: Lewis / Botham French House.

Fothergill, Stephen (2000), *The Last Lamplighter: A Soho Education*. London: London Magazine Editions.

Heath, Michael (1985), *Welcome to America*. London: Heinemann.

— (1990), *The Complete Heath*. London: John Murray.

Heath-Stubbs, John (1988), *Collected Poems*. Manchester: Carcanet Press.

— (1993), *Hindsights: An Autobiography*. London: Hodder & Stoughton.

— and David Wright (eds) (1950), *The Forsaken Garden*. London: John Lehmann.

— (1953), *The Faber Book of Twentieth-Century Verse*. London: Faber & Faber.

Ingrams, Richard (1971), *The Life and Times of Private Eye*. London: Allen Lane.

Lord, Graham (1992), *Just the One: The Wives and Times of Jeffrey Bernard*. London: Sinclair-Stevenson.

Marnham, Patrick (1982), *The Private Eye Story: The First Twenty-One Years*. London: HarperCollins.

Martin, Simon and Frances Spalding (2017), *John Minton: A Centenary*. Chichester: Pallant House Gallery.

Moraes, Henrietta (1994), *Henrietta*. London: Hamish Hamilton.

Muir, Robin (1996), *John Deakin: Photographs*. London: National Portrait Gallery.

— (2002), *A Maverick Eye: The Street Photography of John Deakin*. London: Thames & Hudson.

— (2014), *Under the Influence: John Deakin, Photography and the Lure of Soho*. London: Art Books.

Norman, Frank (1959), *Stand On Me*. London: Secker & Warburg.

— and Jeffrey Bernard (1966), *Soho Night and Day*. London: Secker & Warburg.

Peppiatt, Michael (2012), *Interviews with Artists 1966–2012*. London: Yale University Press.

— (2015), *Francis Bacon in Your Blood*. London: Bloomsbury Circus.

Reid, Michaela (1987), *Ask Sir James*. London: Hodder & Stoughton.

Reid, Philip [Richard Ingrams and Andrew Osmond] (1973), *Harris in Wonderland*. London: Jonathan Cape.

Short, Constance and Tony Carroll (eds) (2005), *Eddie's Own Aquarius*. Cahermee Publications.

Spalding, Frances (2005), *John Minton: Dance Till the Stars Come Down*. London: Lund Humphries.

Survey of London (1966), vols 33 and 34, *St Anne Soho*. London: London County Council.

Thomas, George (1931), *A Tenement in Soho*. London: Jonathan Cape.

Thompson, Harry (1994), *Richard Ingrams: Lord of the Gnomes*. London: Heinemann.

Waterhouse, Keith (1991), *Jeffrey Bernard is Unwell*. London: Samuel French.

Waugh, Auberon (1991), *Will This Do?*. London: Century.

Wilson, Colin (1961). *Adrift in Soho: A Novel*. London: Victor Gollancz.

Wright, David (1969), *Deafness*. London: Allen Lane.

Index

A Note on the Author

Christopher Howse is a writer and assistant editor at the *Daily Telegraph*. He contributes regularly to the *Spectator*, the *Tablet* and the *Oldie*. His previous books include *The Train in Spain* and *Sacred Mysteries*.

A Note on the Type

The text of this book is set in Bembo, which was first used in 1495 by the Venetian printer Aldus Manutius for Cardinal Bembo's *De Aetna*. The original types were cut for Manutius by Francesco Griffo. Bembo was one of the types used by Claude Garamond (1480–1561) as a model for his Romain de l'Université, and so it was a forerunner of what became the standard European type for the following two centuries. Its modern form follows the original types and was designed for Monotype in 1929.